QUARTERMASTERS
OF CONQUEST

QUARTERMASTERS OF CONQUEST

THE MEXICAN-AMERICAN WAR AND THE MAKING OF SOUTH TEXAS, 1846–1860

CHRISTOPHER N. MENKING

UNIVERSITY OF OKLAHOMA PRESS : NORMAN

Library of Congress Cataloging-in-Publication Data

Names: Menking, Christopher Neal, 1988– author.
Title: Quartermasters of conquest : the Mexican-American War and the making of South Texas,
  1846–1860 / Christopher N. Menking.
Other titles: Mexican-American War and the making of South Texas, 1846–1860
Description: Norman : University of Oklahoma Press, 2025. | Includes bibliographical references
  and index. | Summary: "A history of the unsung role of the US Army Quartermaster Depart-
  ment in the US-Mexico War and the rise of the disproportionate Euro-American power in the
  South Texas borderlands circa 1848–1860"—Provided by publisher.
Identifiers: LCCN 2024026877 | ISBN 9780806195308 (hardcover)
Subjects: LCSH: United States. Army. Quartermaster Corps—History—19th century. | Mexican
  War, 1846–1848—Logistics. | Mexican War, 1846–1848—Influence. | War and society—Texas,
  South. | Economic development—Texas, South—History—19th century. | Texas, South—Race
  relations—History—19th century. | Texas, South—History, Military—19th century. | Mexico,
  North—History, Military—19th century. | Mexican War, 1846–1848—Campaigns.
Classification: LCC E409.2 .M465 2025 | DDC 973.6/244—dc23/eng/20241105
LC record available at https://lccn.loc.gov/2024026877

The paper in this book meets the guidelines for permanence and durability of the Committee on
Production Guidelines for Book Longevity of the Council on Library Resources, Inc. ∞

Contents

Introduction

Growing up in South Texas as a white kid with German-American background was a distinctive experience. South Texas is a unique demographic region in Texas. Almost every county within the region has maintained a Tejano or Mexican-American ethnic majority for its entire history. My family first moved to Alice, a small town just west of Corpus Christi, in the late 1800s as part of a Lutheran ministry effort. My great grandfather served as a minister leading settlers from Fredericksburg to Alice to set up a Lutheran church, ostensibly to convert Catholics. As of the 2020 census, the population of Alice is about 84 percent Hispanic and just over 8 percent Anglo, with the remainder being a mix of other racial and ethnic groups. Therefore, the dominant culture when I was growing up was one of Hispanic, particularly Mexican, origin. Nevertheless, one aspect of my youth that always struck me as odd was the disproportionate number of wealthy Anglos despite their being a minority of the population. This apparent paradox always sat as a curiosity in the back of my mind. In college and graduate school, I began studying history and focused my research on the US-Mexican War because I was familiar with many of the locations in South Texas and Northern Mexico where battles occurred. My research eventually led me to the United States Army Quartermaster's Department and its influence on wartime logistics. What I did not expect was the impact the department left on South Texas and the Lower Rio Grande Valley. This book is my effort to help explain the catalyst that propelled Anglos to a place of economic and social prominence in a region where they remained an ethnic minority.

The war between the United States and Mexico is one of the least studied conflicts in United States history despite its significance to the country's development. The conflict represents more than just a territorial land grab justified by Manifest Destiny. While there is no doubt that territorial expansion during the campaign and presidency of James K. Polk (1844–1848) played a crucial role in shaping the nation, the war itself produced significant military, social, and political changes for the United States.

Militarily, the US-Mexican War was the first fought by the United States almost entirely on foreign soil. It also included the United States' first occupation of a foreign capital, the largest amphibious landing to date, and the first large-scale test of West Point–trained officers, many of whom would later come to prominence in the American Civil War. Socially, the war created numerous tensions as political borders shifted in what became the southwestern United States, stretching from the Gulf of Mexico all the way to California. In particular, such changes affected the Tejanos who resided in South Texas and the Lower Rio Grande Valley. The now Mexican-American Tejanos had to adapt to dramatic shifts in the social hierarchy and fluctuating economic opportunities. Such hardship arose from policies developed and implemented during the war by the US Army and its Quartermaster's Department. The land gained from Mexico in the Treaty of Guadalupe-Hidalgo, the Mexican Cession, reignited the national clashes over the expansion of slavery, starting with the Wilmot Proviso, continuing through the Compromise of 1850, and ultimately ending with the Civil War. The US Army faced its own challenges in expanding its new logistical systems into the newly acquired Rio Grande borderland, which in turn underwent a period of dramatic transformations.

This book will analyze the logistical aspects of the US-Mexican War and how the supply networks established in the Rio Grande Valley influenced the greater South Texas region during the conflict and postwar era, 1846–1860. Adequate logistical support was a vital element for the effective operations of American regular and volunteer forces during the war, and it had an equally important and unanticipated impact on South Texas. Wartime logistics, operation level strategic choices relating to logistics, the actions of the US Army Quartermaster's Department, the development of South Texas along the border with Mexico, and the relationship between war and society in the Rio Grande borderland all represent key themes in this region's history.

While the US-Mexican War has gained more attention since 1990, this work will focus on a less discussed aspect of the war: the logistical efforts of the Quartermaster's Department and their effect on South Texas.[1] During the war with Mexico, the US Army operated in three main theaters: present-day South Texas and northern Mexico, central Mexico, and what became the United States' southwestern territories. These efforts represent the largest logistical operations ever undertaken up to that point in time by the US Army—by several orders of magnitude. Despite the United States' military achievement in defeating Mexico, including crossing oceans and vast portions of the continent, there has been virtually nothing written on the logistics that made this accomplishment possible.

Logistics officer and historian Charles R. Shrader wrote in 1992 that a study of "US Army Logistics in the Mexican War of 1846–1848 . . . should be started tomorrow."[2] Likewise, Army historian Samuel Watson has written that, with the exception of a few works by Joseph G. Dawson, "there are virtually no tactical, operational, or strategic analyses" of the Mexican-American War.[3] This book takes the first step toward completing the task set forth by Shrader by creating a thorough account of the logistical efforts during the war for each of the three major theaters. This study will mainly focus on northern and central Mexico since the largest United States armies operated there and comprised most troop deployments. The emphasis on northern Mexico and South Texas supports the larger argument that the department left a lasting mark on the region for years following the war..[4]

The literature on the United States-Mexico War and the related field of the Lower Rio Grande Valley has already made some connections between the United States Army and regional development. This book builds on those works to demonstrate a connection between the wartime actions of the Quartermaster's Department and the postwar development of South Texas. Several historians have demonstrated how the influence of money via US Army contracts alters a region and how these economic changes begin to manifest in geographic ways as towns grow in proximity to the new military installations. Across from every town on the Mexican side of the Rio Grande, the army established a fort or supply depot on United States soil. While Fort McIntosh was already established at Laredo, this was the only city north of the Rio Grande prior to the war. In almost every location, a town developed near the military installation. While it was common across the United States for towns to follow frontier forts and depots, what was unique about South Texas was that the locations chosen paralleled the depots established during the war with Mexico as part of the Rio Grande Line, one of the logistical networks developed by the army.

The nineteenth-century experience of the United States Army on the westward moving frontiers of the country has been thoroughly analyzed. The US Army not only served as a tool to project power, but it also adopted the role of fostering national development. The US Army represented the largest employer in various locations and Army Quartermaster operations, specifically the influx of the

American dollar to support military logistics, was the most significant factor in the progress of economic development in the American Southwest.[5]

The social aspect of this period has drawn more attention from historians than the military's role in the Southwest. The settlement story of the area that would become South Texas follows Frederick Jackson Turner's frontier thesis in many ways. As Spain and then Mexico tried to secure its far northern frontier, the *frontera*, the United States began to expand towards the Sabine River and Texas. The Rio Grande Valley became a point of contention between rival settlers and nations. Be it by environment or American Indians, the Valley tested whether people possessed sufficient bravery to settle the region successfully. This idea of the frontier experience, while not an all-encompassing theory, does help define the determined nature of the region's hardscrabble denizens. One of the first historians to propose the uniqueness of this region and introduce the idea of borderlands was Herbert Eugene Bolton. His work examined how the Spanish influenced the territories that they occupied and, most important, how the territories on the fringes of that empire developed a unique character. These regions fell under Spanish rule but often resided too distantly from seats of power in either Madrid or Mexico City to feel any regular influence or control. This isolation forced them to confine to the more homogenous Spanish culture that developed in societal centers. David J. Weber continued this analysis in a similar vein with his study of the Mexican period, 1821–1846, when Mexico gained independence from Spain. Weber argued that Mexico repeated Spain's inability to settle and fully control its frontier regions. The far-flung regions of Mexican territory developed a unique character defined by their location as a borderland between two competing nations.[6]

Building on the foundation laid by Turner, Bolton, and Weber, the scholarship on the Rio Grande Borderlands has expanded greatly since the 1990s. The mid-nineteenth-century Rio Grande borderlands experienced a period of exceptional change, and the Mexican-American War was at the heart of it. Historians have analyzed the social components of South Texas and the Rio Grande region. The inclusion of the Quartermaster's Department adds another layer of complexity to explanations of why the borderlands became a place of shifting identities, alliances, wealth, and power. The goal here is not to argue that Anglos and Europeans swooped into South Texas in the wake of the war and took advantage of unsuspecting Tejanos. Rather, several prominent Anglos and Europeans already resided in the region, and the war simply accelerated the process of their hegemony. The quartermasters provided a tool that existing residents and newcomers utilized to propel themselves to great social and economic heights. Both Tejanos and Anglo Texans were important actors in the development of Tejano identity. One was not simply the victim of the other, though both did commit physical, social, economic, and political injury to each other. Often the story is one of cooperation as much as it is of conflict and violence. This complicated interrelationship defines the development of the lower Rio Grande Valley. Understanding borderland identity helps shed light on the choices frontier residents made to deal with the ebb and flow of power between the Mexican state and the American market.[7]

The development of the US Army and the Quartermaster's Department organized the nation mechanism that projected American economic influence into the South Texas borderlands. The presence of occupying armies and military instillations brought an influx of currency into the region that bolstered the postwar growth of the Rio Grande Valley.

The Second Continental Congress created the original posts of Quartermaster General and Commissary General of Stores and Purchases on June 16, 1775. During the War of 1812, the Quartermaster's Department experienced only minor changes and expansion. In contrast, during the Seminole Wars, Thomas Sidney Jesup, the most important figure for the Quartermaster's Department, greatly improved the department in important ways, such as increasing the number of regular staff officers and modernizing the bureaucratic management system of money and supplies. Congress further refined the Quartermaster's Department on July 5, 1838, but it was still far from the sizeable agency that would grow out of the Mexican-American War and later the Civil War. The department did not receive a man-power increase again until ten months into the war. Ultimately, the Mexican-American War served as the catalyst for the growth of the Quartermaster's Department.[8]

Quartermaster General Thomas Sidney Jesup became one of the longest serving generals, and his actions guided the department through several wars and shaped its expansion until the American Civil War. He was appointed Quartermaster General on May 8, 1818, by President James Monroe and served until he died in office on June 10, 1860, at the age of seventy-two. Jesup shaped the department to his own design, within the parameters defined by Congress, but he could never imagine the extent to which his actions would alter the course of South Texas history.

Jesup was born on December 16, 1788, the son of James Edward Jesup, a Revolutionary War veteran from Connecticut. Jesup, along with other prominent figures such as Winfield Scott and Zachary Taylor, joined the US Army as part of its expansion during the War of 1812. Enlistment offered the potential for distinction in an upcoming war and provided income for families. Soon after joining, Jesup realized that the American military was in its infancy. The army was woefully disorganized, lacking any regularity or structure for supplying and transporting its forces. He was first assigned as brigade quartermaster under Brigadier General James Wilkinson. Although eager to advance through the ranks, Jesup soon realized the need for political support for advancement. It would take about twenty-two months for him to receive his first promotion to first lieutenant.[9]

Jesup recognized the greater potential of the Quartermaster's Department during the War of 1812. The war provided him with wartime experience and put him on the path to developing and expanding the Quartermaster's Department in ways that laid the foundation for the operations during the US-Mexican War. After the war, Jesup spent time in the capital while John C. Calhoun became the secretary of war and restructured the US Army. Jesup and other officers had long called for such reform. These reforms included a large expansion of the Quartermaster's Department. Although Jesup hoped for the appointment as quartermaster general during this reform, it went to William Cumming instead. A letter reached Jesup, however, on May 24, 1818, informing him that Cumming had turned down the position and that Jesup had finally received the appointment as the quartermaster general. He then reported to Washington, DC.[10]

The assistant quartermaster general, Colonel Henry Stanton, became Jesup's right-hand man, often performing as acting quartermaster general when Jesup was away from Washington. Colonel Trueman Cross and Lieutenant Colonel Thomas F. Hunt were among the first officer appointments issued by Jesup when he became quartermaster general. These three men formed the nucleus of Jesup's department during the early days of the Mexican-American War. All orders and supplies flowed through these men's offices and depots. The war became a trial by fire that forged the army into a battle-hardened force from which many of the leading men in the Civil War emerged.[11]

The Quartermaster's Department used several different methods to support the various armies in the field. It employed a network of supply depots and arsenals that existed before the war, but this network expanded after the declaration of war to support the armies operating far from United States supply centers. The department's supply lines stretched along the East Coast of the United States, around and through many of the Gulf of Mexico ports, and to Veracruz before extending through central Mexico and culminating at Mexico City. Railroads did not play a significant role in the war because of the limited number of American rail lines. Even fewer lines were accessible in Mexico. River transport dominated the transportation of men and supplies across the United States and into northern Mexico. Much of the remaining cargo arrived on sailing and steam vessels crossing the Gulf of Mexico. To support both the river and coastal supply networks, the Quartermaster's Department began to purchase, lease, or charter ships and other vessels. Still it could not completely meet the transportation demands. Overland transport lacked the speed of waterborne transportation, but wagon trains guided by their teamsters proved to be essential to keeping armies moving when not operating near rivers and coasts. Herds of cattle provided mobile sources of food when available, but the soldiers often served as their own supply train, carrying several days rations in addition to their gear. These methods combined to create the largest, most successful logistical operation ever attempted by the United States up to this point.

The twelve postwar years saw the most significant growth of South Texas and the Lower Rio Grande Valley since its initial settlement by the Spanish. The Anglo and European merchants that settled along the river and surrounding region utilized the supply infrastructure and employment opportunities provided by the US Army to greatly expand their businesses. These men used their unique skills, contacts within the Quartermaster's Department, and relationships with Mexican and Tejano families to obtain significant wealth and power in South Texas. Despite remaining an ethnic majority, Tejano elites ended up relinquishing their power to the Anglo and European settlers who propelled their economic wealth into political power for decades to come. As a result of these changes, South Texas became a hybridized culture mixing aspects of Mexico and the United States in a unique way that created a distinct borderland region along the Rio Grande.

This book includes seven chapters conveying the role of the Quartermaster's Department during the US-Mexican War and the interwar period, particularly relating to South Texas and the Rio Grande Valley. Chapter one focuses on the history of the Lower Rio Grande Valley, a region encompassed by what is now South Texas. The traditional borders of South Texas are marked by the Rio Grande to the south and the Nueces River in the north, but Tejano prominence extends to San Antonio as a greater boundary of South Texas. Laredo is the western boundary of this region, and the Gulf of Mexico serves as its eastern boundary. This chapter addresses how the Valley changed from Spanish to

Mexican and then to Texan hands. Each of these nation-states recognized the potential value that the region presented. The struggle to occupy and exert control over the region eluded Spain, Mexico, and Texas because of a combination of political conflicts, environmental obstacles, and Native American actions. Beyond initial colonization by Spain, the region north of the Rio Grande, South Texas, would not begin to grow rapidly until Texas joined the United States and the US Army arrived with American money in the aftermath of the US-Mexican War.

The second and third chapters contend that the invasion of South Texas and Northern Mexico resulted in the establishment of new trade depots and supply networks that laid the groundwork for the postwar socioeconomic shift. The obstacles faced by the army elucidated the need to expand the Quartermaster's Department. Such challenges included long marches south by the US Army crossing inhospitable terrain and a massive mobilization by all branches as a result of the outbreak of hostilities. With the United States' annexation of Texas, General Taylor was ordered first to Corpus Christi, then to the Rio Grande to goad Mexico into a fight or capitulation. The war began, and Taylor began his operations against Mexican forces and cities. New supply routes, supply depots, and forts established along the Rio Grande supported the armies in the field. During this campaign, the foundations were laid for sweeping changes that would alter South Texas in the postwar period.

Chapter four focuses on the logistics of the Western Campaign. The western targets included Santa Fe and California due to the potential for lucrative trade with or through the regions and utilized existing trade lines, such as the Santa Fe Trail. The fifth chapter analyzes the logistical significance of the Central Mexico Campaign. General Winfield Scott invaded central Mexico at Vera Cruz with the goal of capturing Mexico City to bring the war to a close. These two additional theaters meant that the Quartermaster's Department would have to support at least three armies active in the field at the same time. Whether for commerce or to end the war, these two theaters put additional strain on the department and became the first time US military forces ever operated at such great distance from US soil. Despite the army occupation, the economic, demographic, and social changes that occurred in postwar South Texas did not occur in these two theaters. The South Texas borderlands proved to be uniquely ripe for the upheavals seen in the postwar decade.

Chapter six looks at the social and demographic changes after the war in South Texas. At an earlier point in Texas history, all the cities in the territory were controlled by Spaniards and later Mexicans; then with Texas independence, a trend began where Anglo-Americans started to exert more control than the Tejanos. Often Anglo and European migrants established peaceful trade and familial relations with Mexicans and Tejanos. Despite South Texas maintaining a numerical majority of Hispanics in the population, however, after the war Tejanos still lost political and economic ground to Anglos and Europeans, some newly arrived during the war. This inequity is the heart of the Quartermaster's Department legacy on South Texas. The supply depots and forts set up by the department led to new towns. These towns were filled with many new Anglos who were often given preference for the best and most profitable jobs from the army. Such favoritism resulted in a disproportionate amount of power ending up in the hands of the ethnic minority of Anglos in South Texas.

The seventh chapter addresses the economic and geographic results of the war on South Texas. During the war, the US Army became involved with two trade networks to help supply their forts, the Rio Grande Line and the Santa Fe Trail. Each provided a lucrative trade for their respective regions and brought the army dollar in to boost the economy. In addition, along the Rio Grande Line several forts, supply depots, and outposts were set up to support the army. After the war, new towns sprung up along the Rio Grande near almost every one of these installations resulting in an influx of settlers, Anglo-American and Mexican. These migrants came to settle, to work, for adventure, and for numerous other reasons, resulting in an unprecedented boom in the Valley's population. Many men of Anglo and European decent rose to social and economic prominence in South Texas by either replacing or coopting the Tejano hierarchy of the region. The geographical changes brought about by the establishment of towns adjacent to the new military installations provided the foundation for the socioeconomic upheaval during this decade.

Naming conventions for the war and the populations involved vary by histo-riographical field. For this work, I have chosen Mexican-American War most often, but I utilize different versions for variety, such as US-Mexican War, not with any particular agenda to favor one over the other. The region of the Lower Rio Grande Valley ranges from the mouth of the Rio Grande at Brazos Santiago up to Laredo, while South Texas stretches further north to either the Nueces River or as far as San Antonio if one includes the greater Hispanic cultural region. When it comes to naming Anglo, white American, Mexican, Tejano, or European characters, I try to be as accurate as possible as to how they identified themselves or how their contemporaries identified them. Mexican refers to Spanish-speaking residents of Spanish, Indigenous, or mixed decent in Mexico, while Tejanos are a subset of that group that reside in the region of Texas within Mexico. Tejano will also be used to differentiate Texans of Mexican decent in Texas during the Texas Republic and US periods from Anglo or European residents. Texian refers to the Anglo-American residents of Mexican Texas. Identity is complex in a borderlands region; depending on the situation and time period the same person may identify in multiple ways. The naming conventions used are more focused on differentiating the different actors by their nation of birth to demonstrate the changes experienced in South Texas.

This book ties together up-to-now disparate parts of the US-Mexican War historiography. The Quartermaster's Department seems to be the common thread that helps explain the connection between the military presence, rapid population growth, and the socioeconomic change of the Valley's citizens during the interwar period between 1848 and 1860. By pulling the different aspects of the historiography together with a new, thorough analysis of US-Mexican War logistics, this work helps clarify how and why South Texas changed so dramatically after 1846.

CHAPTER I

South Texas before the Mexican-American War

B y the outbreak of the US-Mexican War in 1846, the US Army Quarter-master's Department relied on the previously established depots and towns that existed at the war's start. Building on and improving those networks challenged American logisticians. United States success in the war depended in large part on how well the quartermasters supported the army. The arrival of the US Army and its quartermasters created a rapid and drastic reshaping of this borderland.

The Rio Grande Valley during the mid-nineteenth century lay at the heart of the military struggle between the United States and Mexico. This region long posed challenges to settlement for both Spain and Mexico. Its distance from Mexico City combined with the harsh desert-like conditions surrounding the more fertile valley made settlement daunting. Additionally, the constant threat of American Indian attacks from the Comanche and Lipan Apache who frequently crossed the Rio Grande (often referred to the *Río Bravo* in Mexico) to raid the populated areas of northern Mexico further hindered settlement efforts. The entire Valley represented a significant military theater during the US–Mexican War, but the portion north of the river changed dramatically when it became United States territory at war's end. The area, now known as South Texas, had experienced a succession of diverse local, regional, national, and military governing bodies in the years before ultimately being acquired by the United States. Its development afterward became a focal point for the international struggle between Mexico and the United States.[1]

Prior to the US–Mexican War, settlement in the Lower Rio Grande Valley, which stretched several miles on either side of the river from the mouth of the

Rio Grande to Laredo, remained relatively small compared to that of many other Spanish, and later Mexican, provinces. This area had also fallen under the control of different regional and national governments in the years before 1846. The greatest initial development of the Valley began with José de Escandón's establishment of a new province called Nuevo Santander. The province included much of the Lower Rio Grande Valley and part of the Gulf Coast reaching from the mouth of the river down to towards the city of Tampico. When Mexico gained its independence in 1821, the province became embroiled in a new conflict with the northernmost Mexican province, Coahuila y Texas. Securing the Texas border with the United States represented a paramount concern to the new Mexican nation. Mexico, however, allowed Anglo-American settlers into the region as a method of colonization. This immigration eventually led to the Texas Revolution (1836–1837), which would lead in turn to a border dispute between the Republic of Texas and Mexico over the portion of Nuevo Santander north of the Rio Grande. While the Lower Rio Grande Valley was not historically part of Texas, the republic's new citizens brazenly claimed the river as Texas's southern boundary. With the annexation of Texas, these territorial claims gave President James K. Polk the tenuous foundation he used to press Mexico for the region, leading in part to the outbreak of the US-Mexican War. As a frontier colony, Nuevo Santander resisted Native American raids, was involved in two revolutions, and finally experienced a war between western national powers. It is understandable that it was not heavily settled prior to 1848.

Nuevo Santander and Texas both played important roles in the development of the Lower Rio Grande Valley. Initially, Nuevo Santander, created in 1746, controlled virtually all of the Valley. The leaders of the Texas Revolution in 1836 made the bold, and historically unfounded, claim that the southern border of Texas was the Rio Grande. While it is anachronistic to tie the development of Texas to the Lower Rio Grande Valley prior to 1836, an understanding of the evolution of territorial and provincial control helps to make sense of the potential for future conflict between Texas and Mexico. Although Texas's eventual possession of the northern part of the Valley was never a foregone conclusion, that possibility must be discussed in tandem with the growth of Nuevo Santander. Even in Spain's instructions for governing the Interior Provinces of New Spain, the government often grouped Nuevo Santander (also called *Colonia Santander*), Texas, Coahuila, and Nuevo León together. These instructions illustrate that there is precedence for discussing two of these neighboring provinces, Texas and Nuevo Santander, in tandem.[2]

The Spanish Rio Grande Valley

The Spanish policies that Mexico inherited laid the groundwork for all foreign settlement of the Lower Rio Grande Valley. Spain saw the *frontera*, the far northern frontier, of their American colonies as crucial to maintaining territorial control in New Spain. It thus pursued several methods to protect and colonize these regions. According to historian Oakah Jones, Jr., "Geographic uncertainties and overlapping boundaries blurred jurisdictional matters and led to frequent disputes as well as a lack of unity in Spanish efforts to colonize the region." In particular, the Spanish worried that the English might lay claim to the Rio Grande in the 1680s, sparking the first significant wave of settlement along the northern frontier. The French expedition by René Robert Cavelier, Sieur de La Salle, in 1682 exacerbated this fear and made more urgent the push for colonization. Non-Indian settlement began initially in the regions of what became Central and East Texas, although the population never rose past about five thousand people during the eighteenth century.[3]

Spain's largest colonization effort began in 1746 with the establishment of José de Escandón's Nuevo Santander. Although Escadón was sponsored by the Spanish government, he funded the inspection of the province out of his own pocket. Among the factors driving Spanish support for Escandón were the regular raids into northern New Spain that disrupted commerce. The Spanish hoped that Nuevo Santander would serve as a buffer zone along the Rio Grande to shield the more established provinces. Escandón, however, saw potential for further development of the new colony and undertook the task as much to establish himself and his family in a region that might grow into a significant economic force in New Spain as to support the Crown. Escandón received the support of the Marquis de Altamira and was appointed the personal representative of the viceroy. In addition, he became the governor of Seno Mexicano, a region that stretched from Matagorda Bay to Tampico, including much of what would later become Colonia Santander. This frontier region gradually developed into a borderland as nations coalesced and encroached on either side of the Rio Grande during the eighteenth and nineteenth centuries.[4]

On February 10, 1747, Escandón's expedition of 765 soldiers arrived on the Rio Grande along the coast upriver from present-day Matamoros/Brownsville with the goal of exploring one hundred and twenty thousand square miles of land along the coast on both sides of the Rio Grande. During the exploration, Escandón became convinced that the area could be settled with the help of irrigation fueled by the river. The expedition explored the *salinas*, or rock salt beds, north of the Rio Grande with interest because salt was an important commodity for Spain. The men also noted an abundance of wild horses and cattle along the river. By the end of the expedition, Escandón envisioned a new colony made up of fourteen initial settlements, each situated for trade and communication. None of these settlements included a *presidio*, a Spanish frontier fort, because Escandón concluded that settlers would fight doubly hard to protect their own lands.[5]

To attract settlers from across New Spain to move to the sparsely populated Lower Rio Grande Valley, Escandón offered the best draw of all: free land. In addition, settlers would receive two hundred pesos for supplies and equipment, a bonus to pay travel costs, the potential for irrigation, and no taxes for ten years to help them get firmly established in the new province. Seven hundred families took Escandón's offer and moved to Nuevo Santander. The first settlement established was Nuestra Señora de Santa Ana de Camargo on March 5, 1749, known today as Camargo. Five days later, Nuestra Señora de Guadalupe de Reynosa was established twelve leagues (roughly forty-one miles) from Camargo. Soon Escandón settled two more colonies along the river, Nuestra Señora de los Dolores ten leagues (thirty-four miles) from present-day Laredo and Mier on the Alamo River near the south bank of the Rio Grande about ten miles from present-day Roma. By 1753 the colony had become stable, and interest in the region continued as more settlers migrated north. Escandón granted 100 *sitios*, sites or small land grants, along the Rio Grande. Many of these new settlements embraced ranching as a primary form of economic development.[6]

In 1755 the Marqués de las Amarillas, Augustín Ahumada y Villalón, arrived in Mexico City to take over as the viceroy of New Spain. He began to discourage additional settlement in Nuevo Santander despite the earlier successful colonization efforts of Escandón. Two years later, in 1757, Amarillas ordered José Tienda De Cuervo of Veracruz to lead an expedition to visit and inspect Nuevo Santander. His tour of the new settlements showed growing prosperity in the region. Despite Escandón's colonial success, the Lower Rio Grande Valley's last few years before the US-Mexican War focused on fending off Native American attacks rather than continued settlement of the region.[7]

Cuervo's inspection recorded a total of twenty-four cities, towns, and villages with roughly the same number of missions. The population in 1757 totaled 8,993 with twenty missionaries and 3,473 Indians living in the missions. The conclusion from the expedition was that the colonization efforts had been successful despite regional hardships endured by settlers. Despite, or perhaps

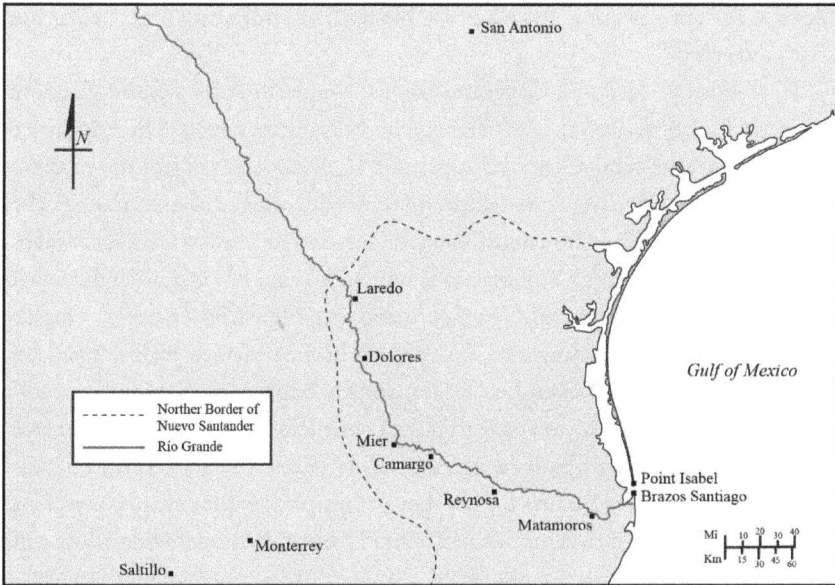

Nuevo Santander and the Lower Rio Grande Valley.

because of, Nuevo Santander's success, the viceroy saw no need to encourage further settlement in the region. He instead decided to let the colony develop at its current pace without governmental intervention. This policy continued under the term of the Marqués de Cruillas, Joaquín de Montserrat, who became viceroy in 1760.[8]

The efforts Spain made to secure this borderland changed dramatically after the Treaty of Paris (1763) with the onset of the Bourbon Reforms. The reform movement in Spanish America sought to centralize the control of government and reduce the power of local elites, giving preference to officials from the Iberian Peninsula. Most notable was the appointment of José Bernardo de Galvéz Gallardo as the visitor general of public finance who conducted a six-year tour of New Spain (1765–1771). Galvéz's office gave him power to make recommendations on general colonial policy and reforms; his powers even superseded the viceroy of New Spain. Several reforms dominated Galvéz's efforts in the colonies, including the Jesuit expulsion, overhauling revenue collection, and strengthening crown monopolies. The most notable result of Galvéz's tour of New Spain was the creation of the Comandancia General of the Interior Provinces of New Spain (Provincias Internas) which included Texas, Coahuila, Nueva Vizcaya, Nuevo

Mexico, Sonora y Sinaloa, Nuevo León, Nuevo Santander, and both Californias (Baja and Alta).[9]

The Marqués de Rubí, Cayetano María Pignatelli Rubí y Saint Climent, Barón de Llinas, arrived in the Veracruz on November 1, 1764. On August 7 of the following year, King Carlos III appointed Rubí inspector of frontier presidios and commissioned him to investigate and remedy economic abuses among other issues. Once he received his commission, he traveled to Mexico City, received his instruction from Viceroy Cruillas, and set out on his expedition on March 12, 1766. Rubí traveled around central New Spain and into New Mexico before crossing the Rio Grande and heading into Texas. Once in the province, he inspected San Sabá, San Antonio de Béxar, Los Adaes, and La Bahía before leaving Texas via Laredo. Rubí inspected no towns within the Lower Rio Grande Valley. Ultimately, he recommended that Spain reorganize its defenses. He argued that beyond the Rio Grande, New Spain's far northern frontier was difficult to control and concluded that only San Antonio and Santa Fe be maintained while advocating for the complete abandonment of East Texas. His final suggestion was a war of extermination against the Lipan Apache to prevent further raids.[10]

Occurring in 1767 was the *visita*—an administrative measure used by the monarch or his viceroys to enforce existing regulations, examine the workings of government, investigate the conduct of officials, or implement reforms—ordered by the Marqués de Croix and Viceroy Carlos Francisco de Croix, who appointed Field Marshal Juan Armando de Palacio and Licenciado José Osorío y Llamas to conduct a *visita general* in Nuevo Santander. The most notable member of the expedition was José Bernardo de Gálvez Gallardo, who served as the visitor general of public finance. His reorganization of the far northern provinces affected Nuevo Santander and the future of Texas in two crucial ways. Nuevo Santander first answered to an intendant at San Luis Potosí regarding taxes amongst other administrative issues and, second, to a comandante general of the Eastern Interior Provinces regarding military matters.[11] Although proposed in 1768, the creation of the Provincias Internas and the commandant general position did not occur until 1776 when Gálvez Gallardo became minister of the Indies.[12] In addition, the commissioners surveyed the land and distributed land to individual settlers at the Rio Grande *villas* (*villas del norte*) of Laredo, Mier, Camargo, Revilla (later Guerrero), and Reynosa. The land was divided into *porciones* (portions), long, narrow lots extending off the Rio Grande. As a result of this visita, some 170 porciones were granted in what is now Texas, representing one of the most significant settlement efforts to establish legal titles to land north of the river in the Lower Rio Grande Valley. Some of the porciones were allotted for civilians, while some were given to soldiers for their service on the frontier. The garrisons that accompanied these towns represented one of the few components of Spanish presence in this province intended to defend against Comanche and Lipan Apache raids.[13]

By the 1760s, Spanish authorities in New Spain found themselves mired in continual wars with the Comanche and Apache, wars that continued into the 1840s and beyond affecting every colonial power staking claim to the region. Between 1771 and 1776, the province of Nueva Vizcaya lost 1,674 people because of Apache raids. The Spanish government calculated that the Apaches also took 154 captives, sixty-six thousand head of cattle, and forced the abandonment of more than a hundred ranches and haciendas. As Mexico City utilized some of the ideas proposed by the Marqués de Rubí, the policy towards the Native Americans shifted towards one of trade over the more costly constant warfare. With the creation of the Internal Provinces, the Apache drew much of the focus of the new regional government, particularly Colonel Don Juan Ugalde, who commanded the troops in Nuevo Santander. Garrisons such as the one located near Laredo, as elsewhere in Nuevo Santander, operated more often as a shield against Native American attacks rather than as a mechanism of Spanish colonization.[14]

Ten years after Gallardo's visit, in 1786, Jose Antonio de Evia pushed for the portion of Nuevo Santander that is now Texas to be broken off to form a new province. In 1795, Félix María Calleja's inspection of the region noted that despite its limited commerce, Nuevo Santander had grown to a population of about thirty thousand residents. While the restructuring of regional command under the Internal Provinces aided Spain's administration of the region, it did not translate into a significant investment therein. For the most part, the new regional government focused on stabilization and defense rather than growth. Much of the stability, however, would be fractured due to the growing unrest that erupted in 1810, when Mexicans began their war for independence.[15]

RISE OF THE MEXICAN RIO GRANDE VALLEY

At the turn of the nineteenth century, Spanish Texas colonization efforts received a severe blow. During the period from 1803 to1821, Spain pursued a threefold strategy toward the region surrounding the Rio Grande borderlands: first, to uphold the historical boundaries of the territory; second, to increase its garrisons and to colonize the frontier with subjects loyal to Spain; and third, to keep out Anglo-American intruders. On April 24, 1807, the Council of the Indies appointed

Manuel María de Salcedo as governor of Texas. When he arrived in Spanish Texas, the territory only had 352 veteran soldiers and a civilian population of 3,122. Salcedo embraced his new role and pushed for new trading houses to placate the Indians and more troops to secure the frontier. Furthermore, he argued that if Texas was to be retained, then Spaniards from Louisiana or Mexico must settle the territory, otherwise there would be no way to ensure effective control. In 1810, he toured East Texas and encouraged foreigners to secure their land titles, though this measure went against instructions from the commandant general. Despite his best efforts to encourage the government to give him the resources needed to solidify the Spanish hold on Texas, his term as governor quickly became dominated by internal strife.[16]

Father Miguel Hidalgo y Costilla declared the Grito de Dolores in 1810, beginning the long fight for Mexican independence, a conflict that carried over into Salcedo's Texas. The most significant event for the settlement of Texas during Mexico's struggle for independence began with José Bernardo Gutiérrez de Lara and Augustus W. Magee's expedition into Texas. Gutiérrez traveled to the United States to seek support for the revolution. This sparked an uprising in Texas during 1813, the same year that Joaquín de Arredondo received his appointment as commandant general of the Interior Provinces. In reaction to the revolt, Arredondo was ordered to Texas to crush the insurrection. Accompanying him on the march to Texas was Antonio López de Santa Anna. Arredondo's policy in Texas was swift and hard, a strategy internalized by Santa Anna. Arredondo's forces greatly reduced the population of Texas, with many Tejanos dying or fleeing to the United States across the Sabine River. The impact on Spanish Texas was clear, according to historian Donald E. Chipman: "A non-Indian population in Texas of fewer than 3,000, largely vacant and dilapidated missions, two fixed presidios, three settlements, and two roads were the only 'memorials of Spain's imperial enterprises in this primeval kingdom.'" The appointment of Arredondo to commandant general of the Interior Provinces shaped Texas and Nuevo Santander during the last few years of Spanish rule. Furthermore, the War for Mexican Independence led to instability in both provinces, but while Texas received further colonization efforts, which strengthened the territory in defining ways, Nuevo Santander never received the same support.[17]

The final attempt by Spain to settle the province of Texas culminated in Moses Austin's proposal to settle some three hundred families in East Texas. Austin initially traveled to San Antonio in 1820 seeking permission to bring his colonists, but he was spurned by Governor Antonio María Martínez. He happened to encounter the Baron de Bastrop, however, whom he had met about nineteen years earlier in New Orleans. With Bastrop's support, Austin returned to the governor's office to request permission to relocate his colonists. On December 26, 1820, Austin received Governor Martínez's endorsement, and the plan was forwarded to Mexico City. This proposal was confirmed by the Provincias Internas on January 17, 1821. On the return trip, Moses contracted pneumonia and died a few months later leaving the colonization project to his son, Stephen F. Austin. The arrangement stated that Austin could offer land to settlers in quantities of 640 acres to the head of the family, 320 acres for a spouse, 160 acres for each child, and 80 acres for each slave. This colonization project began one the most significant movements of Anglo-Americans into the province of Texas. None of the Anglo-Americans settled along the Lower Rio Grande Valley, however; all migrated to areas far east of the Rio Grande Valley because of the fertile lands suitable for plantation agriculture and their proximity to United States markets. While settlement efforts shifted to East Texas, the towns along the Rio Grande focused more on defense from Indian raids.[18]

Mexico finally achieved independence from Spain in 1821, but with independence came the daunting task of managing and protecting an immense country stretching from the Yucatan to Alta California. After independence, Mexico established itself as a short-lived empire under Emperor Agustín de Iturbide, which was followed by a republic. One of the first issues that the new Mexican republic faced was the necessity of securing its northern frontier from the impending threat of Anglo settlers. On December 29, 1821, the Commission on Foreign Relations presented to the National Junta a report stating, "The most important problem is the security of the Province of Texas." The report outlined the three sources from which to draw new waves of colonists for this proposed colonization effort. The first source of colonists was New Orleans and the Louisiana Territory due to the many Spanish connections there and the pre-existing contract with Moses Austin that had been carried over from the Spanish period. Moses, and later Stephen F. Austin, still planned to settle East Texas. The second source required the Mexican government to draw from its own empire to settle Texas. The reports to the National Junta suggested that there were many poor citizens living in central Mexico who could use the frontier Texas land to better their lives. It noted that many Mexican troops had already received land and a pair of mules by the decree of March 23, 1821, and the Mexican government suggested extending this land offer to expeditionary troops who joined the Independence Army during the war. The third method for enticing colonists involved the empire looking to Europe for more settlers. The commission argued that the Irish were the best candidates for settlers because of the poor climate of their homeland and because of their Catholic faith. The report concluded: "If we do not take the present opportunity to populate Texas, day by day the strength of the United States grows until they will leave their center and annex Texas, Coahuila, Saltillo, and Nuevo León like the Goths, Visigoths, and other tribes assailed the Roman Empire." The settlement of Texas represented a desire to protect the more developed provinces such as Nuevo Santander immediately south of Texas. The Rio Grande, paired with the growing town of Matamoros, represented a vital economic component for the Lower Rio Grande Valley and northern Mexico. [19]

The discussion of the various means of colonization began as early as December 19, 1821, during a congressional session. Again, on January 1 and January 11, 1822, the Mexican congress addressed the need to colonize the empire's far northern frontier. As a result of these discussions and the report by the Commission on Foreign Relations, the leaders in Mexico acknowledged what the Tejanos had already concluded: the colonization of Texas was the only viable solution for securing their northern territories. Mexico needed loyal citizens in Texas to secure its holdings, and reports from San Antonio leaders reinforced this concern. "It is absolutely necessary that the nation make some effort to populate it, "argued Antonio Martínez, referring to the northern frontier and further insisting that "admitting foreigners would be the easiest, least expensive, and fastest mode." Despite the desire by some Tejanos to recruit primarily foreign settlers, the leaders in Mexico City remained leery about letting too many foreigners into the territory for fear of their lack of loyalty to Mexico. Despite caution, necessity coerced the Mexican government into relying heavily on foreign settlers instead of trying to move their own population.[20]

In Mexico's first few years as a nation, three colonization laws passed in relatively quick succession. The laws included: the Imperial Colonization Law on January 4, 1823, the National Colonization Law on August 18, 1824, and the Coahuila-Texas State Colonization Law of March 24, 1825. Though passed at different levels of government, these laws collectively showed the begrudging acceptance of the Mexican government's reliance on foreign colonists rather than the movement of poor Mexicans to the far northern frontier as suggested by the Commission on Foreign Relations. The Imperial Colonization Law favored Mexican nationals over foreign settlers, but Stephen F. Austin and his Tejano allies quickly found loopholes in the law. The National Colonization Law began the Mexican government's reliance on Anglo settlers, but it attempted to mold them into model citizens of their own design. The Coahuila-Texas State Colonization Law added new provisions for colonization in the region. This was the first law to offer territorial gains to colonists for integrating themselves into Mexican society through marriage. Another issue relating to restricting slavery in Coahuila and Texas caused an uproar in Texas among Tejanos and Anglos. Article 13 of the state's constitution set an endpoint for slavery in the state, a stipulation that directly opposed many Anglo Texans' view of economic prosperity based on slave labor. Most of the new settlement of Texas by foreign colonists was focused in Central and East Texas, leaving the Rio Grande Valley with few new settlers. The region along the river lacked support for settlement until the 1840s with the beginning of the US-Mexican War. The rapid passing of these laws changed the political environment of the new Mexican nation and increased the uncertainty of Anglo colonists as each law was passed.[21]

The final effort to address the tumultuous issue of Texas colonization began in 1834 with a trip to Texas by Juan Nepomuceno Almonte. He produced a statistical report in January 1835 on the state of Texas that included many of his own impressions. At the beginning of his report, he asked rhetorically if "the condition of Texas is so prosperous what prevents Mexicans from enjoying its prosperity?" This question illuminated the chronic problem that had faced Mexico since its independence. On the precipice of independence, Mexico understood the imperative to populate Texas with loyal citizens, posited Almonte, but once independent it never implemented effective policies to accomplish that goal. He also noted that one of the "objections raised against the colonization of Texas by Mexicans is the distance between Mexico and Texas." He quickly dismissed this obstacle as spurious, citing that it took only fourteen days to go from Mexico City to Galveston or Brazoria. He went on to propose that retired and disabled officers be given lands in Texas in lieu of their pensions and arguing that the settlement of Texas "is an enterprise so noble and patriotic." The bulk of Almonte's report portrayed a mythic land of milk and honey, ripe for the taking for any adventurous Mexican. He described the climate, peoples, land, and economic opportunities in the state, demonstrating yet again how valuable Texas already was and certainly would become to both Mexico City and potential settlers. Clearly, Almonte saw hope for the settlement of Texas by Mexicans, but this pragmatic and optimistic policy came more than a decade too late.[22] While a policy similar to Escandón's might have worked well in the region between the Nueces River and Rio Grande, the Anglo-American settlers in Central and East

Texas disrupted the possibility of renewed settlement of the Lower Rio Grande Valley during Mexican rule.

Sadly, for Mexico City and Almonte himself, these hopes were never realized. With the outbreak of the Texas Revolution in 1836, Mexico lost control of the province of Texas, effectively ending its colonization and nation-building efforts in the region. The policies created by Mexico illustrated the need for Texas and the northern frontier to be settled both to reap the rewards of its resources and to protect it from foreign encroachment. Mexico's most significant error in its policy making was not the policies themselves, but the implementation (or lack thereof). Repeatedly Mexicans recommended that native Mexican citizens be used to colonize the frontier provinces and states. Nevertheless, these proposals were ignored until Anglo-Americans had too great a foothold in Texas. The Anglo Americans were able to achieve such solid numerical control of the territory because the Mexican government chose the most inexpensive and expedient path to populate the state. The acceptance of foreign *empresarios* to settle Anglo-American families ultimately hastened the loss of the territory that Mexico City so ardently tried to keep. It was not until the Law of April 6, 1830, that Mexico took serious steps to hinder Anglo immigration, but even these measures came late, were underfunded, and ineffectively executed.

Clearly, the Mexican government and many of its citizens understood the tenuous hold Mexico had on Texas, repeatedly making proposals to settle it with Mexican citizens. The turmoil of creating a new government after independence in 1821, however, and the continual shifts in power from a monarchy to a republic in 1823, destabilized both the central government and the economy of the nation. Without a focused and well-funded effort from Mexico City to create a coherent, native Mexican-based colonization program, the government had little other alternative than to accept foreigners as empresarios and trust their word that they and their colonists would indeed become loyal, Catholic citizens. Despite some early successes, Mexican reliance on foreign settlers, particularly Anglo-Americans, resulted in first the loss of Texas and then the entire Southwest after the Mexican-American War. Perhaps if the Mexican government had reached equilibrium after independence, it could have focused its efforts and resources on promoting colonization of the far northern frontier. The political and economic instability after 1821 prevented Mexico from pursuing policies that would have allowed it to achieve its goal of settling the Texas and preventing the loss of the territory to the United States.

THE DISPUTED RIO GRANDE VALLEY

The Texas Revolution began in 1835 when Captain Antonio Tenorio arrived in Texas to establish a customs house. Tension began to grow with Anahuac residents when a merchant was arrested and accused of smuggling. William B. Travis quickly raised a small force of armed volunteers and forced Tenorio to surrender the merchant. This action represented an armed rebellion against Mexico. Some Texians appealed to General Martín Perfecto de Cos, the Mexican commander of the Eastern Internal Provinces. Cos, however, believed military occupation of Texas was the only solution. This decision triggered a series of battles in 1835, including the Battle of Goliad and the capture of San Antonio. Initially, the revolution looked optimistic for the Texians and Tejanos, but lack of unity and very little clarity over what exactly the goal of the revolution was left an unstable situation. Mexico promptly sent Antonio López de Santa Anna to Texas to put down the insurrection. This action resulted in the famous Battle of the Alamo, where most of its defenders died, but the battle served as a rallying cry for the Texians. With the success at the Alamo, Santa Anna pushed northeast into the heart of Texian territory, beginning what became known as the "Runaway Scrape" as Texians and Tejanos alike fled eastward trying to escape capture by Mexican forces.[23]

Texas finally achieved independence from Mexico in 1836 after the Battle of San Jacinto, where Texians managed to defeat an overconfident Santa Anna and forced him to sign a treaty granting independence. The new republic claimed its southern boundary rested along the Rio Grande, though Mexico never accepted this claim or Texas's independence. This period saw demographic trends in Texas similar to the previous Mexican efforts to settle the lower Rio Grande Valley, although there was an increase in American merchants investigating the trade possibilities along the river. Texas claimed the boundary, but because it was unable to enforce that claim or settle the region, it remained under de facto control of Mexico. It would take the US Army another decade to enforce Texas's claims. The Republic of Texas failed to establish its control over the Lower Rio Grande Valley for similar reasons that Spain and Mexico had failed to do so. The continuing conflict between Mexico and Texas often involved a struggle over the Lower Rio Grande Valley because of the region's economic value. The frontier along the river proved to be difficult to settle, and thus control. It would take an international war to instigate change.[24]

During the Republic of Texas period, the significance of controlling the Rio Grande was not lost on Texan leadership. The republic's Secretary of State James Mayfield noted that, "the harbor known as Brasos Santiago and its importance to the Rio Grande, as being the only convenient shipping port of that River" was crucial to controlling the trade of South Texas and northern Mexico. He continued, "This harbor is entirely within the limits of Texas. . . . Nothing less than those limits can be accepted for our boundary." The importance of Brazos Santiago lay in the relationship between the port and Matamoros. The nation that controlled Brazos Santiago in the first three-quarters of the nineteenth century possessed de facto control of the international trade flowing in and out of northern Mexico. The Republic of Texas never capitalized on this trade, but the United States had not missed its significance. The United States Consul at Matamoros D. W. Smith noted about the port that "together with the . . . goodness of the roads that facilitate communication with the interior must necessarily give it a decided preponderance in a commercial and military point of view to any other port in the Gulf of Mexico." He continued, noting, "nor have such important natural advantages escaped the attention and enterprise of our citizens."[25]

Similar to Texas's struggle for independence, several northern Mexican states chose to break with Mexico to start their own republics. Federalist leaders in Tamaulipas (formerly Nuevo Santander), Nuevo León, and Coahuila broke from the Centralist Mexican government to create the Republic of the Rio Grande in 1840. The Republic of the Rio Grande claimed the areas of Tamaulipas and Coahuila north to the Nueces and Medina Rivers, as well as Nuevo León, Zacatecas, Durango, Chihuahua, and New Mexico. Even though Texas had several unique driving factors such as slavery for its revolution, the Lower Rio Grande Valley and surrounding states chose a similar path due to frustrations in common that pushed Texas to rebellion. Jesús de Cárdenas was elected president and Antonio Canales Rosillo as Commander-in-Chief of the Republic of the Rio Grande Army. Canales Rosillo met the Centralist Army under General Mariano Arisa on March 24–25, 1840, in battle at Morales, Coahuila. The Rio Grande Army was disastrously defeated by the Centralist forces.[26]

Complicating Texas's relationship with Mexico stemmed from Mexico's abolition of slavery within its borders. Over three-quarters of all runaway slaves in Texas headed toward Mexico rather than to free American territories or Canada. The only other nation in the Americas that had passed a law abolishing slavery as ardently as Mexico was Haiti. The Haitian Revolution occupied a particular place of fear in the American, particularly Southern, mind. Runaway slaves entering

Mexico often found work quickly in one of the towns or haciendas of northern Mexico, a region defined by a shortage of labor. While the debt peonage system in Mexico shared some similarities with slavery, Mexico maintained several legal protections for its laborers that provided a much better environment than slavery. Over four thousand fugitive slaves resided south of the Rio Grande by 1855. As enslaved Texans fled south of the Rio Grande, however, Mexican indentured servants or peons crossed the river north with hopes of escaping their versions of bondage.[27]

As an independent nation Texas did not thrive. Continued conflict with American Indians and Mexico left the fledgling republic in a precarious position. When such conflict was coupled with the growing national debt, Texas looked likely to fail as a nation, as Mexican leaders hoped. As the presidency of Texas vacillated between Sam Houston and Mirabeau B. Lamar, it became evident that the new nation would need support from a larger, more established country. The United States initially rejected Texas's request for annexation in 1836 despite a friendship between Houston and Andrew Jackson, then president of the United States. The fate of Texas changed in 1841 when William Henry Harrison, the recently elected American president, died in office and John Tyler stepped into the position. Tyler began actively trying to secure Texas annexation, but Congress would not support him. His efforts received a second wind during the campaigns for the 1844 election. The rhetoric of James K. Polk, the dark horse candidate, sparked a renewed interest in Texas. Polk called for westward expansion not only with Texas but also with the addition of the Oregon Territory. With visions of Manifest Destiny in the nation's eyes after the election of Polk in 1844, Tyler had the momentum to push for annexation.[28]

With the end of his presidency quickly approaching, President Tyler urged Congress to pass a joint resolution to admit Texas immediately to the Union. Tyler signed the bill on March 1, 1845, and then sent a messenger to Texas to present the Texas Congress with the annexation documents. Gaining Polk's and the Texas Congress's acceptance of the joint resolution, the Texas government wrote its state constitution by February 14, 1846, officially joining the United States.[29]

~

The colonization of Nuevo Santander started by José de Escandón settled the Rio Grande Valley successfully in the first few years of effort. After the initial wave of settlers, the Spanish government did not continue supporting further colonization efforts. This neglect left the region at risk from the harsh environment and hostile Native Americans. Numerous tours and visitas attempted to address the issues along the frontera, but other issues in New Spain continually prevented resources from supporting more settlement. Spain and the local governance from the Provincias Internas focused on stabilization and security rather than growth of the Valley. The Mexican War of Independence ended Spanish rule, but the Mexican government still considered settling the region an essential part of the new nation's border security.

Spanish policies and their continuation under Mexican rule allowed a relatively seamless governing the region. The porciones grants were given to Mexican families who lived in towns along the river. These early settlers made up the most dominate ethnic-Mexican stronghold in the state. Settlers obtained most of the grants as part of Escandón's early efforts at settlement of Nuevo Santander. The Mexican government pursued a policy of contracting foreign empresarios, which brought numerous European and Anglo-American settlers to Texas. Many of these settlers, particularly the latter arrivals, never assimilated into Mexican society. Even with increased Anglo-American settlement, Tejanos maintained a numerical majority along the Rio Grande despite the loss of political and economic power in the region. The only reason these superior numbers were possible was because of early settlement under Spanish and Mexican governments. Mexico could not translate these early successes into repeatable efforts elsewhere in the state, however. With the Texas Revolution and the establishment of the Republic of Texas the political landscape changed and began pulling the United States into the conflict over what became South Texas.[30]

The war between the United States and Mexico did not stem from single-minded land-lust on Polk's behalf, but rather was the result of numerous fractures among the nations, societies, and cultures mingling along the borderlands of the Lower Rio Grande Valley. The influence of Texas annexation, Comanche raids, a desire to control markets, jingoism, racism, and ideas like Manifest Destiny created the perfect storm and served as a catalyst for the roughly two-year-long war and the decade of social, political, and cultural upheaval that occurred in South Texas after the war. The quartermasters faced many of the same difficulties plaguing the colonization of the Rio Grande Valley prior to the war. At the heart of both the American war effort and the changes that occurred in the Valley was the US Army Quartermaster's Department. The men found themselves devising methods to overcome the obstacles that had thwarted first Spanish, then later Mexican, efforts at settlement. The trade networks and military bases established by the department laid the foundation for the coming changes. However intentional or unintentional the actions of the army on South Texas were, the department served as the mechanism to project United States culture and wealth, which radically altered the region's trajectory. The Mexican War brought the army with its Quartermaster's Department, which often out of necessity absorbed and expanded the existing trade networks, building new outposts that grew into towns drawing both Anglo and Mexican settlers. This war with the arrival of the Quartermaster's Department to the region was the pivotal turning point for South Texas.

CHAPTER 2

South Texas and the Nueces Strip

1846–1847

The war between the United States and Mexico is most often divided into three theaters of operation: northern, western, and central. The next three chapters will look at the logistical efforts in each of these theaters and the results they had during the postwar era, 1848–1860. The northern campaigns led by General Zachary Taylor had the greatest impact on South Texas. The US Army's march into the area allowed the Quartermaster's Department to rapidly gather information and establish trade networks to supply the troops in the field. These supply lines stretched from the northeastern United States to New Orleans, then terminated in South Texas or later Mexico as more territory was occupied.

This occupation of South Texas and northern Mexico began to radically change the newly redefined borderlands in the Rio Grande Valley. Local trade networks along the river existed before the war, but the Quartermaster's Department greatly expanded these pathways to meet the growing needs of the US Army. The building of new forts and depots laid the groundwork for economic growth in the years after the war. The demand for goods, skilled and unskilled labor, and potential for profit brought many entrepreneurs into the region to take full advantage of the opportunities presented by the presence of the army during wartime. Anglo-American and European merchants had settled in South Texas and northern Mexico since the 1820s, but additional traders flocked to the region during wartime. They took advantage of the relative free-trade zone along the Rio Grande established by the US Army during the occupation. The relationships these entrepreneurs established with Quartermaster's Department officers during the war persisted in the postwar years. Preference for supply contracts was often given to businessmen with previous army connections, most of whom were Anglo-American immigrants. As their numbers grew, they began to supplant the Mexicans and Tejanos from their previous dominance along the Rio Grande.

While the Texas border dispute over the Nueces Strip—the piece of land between the Rio Grande and Nueces Rivers—acted as the ostensible catalyst for the war, there were many additional underlying causes. The United States annexation of Texas and the pressures of Manifest Destiny—the belief that American possessed a God-given right to expand westward—fueled the fires of war. The fact that much of the land that lay between the United States and the Pacific coast belonged to Mexico furthered tensions. The refusal of Mexico to sell any of this land and settle the border dispute further agitated those already prone to hostile action. Expansionists like President James K. Polk found further cause for war after the Mexican army killed dragoon Captain Seth Thornton and several of his men along the Rio Grande as they scouted for Taylor's army. Polk declared that "we must take redress for the injuries done [to] us into our own hands, that we had attempted to conciliate Mexico in vain, and had forborne until forbearance was no longer either a virtue or patriotic; and that in my opinion we must treat all nations, whether great or small, strong or weak, alike, and that we should take a bold and firm course towards Mexico." The expansionists were not willing to use *any* means necessary, but they did not shy away from force if that meant successful expansion.[1]

This desire for expansion across North America, fueled by Manifest Destiny, led the United States into its first imperialistic war with a non-Native American nation. With the conclusion of this war, the United States almost doubled in size with its addition of the vast lands gained from Mexico. The fighting itself drew much attention from the rest of the world because it was the first time that the fledgling United States had fought a foreign power aside from its estranged political parent, Great Britain. Not much was expected of the young country with its little army, certainly not against a potentially more powerful rival such as Mexico. Many European onlookers assumed Mexico's longer history of settlement gave them an advantage. The United States soon proved it could hold its own in an international conflict.

Not all rejoiced for Texas annexation. Mexico saw it as a blatant theft of a territory in rebellion rather than the annexation of a sovereign nation, raising the prospect of war over the entire region, including, but not limited to, the contested Nueces Strip. Furthermore, the annexation treaty was vague about the southern border of Texas. Texans claimed the Rio Grande, while Mexicans argued for the more historical boundary of the Nueces River. The United States and Mexico both claimed all the land between these two rivers. Polk would again let his desire for land drive his actions. He insisted on the Rio Grande boundary and sent General Zachary Taylor from Fort Jesup on the Texas-Louisiana border to Corpus Christi to stake claim to all but the contested territory. Taylor received orders to stop at Corpus Christi until news was heard from the minister to Mexico, John Slidell. While in town, Ulysses S. Grant, a quartermaster in Taylor's army, bought mules from Mexican merchants for between $8 to $30 in preparation for the invasion. Silver bars from Monterrey arrived regularly, facilitating the trade between Mexican and Anglo merchants and the US Army.[2]

Polk's administration instructed Slidell to pursue more territorial concessions from Mexico in exchange for financial compensation. He requested that the Rio Grande boundary be accepted, the western half of New Mexico, a boundary giving San Francisco to the United States, and a settlement including California north of Monterrey. His financial limit to promise Mexico for all the enumerated territories was $50 million. When Slidell arrived in Mexico and attempted his negotiations, he was met with sharp disapproval, particularly regarding California. Mexicans contended that Texas had been stolen, and they would not give up California. Instead, the Mexican government ordered troops to reinforce Matamoros along the Rio Grande and gave instructions to resist any American attempt to claim the Nueces Strip.[3]

Zachary Taylor Occupies South Texas

In early June 1845, General Taylor received orders to mass two thousand troops at Fort Jesup, Louisiana, just across the Sabine River from Texas. By July 31, his Army of Occupation had arrived in Corpus Christi. On May 26, 1846, Quartermaster General Thomas Sydney Jesup, for whom the fort was named, had already requisitioned three hundred wagons with harnesses to be shipped to Texas for the army's movement. As Taylor and his army arrived, Captain George H. Crosman, as acting assistant quartermaster, worked to acquire wagons for the supply train. Having graduated from the United States Military Academy at West Point in 1823, he served across the various midwestern posts until rising to prominence in the Quartermaster's Department during the Seminole and Mexican Wars. Crosman estimated at least one hundred wagons would be needed to have a train capable of supporting a movement to the Rio Grande. As Crosman gathered what wagons he could in Texas, Assistant Quartermaster General Henry Stanton ordered fifty more wagons shipped from the Schuylkill Arsenal in Philadelphia.[4]

The Philadelphia Depot—built in 1800 and originally named the Schuylkill Arsenal—manufactured, housed, and shipped most of the supplies for the army. The demand during the Mexican-American War vastly exceeded its production capabilities. If they were not manufactured here, most supplies from the northeastern United States passed through this depot after purchase. The Philadelphia Depot also had the important role of storing supplies for both the navy and the army. Its proximity to Delaware Bay contributed to its importance because it could easily send manufactured or purchased goods by ship to another appropriate depot. This central depot demonstrated the growing industrial strength of the United States and allowed the army to harness that strength to better wage war. A supplemental depot was the Allegheny Arsenal—established on April 9, 1814, in Pittsburgh, Pennsylvania—which became a major production point for leather goods, rifle and pistol ammunition, and the storage of large artillery pieces manufactured at nearby Fort Pitt Foundry.[5]

Jesup appointed Colonel Trueman Cross to serve in the Southwest as the chief assistant quartermaster and assigned him in August 1845 to General Taylor's headquarters. The Maryland-born soldier served under Andrew Jackson in 1814 and Winfield Scott as he rose in rank through the Quartermaster's Department. Cross directed logistical affairs in Texas and its vicinity. By September 1845, Stanton concluded that "the concentration of troops, and the probability of active field operations on our Texas frontier, impose upon this office the obligation of increasing the number of officers of the quartermaster's department on duty with the 'army of occupation.'" But Cross, under Stanton's orders, received few additional personnel to stockpile supplies for a possible war. He did receive orders to "have 85 four-horse wagons built for the use of the army serving in Texas" as well as to procure harnesses for mules and horses. Cross also employed wheelwrights and smiths to produce extra "spokes, fellies, and hounds" for wagon field repairs. He concluded that a total of 265 wagons would be necessary to move the army to the Rio Grande, including the seventy-six companies of regulars, professional soldiers who are part of the armed forces during peace and war, in or on their way to Texas. While steamships carried the supplies to the coastal depots such as Victoria, Corpus Christi, and later Brazos Santiago, long wagon trains supplied the armies in the field.[6]

The small trading post city of Corpus Christi, established by Henry Lawrence Kinney and William P. Aubrey in 1839, blossomed with the arrival of the US Army. The Pennsylvania native Kinney arrived in Texas after failed land speculation in Illinois and ingratiated himself in Rio Grande society due to his ease in speaking Spanish and communicating with many of the Native Americans in the region. Kinney was willing to work with anyone—Anglo, Mexican, or Native American—if it meant he could improve business. Such a mindset served many who sought to overcome the harsh environment of the Rio Grande frontier. Many of the merchants and laborers of Corpus Christi were of Mexican decent, but they still seemed willing to trade and work for the army camped near the burgeoning town of Corpus Christi. Several Anglo merchants already settled in the Rio Grande borderlands were primed to supply Taylor's army when it arrived. They knew the terrain, markets, and established trading routes to and across the river. The influence of merchants like Kinney, Henry Clay Davis, and John Kelsey aided the quartermasters in securing trade routes.[7]

Overland Transport and Supply

Wagons and draught animals became some of the most valuable commodities for the Quartermaster's Department during this period. Without them armies would be crippled, unable to advance into the field. The department estimated that one wagon per company was needed, eight for field staff, and six for the general headquarters. Taylor's army of roughly twenty-five hundred to four thousand, depending on the engagement, required a minimum of fifty wagons. These numbers accounted only for the baggage of an army, not the perishable foodstuffs and fodder. One hundred seventy-five additional wagons were needed for fodder, artillery, and other supplies that an army should take into the field. Wagons accompanying the army often numbered in excess of two hundred, but hundreds more traveled the various supply routes to resupply the armies as they marched. The depots in the northern United States built some of the wagons that were sent to the fronts, but many more were purchased to keep up with army needs. The Department paid around $110 per "quality" wagon. By January 29, 1847, the Schuylkill Arsenal had four hundred wagons and two thousand mule harnesses awaiting further orders. The department calculated how many wagons would fit on a ship to help determine whether a vessel should be chartered or purchased. By September 5, 1846, the initial procurement of wagons reached its apex. Jesup confessed, "We have now a greater number of wagons, than the service requires.[8]" Without this emphasis on wagon procurement, the movement of troops would have suffered.[9]

The quartermasters purchased horses, mules, and oxen in huge quantities from across the southern United States and sent them south to help supply the army. Deputy Quartermaster General Colonel Thomas F. Hunt, who commanded

New Orleans Department, ordered Major Nathaniel Anderson to purchase two hundred horses, one hundred for draught and one hundred for dragoon service, from Memphis, Tennessee. General Jesup directed the purchase of several hundred mules from western Georgia and southern Alabama to be sent to Colonel Hunt in New Orleans. These were to be held in reserve should the need for mules arise suddenly from the Rio Grande. Jesup also directed a selection of horses by the Second Regiment of Dragoons for their own use from those belonging to the public, paying the original cost of the horses. By January 1846, Cross had 592 oxen with the army, with almost half of these used daily to haul grass for the animals and wood for the regiments and depot. The Quartermaster's Department often purchased cattle to travel with the marching armies and be slaughtered as needed to feed the troops. Armies in every theater used this method to provide for the soldiers while far from supply lines. The quartermasters purchased hundreds, if not thousands, of animals throughout South Texas and Mexico during the war. Without these animals, the progression of the war would have stalled.[10]

New Orleans operated as the center of logistics for the Mexican War. Even though Jesup and Stanton kept the main quartermaster's office in Washington, all major logistical maneuvering occurred at New Orleans. Most of the supplies

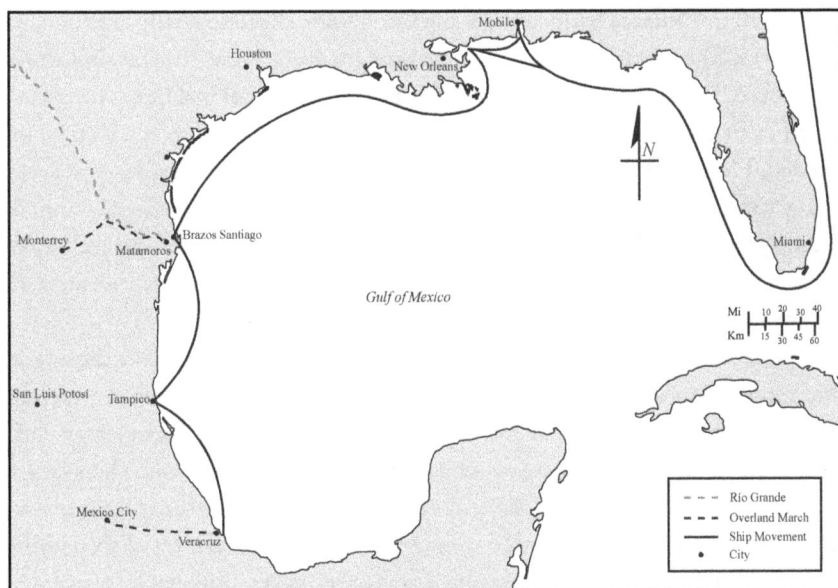

Quartermaster Gulf Transport and Supply Routes

and troops headed to Mexico to join either Taylor's or Scott's armies passed
through New Orleans, making the port city a central gathering point for the
war. Situated on the Mississippi River, which connects to the Ohio River, New
Orleans received most inland river travel before it reached the sea. Its proximity
to Pensacola, Florida, and Mobile, Alabama, also made it an ideal command
location to direct the transports from those nearby ports. The depot also acted
as the major coaling station after Key West, making it a necessary stop for most
steamships. Mobile also served as a supplemental gathering point for men and
vessels destined for Mexico.[11]

Horses and other draught animals were a double-edged sword for the army.
They made supply trains possible, but the quantity of fodder they ate greatly
increased the length of trains, necessitating more animals to pull wagons of
fodder. The Quartermaster's Department ordered twenty-five thousand bushels
of oats shipped monthly to Brazos Santiago from New York. Thousands of
bags of oats in gunny sacks traveled from the northern United States to New
Orleans and on to Brazos Santiago every month. Additional forage obtained at
New Orleans was also shipped across the Gulf. In South Texas and Mexico, the
army utilized what forage grew in the operations theater and purchased more
from Anglos, Tejanos, and Mexicans throughout the war.[12]

Even more difficult than procuring draught animals was recruiting wagon
drivers. In the Nueces Strip, labor was a rare commodity, especially experienced
teamsters. Therefore, drivers had to be brought from New Orleans, but these
men often lacked the experience they claimed to have. Colonel Cross proposed
an efficient corps of enlisted drivers, ready to join the army in the field when
needed. He feared that the existing voluntary system could paralyze the army
at any time. Here Cross pushed, unknowingly, toward a more modern system of
military logistics. He saw the need for a reliable, cost-effective solution and began
working toward that goal, which would ultimately result in the recruitment of
future soldiers for the purpose of transport and logistics.[13]

The department recruited teamsters as the last component to make the wagon
and mule trains work effectively. Teamsters initially were civilian contractors
with the army. The basic contract teamsters received was a form letter with
some blanks to fill with details such as name and date of service. The average
teamster "agree[d] to serve in the United States Quarter Master's Department,
as a *Teamster* with the Army in Texas or Mexico" for a typical term of six months
and received deck passage to and from Texas or Mexico on any public transport.
They received twenty-five dollars per month, a sizeable sum, and were supplied

one ration per day. This recruitment presented a lucrative opportunity for the adventurous American.[14] Teamsters were also hired at four or five dollars a day, if they had their own wagons with horses or mules. Mexican muleteers could be hired for fifty-five cents per day. Even though the United States was at war with Mexico, many Mexicans chose to work for the American army because of reliable employment and steady pay. This decision was particularly common in northern Mexico on the frontier of Mexican territory where the influence of Mexico City was the weakest.[15] This workforce later became a factor in the reshaping of South Texas during the immediate postwar period.

Despite the harsh environment of South Texas and northern Mexico, opportunities existed to live off the land. Commanders and quartermasters often turned to the area of operation to obtain goods. Even if these goods cost a premium compared to their purchase price at home, the savings from transportation costs as well as their immediate availability made such goods desirable. Many Mexican citizens were more than willing to trade with the American army, primarily because quartermasters brought dollars to purchase goods. The American "silver eagles" represented a persuasive tool for acquiring goods while far from established supply lines. Furthermore, on the frontera of Mexican territories, the loyalty of citizens had weakened over the preceding decades. This sentiment was particularly evident in Santa Fe and the California territories that were far removed from the influence of Mexico City. Mexican officials in the Rio Grande Valley often cooperated with the army for the dual reasons of greater economic benefit and control of their citizens. At the same time, American merchants often traveled with the armies, providing supplemental resources and trading with Mexican citizens along the way. This trade with Mexicans established new ties between American and Mexican markets. All three theaters managed to provide local resources to supplement what the department provided at the outset of a march or during a campaign via supply lines.[16]

While Cross and other quartermasters struggled to furnish Taylor's army, Hunt shouldered the burden of quartering the troops arriving in New Orleans. They awaited Taylor's orders about their destination in Texas. He had to find lodging for them and procure sea transport to Corpus Christi. Taylor preferred steamships, which operated more reliably than sail. When soldiers arrived in New Orleans from their respective states, the quartermaster directed them to Andrew Jackson's old battleground for encampment until ships arrived for embarking. Private J. Jacob Oswandel wrote about his excitement at being at the same place where Jackson once fought the British. Many of the men who invaded Mexico at

Veracruz, such as Colonel George T. M. Davis—an aide-de-camp for General Scott—explored New Orleans while they waited to be transferred to transports that carried them to Mexico. New Orleans was the beating heart at the center of the lifeline that supplied and manned the United States invasion force.[17]

Seaborne Logistics

With tensions mounting between the United States and Mexico, the Quartermaster's Department began buying and chartering many sail and steamships. Finding enough satisfactory ships posed a problem for the department, especially after the added transportation demands of General Winfield Scott's expedition to Veracruz in 1847. Purchasing or chartering vessels proved to be difficult, but finding experienced pilots to guide the river steamers up the treacherous Rio Grande became a primary task. The Rio Grande was marked by ever shifting sandbars that regularly threatened to run steamers aground. It required a skilled pilot to navigate the constantly changing, shallow river and carry supplies to the newly established depots. The only way the Quartermaster's Department could acquire skilled pilots from elsewhere in the United States was to hire them as private contractors. Men like Mifflin Kenedy and Richard King filled these roles well and successfully managed the river, keeping goods flowing during the war. Kenedy and King would capitalize on their relationship with the department after the war to establish their own shipping and ferrying monopoly on the Rio Grande. This effort provided them with the money necessary to expand into real estate and ranching across South Texas.[18]

The primary mode of transportation was the sea, both by sail and by steam. With the onset of the war, the Quartermaster's Department began chartering or buying as many vessels as it could reasonably manage. Finding enough vessels (most sailing ships had three or more masts) posed a problem for the department. The army quartermasters sought "vessels of suitable charters at competitively low rates to be taken up at New York and Philadelphia . . . in the first instance with the understanding that their monthly services can after the discharge of their outward cargo be commanded at stated rates should the Department think proper to employ them under such conditional agreement." Some charters offered the option to be renewed for three months after the initial delivery if the shipping was acceptable. Many shipping contracts originated in Philadelphia, where the Schuylkill Arsenal was located.[19]

Steamships presented a new tool for the army and navy. Steam power allowed ships to travel without being completely reliant upon the whims of the wind to carry them to their destination. They fulfilled the same basic roles as sailing ships in troop and supply transportation. Shallow draft steamboats allowed the movement of men and supplies to inland locations such as Camargo, Mexico— opposite of what is now Rio Grande City—along the Rio Grande. Armies gained new flexibility and mobility thanks to steamships. Furthermore, many of the men in Scott's army, as well as Scott himself, made their way to Mexico aboard steamers.[20]

The terms of the charters were similar for all steamships. The basic language included the following provisions: $220 per day (deducting $100 each day the engine was not used) to be paid upon delivery of the cargo, up to about $5,400, and the owner had to furnish all coal. The contract for one ship, the *Endora*, followed very similar lines but included other provisions. It had to be officered, manned, and kept in good repair at all times. The charter included stipulation that the "United States [had] the privilege to purchase the vessel at the end of her charter for $20,000 deducting from that sum $100 per day for the whole period for which she may have received full pay ($220) on her charter." The *Ocean* and *Ashland* were each purchased for $17,000, a similar sum as specified in the *Endora*'s charter, except that these were bought outright. A particularly interesting purchase by the department was the steamer *Massachusetts*. It became Scott's flagship, from which he led the Veracruz invasion, although it was initially acquired to move troops from New Orleans to Brazos Santiago. The difficulty in financing such contracts is clear: the contract for the purchase was made in New Orleans, with the ship being transferred to Hunt's possession, but the bill was paid by Stanton in Washington.[21]

To feed their voracious engines, steamships had to ensure that they carried enough coal for their voyage or that there were coaling stations along the way, where they could resupply. Maintaining the supply of coal for the army trans-ports and navy ships became one of the major tasks for the Quartermaster's Department. The department bought two types of coal—general anthracite and Cumberland—to fuel steamships and supply depots. On September 25, 1846, General Jesup directed one of his quartermasters in Louisville, Kentucky, to contract with the Louisville Coal Company for fifty thousand barrels of coal for steamboats to be delivered to New Orleans. In Philadelphia the quartermaster ordered two thousand tons of "the best anthracite" at $4.25 a ton and freight at $4.50 and $6.50 to Key West and Brazos Santiago, respectively. Purchases such as these continued throughout the war to keep men and supplies flowing to the frontlines. Despite the burden of supplying coal to the depots, the advantage gained in both speed and reliability of movement was essential to the war effort. Steam power kept the vessels moving forward regardless of the fickle Gulf of Mexico weather.[22]

River transport was essential in both preparing goods to ship from the depots and carrying supplies to Mexico, particularly along the Rio Grande. The Quartermaster's Department already used private contractors to carry men and goods along rivers such as the Ohio, Monongahela, and Mississippi. The river transports were usually shallow-bottom steamboats that performed well on wide rivers like the Mississippi. Supplies had to be transferred to larger ships with a deeper draft to make the ocean portion of the journey. One of the significant problems facing the department became moving some shallow-draft river steamers from the inland waterways across the Gulf of Mexico to the Rio Grande. The storms that arose within the Gulf caused many delays and damaged many of the vessels on their journey. Once on the Rio Grande, the boats faced the troubles of a far shallower river than the main American waterways, worsened by ever-shifting sandbars. The shipping along the Rio Grande improved over the course of the war, which translated to an increased trade network in South Texas after hostilities ended in 1848. The initial trade contract went to M. Kenedy and Company (owned by Mifflin Kenedy, Richard King, and Charles Stillman), but another competing riverboat company contested their trade monopoly.[23]

Taylor Crosses into the Nueces Strip

It took weeks of preparation to ready Taylor's Army of Occupation for its trip by land and sea to the Rio Grande. One of Taylor's officers, John Robinson, wrote about receiving the orders that "the whole Army is now bound for the Mexican Frontier." Robinson expanded on the orders received, relating to his brother that, "Genl. Taylor has received orders to go to the Rio Grande. . . . We shall be on our way to that river alltho he is authorized to take his own time for the movement." He added, "This I think will soon bring matters to a crisis and I presume our ministers to Mexico will then be treated with some respect." [24] Many like Robinson concluded that the presence of the army on the southern border would persuade Mexico to yield to American desires, but that did not prove to be the case. Fortunately for Robinson and his comrades, the preparations included gathering supplies, wagons, and ships for the waterborne portion, as well as vitally important water rations since there was little access to fresh water between Corpus Christi and Matamoros. Lieutenant John James Peck recalled what the army brought on their march south. "We have horses, oxen and wagons, and the rainy season is about coming on. We have four thousand troops of the best kind, thirty odd pieces of artillery, and the strong desire to go. In addition to this force, the general is authorized to call out three thousand Texans who are already enrolled."[25]

The department's lack of intelligence about the Lower Rio Grande limited its ability to formulate practical logistics. The United States planners had virtually no maps of the border regions nor solid information concerning what resources could be foraged or purchased along the Rio Grande. Slow communication accentuated the reluctance of some commanding officers to work together, most notably Taylor and Jesup, and thus the army often struggled to stay fully supplied. Urgent requests such as boats to cross a river rarely could be answered in time, and so officers often found other options to complete their tasks, such as acquiring boats or supplies from locals, often through purchase with US currency. Although the telegraph revolutionized communication by 1845, the technology had not made it to the Southwest and was not used tactically during the war.[26]

On January 13, 1846, General Taylor began leading his army from Corpus Christi to the east bank of Rio Grande, near Point Isabel to capture Brazos Santiago. Taylor declared that "the occupation of Point Isabel or Brazos Santiago as a depot will be indispensable." Once taken, this base acted as a supply depot for Taylor's army, receiving its supplies directly from New Orleans. The "necessity of having our movement and position at Brazos Santiago covered by a small armed vessel" was "vitally important" to Taylor. Commodore David Conner of the Home Squadron provided these ships. Taylor's force consisted of 3,550 men and officers, followed by a supply train of 307 oxcarts and mule-drawn wagons. The supply train had not received all the wagons Cross requisitioned in September 1845, but enough traveled with the army to prevent delay.[27]

While the march towards Brazos Santiago started pleasantly enough, it soon turned hot and dry, with the army going without water for thirty-six hours. A total of nineteen hundred horses and mules and five hundred oxen moved with the troops. When the army approached the Arroyo Colorado, northeast of present-day Harlingen, Texas, some of the Mexican cavalry made it known that crossing the river would be "an act of hostility." In response, Taylor readied for a full-scale river assault the next day. The "crossing was then commenced and executed in the order prescribed. Not a shot was fired." On March 24, 1846, Taylor inspected Point Isabel and saw that his seaborne units had arrived. Quartermaster Charles Thomas received the task of establishing the Brazos Santiago Depot. Born in Philadelphia in 1797, Thomas switched army branches several times before settling in the Quartermaster's Department in 1826. Thomas conducted the fleet transfer of supplies and troops to Point Isabel and began setting up the new depot. It was backbreaking work to get the supplies ashore. The cargo had to be transferred twice to get it ashore because vessels drawing more than four and a half to five feet of water could not make the landing. The supplies had to go from the seagoing transports to the department's light steamers, and then from the latter to flats and light boats. Colonel Cross hoped to alleviate much of this tedium once his men built a wharf with the supplies from New Orleans. Sadly, Cross never saw his plans come to fruition. Banditti killed him outside the camp at Matamoras, and Thomas replaced him as chief of the Quartermaster's Department with the Army of Occupation.[28]

Regardless of the change of quartermasters, Taylor's army began to feel the tension before the full outbreak of war. Lieutenant Peck concluded, "We are to march to the boundary of Mexico and take our position on the Rio Grande. We shall move to a point called San Isabel, about twenty miles from the Mexican city of Matamoros. We shall go in sight of Mexican troops and their defenses. This will bring matters to a crisis. We shall either have to fight them, or they will come to terms and negotiate."[29] The hope that the movement of the army to the Rio Grande would prod Mexican diplomats to concede to American demands was not fulfilled, however. Instead of the army's forward movements acting as a political nudge, they became a catalyst for war.

Taylor and his army advanced to Palo Alto, catching their first glimpse of Mexico and the Rio Grande on the afternoon of March 24, 1846. In response to an ultimatum presented to Taylor by Mexican General Pedro de Ampudia to return north of the Nueces River, on April 14 Taylor ordered the navy to blockade the mouth of the Rio Grande and seize any supplies destined for Matamoros. Robinson reported to his brother that "fifty men commanded by Capt. [Seth B.] Thornton who were out on a reconnaissance were surrounded by about two thousand Mexican Lancers [and the] infantry [were] captured with the loss of one officer." He added, "Two wounded men were sent into our camp by the Mexican Commander. . . . You see by this that the war has fairly commenced. Mexico has stricken the blow that will cause her downfall & I hope to see the star spangled banner waving over the city of Mexico." With the killing or wounding of sixteen of his soldiers and the capture of some fifty more on April 26, Taylor sent a dispatch to President James K. Polk that "American blood has been shed on American soil," giving Polk the formal justification to ask Congress for a declaration of war. Polk, just as many of the soldiers, seemed primed to wage this war.[30]

The decision to declare war on Mexico in May 1846 resulted from the president's speech to Congress claiming, "The cup of forbearance had been exhausted even before the recent information from the frontier of the Del Norte. But now, after reiterated menaces, Mexico has passed the boundary of the United States, has invaded our territory, and shed American blood on American soil. She has proclaimed that hostilities have commenced, and that the two nations are now at war." Polk minced no words and made his point of view clear to Congress, which quickly voted for a declaration of war against Mexico on May 13. Despite resounding support, some in Congress did eventually speak out against the war with the Spot Resolutions in December 1847, including a young politician named Abraham Lincoln.[31]

The war against Mexico appeared as a war of aggression to some on both sides of the Rio Grande. The Nueces Strip, the land between the Nueces and Rio Grande, had inherently little economic benefit before the start of the war. It had always been sparsely settled by the Spanish, Mexicans, and Texans. However, Daniel W. Smith, the United States consul at Matamoros, and James Shannon Mayfield, the Texas secretary of state made clear, the wealth of northern Mexico flowed through Matamoros. Therefore, to control the economy of northern Mexico, it was essential to control the port of Matamoros: Brazos Santiago. It is certainly too reductive to claim that Brazos Santiago was the cause of the Mexican War, but it is undeniable that the United States took the economic interests in Matamoros and Brazos Santiago into consideration before deciding to go to war. The possession of Brazos Santiago placed control of San Luis Potosi, Saltillo, and Matamoros markets firmly in the hands of the Americans. The war against Mexico also served as a catalyst for settlement in the Rio Grande Valley for Mexicans, Tejanos, and Anglo-Americans, but the Anglos slowly came to dominate the region due to the influence of the military installations. While many factors influenced President Polk's decision to go to war, reaping the economic rewards of controlling northern Mexico's import and export economy certainly had not been overlooked.[32]

The Seventh Infantry held Fort Texas across from Matamoros while Taylor moved the rest of his army back to Brazos Santiago for supplies. Fort Texas was "a strong bastioned field fort, for a garrison of 500 men . . . laid out by the engineers in rear of the battery." Taylor initially established this fort to "enable brigade to maintain this position against any Mexican odds, and will leave me [Taylor] free to dispose of the other corps as considerations of health and convenience may render desirable." Taylor made sure that his army "cover[ed] its supplies at Brazos Santiago." Even over the short distance from Brazos Santiago to Fort Texas, Taylor guarded his supply lines and established a small fort to protect his main force's movements away from Matamoros. Major Jacob Brown held Fort Texas against ineffective Mexican artillery, allowing Taylor's Army of Occupation to begin moving back towards the post from Brazos Santiago. At Palo Alto, Taylor's scouts discovered General Mariano Arista's soldiers in position, blocking the road to Matamoros.[33]

On May 7, 1846, Taylor wrote a dispatch to army headquarters in Washington stating that he would "march this day with the main body of the army to open a communication with Major Brown, and throw forward supplies of ordnance and provisions." In the same dispatch, he noted that the first "recruits under Lieutenant Daniel H. McPhail arrived" at Brazos Santiago; they could serve as a garrison and allow his main force to depart for Matamoros. Taylor's march towards the Rio Grande marked the beginning of the Mexican-American War in earnest. Taylor would take the city of Matamoros without much bloodshed, making it the first Mexican city occupied by American forces. This point also marked the beginning of the troubles that the Quartermaster's Department had to overcome.[34]

As Taylor marched south towards Matamoros, Brigadier General John E. Wool organized his regulars in San Antonio de Bexar. Those soldiers included one squadron of the First Dragoons, one squadron of Second Dragoons, three companies from the Sixth Infantry, plus volunteer units—a regiment of Kentucky horse, one Kentucky infantry company, and two regiments of Illinois infantry, roughly thirty-four hundred troops in total. With supplies already shipped to Brazos Santiago to support Taylor, the Quartermaster's Department also shipped goods to the port at Lavaca to supply San Antonio. Ships carried goods from the United States to Lavaca, where they were loaded on pack mules or into wagons, which transported the goods overland to San Antonio. Eventually, the supply line extended to Camargo, Mexico. The quartermaster position at Lavaca transferred from Massachusetts born Lieutenant Colonel Henry Whiting to Thomas. Whiting traveled south to support Taylor's operations more directly, while Thomas was assigned to serve as the quartermaster in charge of departmental operations with the division under Wool's command. As Whiting and Thomas worked in Texas, Jesup sent regular orders to Hunt in New Orleans to continue and expand supply shipments to Texas in preparation for expected operations in northern Mexico.[35]

WARTIME FUNDING AND LOGISTICS

By May 13, 1846, Congress passed an act to provide for the prosecution of the war between the United States and Mexico. The primary clause of the act gave the president the ability to call into service up to fifty thousand volunteers to serve twelve months. At the start of the war, the army included 637 officers and 5,925 enlisted soldiers (total 6,562). The number of regulars increased to over 36,000 with an additional 73,500 volunteers. About 116,000 men saw service during the war, but only a fraction of that number was active in the field at any given moment. The short-term enlistments of three- and six-months meant that some soldiers only briefly participated in the war. The act also appropriated $10 million to fund the war. This allotment of money quickly proved inadequate, forcing Congress to approve new funds to continue the war. A few of the provisions aided the Quartermaster's Department's effort to supply the new volunteers. The act expected the new volunteers to "furnish their own clothes, and if cavalry, their own horses and horse equipment; and when mustered into the service shall be armed at the expense of the United States." This stipulation put much of the initial outfitting burden on the individual soldiers, particularly in the procurement of clothing. Volunteers received a stipend for clothing rather than a uniform provided by the department.[36]

Jesup struggled to ensure that his department met the growing needs of the army. Increasing the number of staff certainly helped, but having enough currency to keep the Quartermaster's Department in New Orleans functioning proved to be a challenge. Given its position as a central hub for the logistics network, much of the purchasing and payments for the entire Quartermaster's Department occurred in New Orleans. To meet the needs of the military, the department made sure to keep enough money on hand to pay its contracts. One exchange of letters illustrates the vast sums of money the department moved to pay for the war. Stanton, while Jesup was inspecting various depots, sent Captain Michael M. Clark, an assistant quartermaster from Washington, DC, to New York to withdraw $500,500 from the assistant treasurer, which was "destined for the service of the Department at New Orleans." Clark was ordered to take the "most expedit[ed] route from New York to New Orleans in the execution of the order." This entry was particularly interesting given that the withdrawal would most likely have been made in specie. This huge sum was put aboard a ship with Captain Clark, who then sailed to New Orleans. The withdrawal was made on November 24, 1846, twelve days after General Winfield Scott's proposal to invade Mexico at Veracruz was presented to President Polk. It is apparent that this transfer was made in preparation for the additional demands that Scott's expedition placed on the Quartermaster's Department.[37]

The Secretary of the Treasury, at the urging of President Polk, sought to keep the cost of the war manageable by utilizing Mexico's own import and export duties as a revenue source. When the army or marines captured a port, it became American policy to reopen the port under American administration and collect the prescribed duties, giving the standard portion to the local government, but keeping what normally went to Mexico City for wartime use. Over the course of the war, Winfield Scott managed to extract about $4 million from Mexican sources. Quartermasters used at least a portion of that revenue to supplement the procurement of supplies while in Mexico.[38]

Despite a growing stream of supplies and animals into Texas, Jesup worried about the horses and mules available for army use. He received requisitions from dragoon units requesting replacement mounts for ones lost in battle. Jesup lacked the knowledge of whether horses and mules could be reliably procured in northern Mexico, so he began shipping as many south as he could. In addition, he ordered his quartermasters in Texas and northern Mexico to begin purchasing any such available animals. To ensure enough animals were available for the army's needs, Jesup sent several quartermasters and agents to procure horses and mules in the Mississippi Valley. Quartermasters loaded the purchased animals onto river steamboats and sent them to New Orleans where they were transferred to ocean steamers to travel to Mexico.[39]

The mustering, supply, and movement of troops fell heavily on the shoulders of the Quartermaster's Department. When the war officially started on May 13, 1846, the United States Army was a small force, given the significant disarmament it had undergone after each war, in part due to the American fear of large standing armies. Waging a large-scale war against Mexico meant mustering volunteer citizen-soldiers to fight. Each of the regiments included a theoretical total of 948 men. Not many volunteer regiments maintained this exact number of men, but the Quartermaster's Department used this number when allotting supplies and obtaining transportation for each regiment.[40]

After the individual officers recruited their companies and regiments, it fell to the Quartermaster's Department to manage and move the hordes of volunteers from the various states. Usually, the troops traveled first to New Orleans.

Joel Oswandel and his company made their way to the Ohio River, where they boarded a chartered steamboat that took them to the Mississippi River and on to New Orleans. The Quartermaster's Department organized transports to take the regiment of Gaines's Georgia volunteers from Montgomery, Alabama, by way of the Alabama River to Mobile to await further orders. This was just the first leg of the three- to four-month journey to Mexico for the new volunteers. This task was easy for the quartermasters because there were many ships along these rivers that could be chartered to move troops. With each movement of troops, the quartermasters assigned to the respective areas requisitioned supplies to be prepared at the various central gathering points, such as New Orleans. Thus, for every movement a group of troops made, the Quartermaster's Department had to coordinate with its various branches by letter to prepare supplies to outfit these men before sending them to their respective theaters.[41]

As more volunteers answered the call to arms, the department provided each of them with supplies and transportation to Mexico. When news reached Jesup of the outbreak of war, he quickly began procuring the supplies needed to support the army. This became the first war for the US Army in which the telegraph expedited wartime procurement orders, though as previously mentioned the technology was not available for tactical use. Just two years before the war, the government had financed a line between Washington and Baltimore, while private enterprises added telegraph lines between New York and Philadelphia. This development allowed Jesup to submit his requisitions from the Schuylkill Arsenal in Philadelphia with unheard of ease and speed. It became standard procedure to follow telegrams with letters the next day to ensure the officers received the orders, which was another clear example of technological advances being followed by policy innovations in the modernizing army.[42]

One of the first requisitions issued by Jesup was for camp equipment to support the new recruits on their way to Mexico. General Scott recommended some twenty thousand men be mustered in as volunteers for the war. Jesup quickly acted, sending procurement orders to Stanton for 650 wall tents, 3,523 common tents, 800 spades, 1,760 axes, 4,082 hatches, 3,523 camp kettles, 7,045 mess pans, and 20,000 each of tin canteens, haversacks, and knapsacks. Jesup directed these supplies to New Orleans as the main gathering point for the new volunteers.[43]

The onset of war brought for the department another problem of procuring enough transport vessels to carry more men and supplies to Mexico. Many of the volunteers gathered at New Orleans and waited impatiently for the procurement of their transports to Brazos Santiago. Colonel Hunt worked diligently to arrange their transportation. He purchased seagoing vessels at prices ranging from $3,000 for a small schooner to $85,000 for the steamer *Massachusetts*, and he chartered many others. He also established a coal depot at New Orleans of sufficient size to meet the needs of all probable demands for transportation of an army of twenty to twenty-five thousand men. Hunt received key support in purchasing and chartering from Colonel Stanton in Philadelphia and Lieutenant Colonel Whiting in New York before his transfer to Taylor's army.[44]

A lack of accurate knowledge of how many men needed to be fed, equipped, and transported complicated efforts to supply them. Taylor's army was particularly difficult in this regard. The volunteers responded so quickly that it initially overwhelmed Taylor and his logistical network. The flood of men stemmed from a combination of good intentions, poor instructions, and army regulations. Congress instructed Taylor to call upon the governors of Texas and Louisiana for nearly five thousand men as soon as hostilities began in April. Major General Edmund P. Gaines further complicated the situation by taking upon himself the mustering of more than eight thousand troops before the War Department could manage his recruitment efforts. Posted at New Orleans, he was instructed to assist in organizing and supplying these volunteer regiments but instead recruited thousands more without direct approval. His actions were deemed illegal, resulting in many of these volunteers being returned home without having seen action. Despite the effort at recruiting volunteers, the bulk of the army remained regular troops.[45]

After his victory at Palo Alto, Taylor advanced and took Matamoros, the first Mexican city south of the Rio Grande occupied by American forces. While securing Point Isabel and Brazos Santiago, the force Taylor left at Fort Texas across from Matamoros came under siege on May 3, 1846, for 160 hours. The bombardment injured thirteen soldiers, two of whom died, including Major Jacob Brown. Following his death the fort was renamed in his honor with the future settlement of Brownsville adopting his name as well. When Taylor's forces returned to the Rio Grande after the two battles in South Texas, they relieved the siege on Fort Texas (Brown). Shortly after, the Mexican General Mariano Arista agreed to withdraw from Matamoros and accepted Taylor's offer of allowing Arista's wounded to stay in the city. When the Americans crossed the Rio Grande, Matamoros became the first foreign city occupied by American forces.[46]

While the initial confrontations of the war were won by the United States, Taylor and his army began facing logistical obstacles. The Quartermaster's

A Camp Kitchen.

Many soldiers, particularly volunteers, had a rude awakening when joining the army and adapting to camp life. For the first time they did not have women, servants, or slaves to help them prepare food, clean, or mend clothes. They quickly learned these skill or spent what little pay they received in the field on such services. Image courtesy of the University of Texas at Arlington.

Department and Taylor did not know how to handle the large influx of volunteers into his camps. Rapid volunteering from Texas caused immediate problems, while more arrivals from across the country left the department unsure of how many soldiers they needed to equip and transport. Taylor himself was unsure how to handle so many new recruits within an army destined for the front lines of a war. These men came with little training and equipment, although the Texans did have some experience from the Texas Revolution and subsequent conflicts with Mexico. Recruits began arriving just as Taylor began his occupation of Matamoros. To compound the supply problems, Congress's call for volunteers resulted in some of the first twelve-month regiments arriving on the Rio Grande in June. The number of troops drastically increased, but the department had not had time to expand its capabilities for supplying and transporting them. The quartermasters hurriedly began purchasing and chartering vessels to carry men and supplies to Brazos Santiago, the island depot occupied by Taylor.[47]

Taylor's march to Corpus Christi brought the US Army into first contact with the Mexican, Anglo, and European settlers of South Texas. The connections established with these merchants, such as Kinney and Stillman, created ripples throughout the next decade. These merchants, Anglo, Mexican, and European alike, welcomed the opportunity to trade with the US Army and to use the war to expand their trade routes further into Mexico. As the Quartermaster's Department needed supplies, labor, and information, these merchants proved more than happy to share their expertise. The quartermasters worked diligently to supply and transport the new recruits to South Texas as the declaration of war followed the Thornton Affair. Existing supply lines expanded, and the department established new ones to meet the needs of the expanding conflict. Jesup and his officers utilized all their resources, including the merchants of South Texas to achieve their goal of supplying Taylor's army.

Taylor's battles at Palo Alto and Resaca de la Palma along with the siege of Fort Texas and occupation of Matamoros began the war in earnest. The quartermasters managed to provide Taylor and his force with the necessary equipment and vittles to defeat the defending Mexican forces twice and push Arista to surrender Matamoros without a bloody fight. The first occupation of a foreign city brought American culture, merchants, and money into Matamoros, permanently changing the city. As the army settled into its role as occupier, the Quartermaster's Department began preparing the push deeper into Mexico. Moving men and supplies along the Rio Grande seemed the most advantageous, but the department still had much to learn about the fickle river. The greater question became could Taylor end the war with this campaign in the north or would the war continue until Mexico City fell?

The occupation that started in the early days of the war became the foundation for new towns, depots, and military bases along the Rio Grande for decades to come. Brownsville was the best example of a new town accompanying a fort, Fort Brown (Texas). The merchant Charles Stillman, who originally called Matamoros home, helped establish the new town of Brownsville. He and likeminded merchants capitalized on the US Army presence to build a new trade hub north of the Rio Grande that grew in size and economic power over the next decade.

Without the establishment of the new fort and the use of the site by quarter-masters who needed to supply the fort and the subsequently established bases and depots along the Rio Grande, the growth of Brownsville would have been almost nonexistent. It is the presence of the military and the Quartermaster's Department that served as the catalyst for the new wave of settlement and immigration to the Rio Grande Vally over the next twelve years.

CHAPTER 3

Northern Mexico and
the Army of Invasion

T he capture of Matamoros set the Quartermaster's Department into motion. The officers began to examine the feasibility of using river steamboats to transport goods and men upriver from Matamoros and Fort Brown to Camargo and the future site of Rio Grande City and Ringgold Barracks. From Camargo Taylor planned to march his army southwest to Monterrey, the center of wealth and power in northern Mexico. Much of the wealth that flowed out of northern Mexico passed through Monterrey, and it was a prized target for Taylor and the merchants who accompanied his army south of the Rio Grande. The Battle of Monterrey presented the first significant test of Taylor's army and stretched the Quartermaster's Department's supply lines to the limit.

The merchants that followed the army, Anglo and European alike, took advantage of the new policies set in place by the occupying US Army. Beneficial tariffs, army protected trade routes, and economic support of the burgeoning river trade route, the Rio Grande Line. River trade along the Rio Grande existed before the war, but the quartermasters knew the usefulness of river travel across the United States and sought to implement the same level of navigation along this great river. The Rio Grande proved to be a far greater obstacle than the Ohio or Mississippi Rivers, but undeterred and benefited by several years of heavy rain, the quartermasters greatly expanded the riverboat trade route. Merchants and contractors took advantage of the growing waterborne route establishing new towns such as Brownsville and Rio Grande City that grew quickly because of the new route and labor demands of the US Army.

As the war progressed, the Quartermaster's Department established depots in addition to the new US Army installations along the river. These bases served

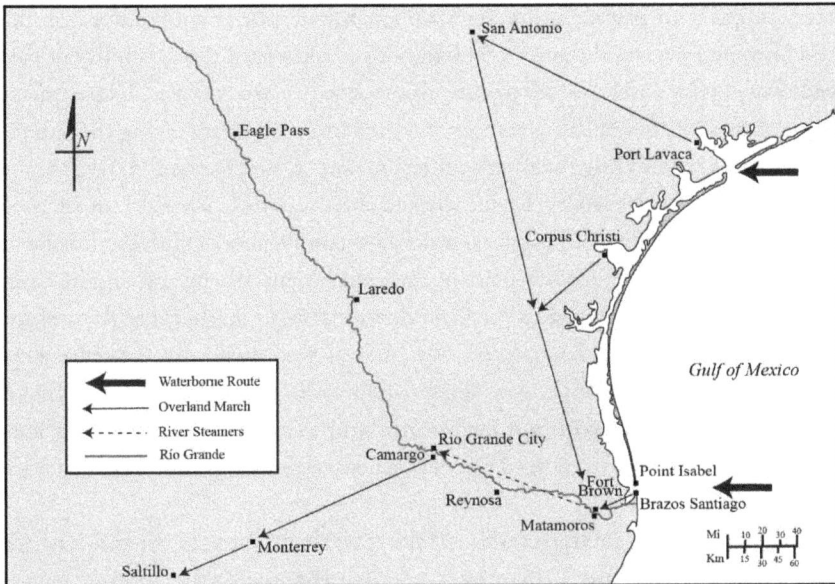

Northern Mexico Campaign Logistics

as a backbone to support Taylor's army as it marched to Monterrey and as the foundation for the postwar military establishment in South Texas. The flow of US currency into the region coupled with the availability of potential water and overland trade contracts with the US Army brought thousands of immigrants to South Texas during the twelve years following the war. Americans, Europeans, and particularly Mexicans flooded into Rio Grande Valley looking for work and opportunity. The merchants that established themselves just before and during the war profited the most, but even laborers achieved an improved lifestyle due to the economic growth north of the river.

Taylor Marches for Monterrey

After taking Matamoros, Taylor set his sights on Monterrey. Monterrey served as the central economic and political hub of northern Mexico. Taylor understood that his forces must first capture Monterrey to have any hope of ending the war with the Northern Mexico Campaign. To reach the city, Taylor worked to establish and secure his supply lines. To do so, he had to take Camargo, a city upriver from Matamoros some ninety-eight miles, to serve as a midway supply depot between his army and Brazos Santiago. He planned to use steamers to carry supplies upriver from Brazos Santiago, but despite having camped on the Rio Grande for several months, he had not yet addressed the feasibility of this endeavor. Taylor's oversight led to difficulties for the Quartermaster's Department. A paralyzing dearth of river steamers resulted in Taylor denouncing the federal government for sending men without the means to supply them. Requisitions for river steamers issued by Taylor worked their way to Colonel Hunt in New Orleans, but Hunt found filling these orders difficult because of the lack of shallow-draft steamers in the area. Eventually, the department procured steamers from Cincinnati, but the trip to the Rio Grande was treacherous because these ships were not designed for the open sea. By July 23, 1846, twelve steamboats were at work on the Rio Grande, conveying the three hundred thousand rations to Camargo that Taylor required for his overland march to Monterrey. Taylor's delay in sending information to the department deprived Jesup of the logistics intelligence he needed.[1]

The journey to Camargo continued the travel hardships for the soldiers. An enlisted soldier, Edward T. Blamire, a first lieutenant with the Virginia volunteers, recounted part of his journey in a letter to a friend. Once his unit arrived in Brazos Santiago, it camped there for four days, then proceeded to Matamoros. After about a day in Matamoros, Blamire and his unit boarded river steamers used by the army to make the three-day trip up the Rio Grande. He reported that the boats moved slowly because "the river is so low at this time that the Boat cannot go at night for fear of getting a Ground." The Quartermaster's Department bought many of the river steamboats that usually traveled the much deeper waters of the Mississippi and Ohio Rivers. Because the Rio Grande was far shallower, the department also tried to attach inflatable bladders made of rubber to the bottom of its ships to make them float higher up in the water.[2]

Many Anglo-American and European merchants accompanied the army into Mexico. This group included newly arrived merchants as well as prewar residents who already had established trade with the Mexican states south of the Rio Grande. Allowing the American merchants to accompany the army into Mexico and to continue to sell nonmilitary articles like tobacco or other dry goods stemmed in part from a recommendation of the Quartermaster's Department. Selling these goods in Mexico created a specie reserve for quartermaster officers in the area. They could exchange the specie acquired by these merchants for treasury notes or drafts without the expense or risk of transporting specie from the United States. The storms along the Gulf of Mexico often jeopardized the vast sums of money, almost always hard coinage, that moved from Washington to

New Orleans and then finally to the various theaters in Mexico. The merchants also served as intermediaries between the army and the indigenous markets for goods and labor. A side-effect of allowing private merchants to do business in tandem with the military's movements was the establishment of American business interests in Mexico, especially the northern regions, that continued after the war ended.[3]

The merchants that accompanied Taylor's army into Mexico benefited from advantageous tariff policy under the occupying army. Rather than allow Mexico to continue collecting tariff duties on trade goods along the Rio Grande, the US Army and government imposed its own tariff that favored Anglo and European merchants. This policy allowed merchants to make inroads into the Mexican economy and establish new trade connections. Small merchants still struggled, particularly after the passing of the Walker Tariff, which leveled out the playing field for American, European, and Mexican merchants. More important, goods brought in by American merchants through Brazos Santiago evaded any tariffs because the port fell under the American flag. Merchants brought in goods at this American port north of the river, then smuggled them across the Rio Grande avoiding tariffs altogether. The great American pastime of smuggling even found its way to South Texas during and after the war. By the end of the war, many imported goods remained unsold. The treaty of Guadalupe Hidalgo made accommodations for these merchants stating that any goods brought into Mexico prior to the war's conclusion would not be subject to import or sale duties or confiscation. Thus, the merchants following Taylor benefited greatly from the invasion during and after the war.[4]

The practical situation on the Rio Grande left much to be desired in the way of logistics. Taylor informed the War Department that he intended to use the river as a supply line to keep his wagon train free to move with his troops towards Monterrey. There is no evidence, however, that Taylor took the time to requisition or plan for this supply line on the Rio Grande. He neither investigated what type of vessels would be necessary to go upriver, nor did he investigate whether or not the steamboats the department used at Brazos Santiago would work upriver, though he assured the War Department he would do so. Left in a quandary, the quartermasters eventually concluded that the river steamboats could only draw about six feet of water and still navigate the river. This discovery did not come until after Taylor sent numerous letters blaming the department for the lack of steamships and supplies to support his army. Taylor became one of the department's greatest obstacles in northern Mexico.[5]

Thomas, the quartermaster at Point Isabel, requested two river steamboats from Jesup to support Taylor's troops upriver at Camargo. As the number of troops traveling along the Rio Grande continued to grow, Taylor quickly expanded the requisition to four steamboats. Hunt worked with Colonel John Winthrop, an aide-de-camp of the Louisiana governor, to scour the Mississippi River towns looking for suitable river steamers. Taylor sent Captain John Sanders of the Engineering Corps to help Hunt locate more steamboats as well. Hunt decided to double the number of requested steamships, perhaps anticipating yet another upswing in demand; Jesup approved this action and authorized a further increase if necessary. Jesup went out of his way to support Taylor, even applying "large amounts of the balance on hand to the needs of the active service, transferring these funds from the specific items for which Congress had made the appropriation." When the department learned that shallow-draft river steamers were available on other rivers such as the Ohio and Chattahoochie in Georgia, Jesup dispatched quartermasters to procure these ships for service. By mid-June 1846, several river steamers were chugging toward Brazos Santiago and the Rio Grande, a perilous journey for these fragile boats, whose design was not suited to the tumultuous open waters of the Gulf of Mexico. By July 23, twelve steamboats worked on the Rio Grande, conveying the goods needed for Taylor's march to Monterrey. The ships managed their task, but the shallow river with its swift current continued to be a daunting obstacle worsened by the lack of wood to serve as fuel.[6]

As the Quartermaster's Department continued to gather supplies for Taylor's campaign in northern Mexico, sizeable amounts of American currency also entered the region. Henry Whiting, promoted to colonel, received appointment as assistant quartermaster general at Camargo; he arrived there on August 23 to assume his duties. Jesup allotted him several accounts to fund the department's activities in northern Mexico, and he also arranged for $200,000 of credit in the Canal Bank, a prominent New Orleans bank. Whiting could not simply draw out money as needed, however. Jesup created several checks on his quartermasters to ensure honesty with such large sums while Congress passed the Sub Treasury Law, which imposed further limitations on the department. The law required that all deposits must be in "banks to the credit of the offices of this Department, as heretofore. All remittance for your use must therefore be made to Lieut. Colo. Hunt, who will hold them subject to your orders." The restrictions from both Jesup and Congress helped hold the department accountable, ultimately reducing some of the corruption that had plagued it in earlier years.[7]

Jesup maintained thorough records of the supplies flowing into northern Mexico to support Taylor's army. He requested on September 19, 1846, that Major Samuel McRee, another quartermaster at Brazos Island, send him regular reports on "the number of steamers, sail vessels, and small craft of every description, wagons, horses, mules, oxen, carts . . . in any way connected with furnishing transportation for" Taylor's army. Jesup was careful to exclude ships carrying goods between Brazos Santiago and New Orleans because Hunt's records already included those ships. Hunt received similar orders instructing him to advise Jesup on "the number of vessels employed in transporting troops and supplies from New Orleans to La Vaca and Brazos Island." Jesup also requested up-to-date information about the forage and coal that was available in New Orleans, where Hunt was the quartermaster, because New Orleans served as the major coaling station on the Gulf Coast. The department thus grew into a more finely tuned, bureaucratic machine that effectively kept track of mustered resources and their location, an impressive feat since news traveled only as fast as a ship could carry letters from one quartermaster office to another.[8]

When leaving Camargo, Taylor took only a portion of the force he had with him because many of the troops lacked the necessary training to be of military use. His army consisted of two divisions of regulars and a field division of volunteers, totaling about six thousand men. The rest of the volunteers remained at Matamoros and Camargo to drill and train. Taylor concluded in a letter to President Polk that the influx of twelve-month volunteers had impeded his forward progress by consuming all the Quartermaster's Department's resources in transporting and supplying the recruits. Taylor's main force lacked the quartermaster support desired because it was distracted and overwhelmed by the new soldiers.[9]

Captain George H. Crosman, a career officer in the regular army who served primarily with the Quartermaster's Department until he retired in 1866, worked diligently to prepare for Taylor's march south toward Monterrey. By August 23, 1846, the Army of Occupation had about fifteen hundred pack mules forwarding supplies to Cerralvo, where some guard troops protected a temporary depot. The pack mules cost about fifty cents per day for each mule, packs, and driver, so they represented a significant investment. By early September, Taylor departed with his army to Cerralvo. The number of hired pack mules increased during the interim to nineteen hundred mules, while about one hundred eighty mule and horse wagons also supported the troops. Each section of Taylor's army had an allotment of wagons or pack mules for the march: eight noncommissioned officers and privates shared one pack mule; company officers had three; and the regimental headquarters had four. Each brigade and division headquarters received one wagon, while each regiment had three: one to transport water and two for articles that mules could not carry. The Ordnance Department received fifty-three wagons, the Engineer Department one, and the Medical Director four. The support of an army on the march rivaled the size of the army itself, much to the distress of many quartermasters.[10]

The Battle of Monterrey and the Monterrey Armistice

The Battle of Monterrey created a new logistical dilemma for Taylor and the quartermasters. Ammunition expenditures, depletion of provisions, and battle casualties were far greater than in any previous confrontation in the war up to this point. When the battle was fought in late September 1846, many of the problems of supporting armies in the field had already arisen and been met by the Quartermaster's Department. But with the Monterrey campaign, the difficulty of logistics so far from the base of operations demonstrated the need for a well-organized and effectively supervised department. The new problems laid the foundation for institutional changes in the department under Jesup and his successors that pushed them even further down the path of modernization.

As the army pushed deeper into Mexico, more quartermasters were needed to maintain the supply lines and depots supporting the armies. One such quartermaster received orders on September 1, 1846, Captain Theodore O'Hara, assistant quartermaster, who traveled first to New Orleans, then found passage to Brazos Santiago. Once O'Hara arrived at the island depot, Jesup ordered him to "report to the principal officer of the Quarter Master's Department at that post, and should he require it you will take charge of either money or property, or both." Jesup continually tried to improve support for the army and provide necessary resources to forces in the field while also building an effective bureaucracy to manage these same resources. Placing qualified officers in the field to manage the reception and distribution of supplies was a significant prerequisite for establishing a supply chain that stretched thousands of miles across the Western Hemisphere.[11]

In September 1846, Jesup issued orders to the quartermasters stationed at the depots in Lavaca and San Antonio, Texas, to send him monthly reports detailing the number of "sailing vessels, small craft . . . horses, mules, wagons, carts, etc." currently at each of their two depots. He also wanted to know the contents and number of any supply trains currently en route to other locations from either of these depots. Jesup was beginning to develop an information network to keep himself informed of the supplies available and their movement. At a time before instant communication, it could take a month or longer to deliver a letter from San Antonio to Washington, DC. Only by creating a regularly scheduled up-to-date system could Jesup maintain a reasonable approximation of what resources he had at his disposal and what he could send to armies in need. This expanding communication network became a crucial component of the growing Quartermaster's Department and continued to improve throughout the war.[12]

To improve steam transportation along the Rio Grande, the department procured two river steamers, the *Gopher* and the *Dragon*, from the Topographical Department of the army. Once turned over to the quartermasters, the boats traveled from Louisville, Kentucky, to Colonel Hunt in New Orleans. Once there, Jesup ordered the vessels sent "to the Rio Grande with as little delay as possible." Taylor's Monterrey campaign progressed with Jesup's aid, and the new ships helped supply his army effectively.[13]

As the army mustered more troops to serve in northern Mexico, including a new unit of dragoons, the Quartermaster's Department gathered horses and equipment to outfit the newcomers. Major Nathaniel Anderson, the quartermaster at Memphis, Tennessee, received orders on September 22, 1846, to procure two hundred new horses, one hundred for draft and one hundred for dragoon service. In addition, he organized approximately fifty teamsters to transport the horses from Memphis to New Orleans for deployment. The teamsters received contracts for a minimum of six months unless ended earlier by the department. Jesup ordered that one third of their pay be withheld until the contract was completed. This last clause reflects the type of civilian contractors that the department encountered during the war. While these men might have been qualified teamsters, they often presented a potential risk of wandering off if paid up front in full.[14]

While Anderson procured horses, Captain David Hammond Vinton prepared eight to ten wagons with complete sets of harness to accompany the dragoon horses to Texas. Ships left New York filled with wagons and harnesses, then resupplied in New Orleans and picked up the draft and dragoon horses, finally continuing on to Point Isabel, Texas. Since horses were going to northern Mexico, hay, oats, and other forage needed to accompany them. Jesup ordered "twelve hundred bales of hay and any quantity of oat not exceeding twenty thousand bushels and that quantity if possible." Vinton worked to have the forage gathered in New York and shipped to Brazos Santiago. Jesup gathered resources from across the country and managed to move them to intersecting points with surprising accuracy.[15]

Jesup carefully coordinated the movement of men and supplies to ensure each arrived as close to the appropriate time and place as possible. Captain Michael M. Clark, the assistant quartermaster to Stanton, received instructions on September 24 to hold the remaining wagons gathered in New York until "we know the points at which they will be required." While the department often managed to deliver supplies from across the United States to positions on foreign soil thousands of miles away with a respectable degree of timeliness, the quartermasters also knew when not to ship goods. Being able to muster supplies and deliver them rapidly is important, but knowing when to hold material in reserve rather than ship it to the last known point of operation is just as beneficial. Until Jesup received word from the secretary of war or Taylor, he at times chose to hold supplies currently in depots. Jesup wrote that depots such as Brazos Santiago and Point Isabel already had a sufficient inventory to last the army until quartermasters received any new requests. This reserve of war material could be quickly shipped if the conflict continued once quartermasters received word of the next operation.[16]

The war continued, and Taylor arrived outside Monterrey with his Army of Occupation on September 21, 1846. His supply lines stretched overland about one hundred twenty miles back to Camargo on the Rio Grande. The Battle of Monterrey pitted sixty-five hundred American regulars and volunteers against seventy-three hundred Mexican soldiers in an urban battlefield filled with twenty thousand Mexican citizens. Taylor sent General William Worth to flank the city and seize the heights behind Monterrey to cut off any escape route. The battle was an all-out brawl through the streets, and brutal hand-to-hand fighting took its toll on both armies. Eventually, attrition forced Mexican General Pedro de Ampudia to ask for a parlay, resulting in what became known as the Monterrey Armistice. Ampudia gave the city to Taylor in exchange for the American forces not pushing more than fifty miles south of the city for the next eight weeks.[17]

As Taylor rested his Army of Occupation at Monterrey, Jesup worked to ensure vital supplies could keep flowing from the United States to Mexico. Most important, he needed to guarantee that his department's new steamships, chartered or owned, did not deplete their fuel supplies. He delegated this task to Captain Samual B. Dusenbury, stationed at Baltimore. His orders stated he needed to prepare "for the delivery of Coal at Key West, Brazos Island and La Vaca. You will give your attention to see that the contracts are properly executed as far as respects inspecting the Coal and seeing it put on . . . suitable vessels." Without coal, a sizeable portion of the department's fleet would be greatly slowed or idled, thus retarding the shipping process. Goods that did not arrive within an acceptable time frame could mean the starvation of soldiers or the loss of a key battle due to lack of munitions.[18]

ARMISTICE RESUPPLY

The call for more supplies came to Jesup's office by the end of September. Quickly, Jesup ordered Colonel Hunt in New Orleans to organize four trains filled with one hundred wagons each. The department records showed that enough wagons and harnesses were on hand at Brazos Santiago to form these trains, but if not, it fell to Hunt to secure the difference and make the trains ready for service as soon as possible. In the letter to Hunt, Jesup noted, "The Army I understand, is impeded for want of sufficient horse shoes." The trains played a crucial role in keeping Taylor's armies moving, but something as basic as a shortage of horseshoes could bring a train to a halt. Hunt procured and shipped some ten thousand sets of four horseshoes along with nails. Jesup also requested that blacksmith tools be included with each train to ensure the horses could be more easily shod in the future. Most army units of any size included at least one trained blacksmith.[19]

Hunt also began procuring mules to pull the wagon trains. In New Orleans at the end of September 1846, the department had about one thousand mules ready to ship. Quartermasters held the animals in reserve, however, because the mules could forage easier near the city than they could in Brazos Santiago. The latter depot was effectively a sand bar and provided little in the way of pasturage. The animals would be sent only when the trains were ready to leave with supplies from Brazos Santiago, rolling inland to Matamoros and then upriver to Taylor's forces at Monterrey.[20]

In a letter between Stanton and General George Gibson, commissary general of subsistence, Stanton estimated that the Quartermaster's Department employed about five thousand persons at various depots. This included "teamsters, ostlers, muleteers, laborers at the depots, mechanics, boatmen, steam boat hand[s], etc." This number, however, fluctuated due to "the emergencies of the service." Zachary Taylor's Army of Occupation rarely had more than five thousand active soldiers. The number of men needed by the department almost equaled the number that was engaged in a combat role under Taylor.[21]

By September 28, 1846, Major General Robert Patterson prepared to lead his roughly one thousand volunteers to the Rio Grande to join Taylor's forces. He commanded the Second Division of the Army of Occupation and, once in

Mexico, earned distinction in the Tampico Expedition. Hunt organized the required transportation for Patterson and his men to the Rio Grande. Jesup also instructed Hunt that a sufficient supply train should be available at Brazos Santiago but that they should be prepared to supply any pack mules or train components should Patterson request them. The department did its best to prepare for any unforeseen material needs of the troops going into the field. Its quartermasters could not predict the future, but they did ensure that they usually had the supplies on hand to provide to the troops or to dispatch to an army in the field.[22]

As troops and supplies continued to be transported to Mexico to support Taylor's army via the coastal depots, Jesup directed other supplies to be shipped from San Antonio. Captain Simon H. Drum served as the assistant quartermaster for the city and directed the trains traveling from San Antonio to Camargo. Jesup left the route up to Drum. He could either send the train to the coast at Lavaca and ship it to the Rio Grande, or he could march overland directly to Camargo. Colonel Humphrey Marshall was expected to be marching along the same route with a mounted regiment, so Jesup suggested that the overland route might be safest if Drum could join Marshall for the march southward to the Rio Grande.[23]

The new troops headed to northern Mexico and the California Expedition, the new campaign to secure New Mexico and California. Ships were scheduled to set sail by late September. Simultaneously, Jesup toured several of the Quartermaster's Department's active depots. He started with the New Orleans Depot because it represented the largest hub for both men and supplies flowing from the United States to Mexico. The tour began with Jesup's departure from Washington, DC, on October 1, 1846, and he expected to be in New Orleans by the end of the first week in October. While Jesup toured the depots along the Gulf of Mexico and the Rio Grande, Stanton supervised the Quartermaster's Department. Leaving the department in Stanton's hands for several weeks reflected the high level of trust that Jesop held for his subordinate.[24]

In early October, two companies of artillery from Fort Moultrie in Charleston, South Carolina, prepared to travel to Point Isabel to begin moving to join Taylor. Lieutenant E. F. Steplie, acting assistant quartermaster at Charleston, began organizing transportation for "their baggage, subsistence, arms" to Mexico. Steplie worked in conjunction with Captain Dusenbury from the Baltimore depot to help move these two companies of about ninety-five men each. The companies were expected to embark by October 10. To ensure the timeliness of their departure, Stanton informed Colonel J. B. Malbach, the commanding officer at Fort Monroe, to have the two companies of artillery "in readiness" by October 9 to join the army in Mexico. On October 8, Stanton requested that Dusenbury try to fit a detachment of Eighth Infantry recruits on the ship with the two artillery companies from Fort Moultrie. At the same time, Stanton ordered Captain Vinton to prepare transportation for two additional companies of the Fourth Artillery from Fort Columbus to Point Isabel. Like Steplie, Vinton worked with Dusenbury to outfit the ships for the voyage.[25]

Jesup purchased another steamer for Quartermaster's Department's use, the steam barque *Edith*. In combination with the *Massachusetts*, these vessels were among the largest in his department's fleet. The *Edith* had a gross tonnage of four hundred tons, and the *Massachusetts* could hold seven hundred tons, making it the single largest ship in the fleet. The purchase of these two ships greatly increased the amount of material and men that could be transported. Once Stanton purchased the ships, he ordered Vinton to review copies of the contracts and have them "thoroughly inspected by competent engineers and ship carpenters or builders" before accepting delivery. Everything on board the ships, including machinery, tackle, and apparel, had to be in perfect order, and all the cabin and table furniture and accessories had to be on board when received, in accordance with the terms of the purchase. Once inspected and received, Vinton had orders to report the ships' arrival immediately to Stanton's office. By October 13, the secretary of war decided that the department would not purchase any more steamers for the time being. Stanton suggested that the crew of the *Massachusetts* could be retained in service to the department if Vinton found them suitable.[26]

By the time the secretary of war decided to stop acquiring ships, the *Massachusetts* was already being prepared to carry troops to Brazos Santiago. Captain Vinton received instructions to gather rations for the soldiers and the crew of the ship from the Commissary Department. This requirement is different from when quartermasters victualed a chartered vessel. For the latter, the department only had to load supplies and provide rations to the army's soldiers; the crew of the ship prepared their own rations drawn from the money paid to charter the ship. While purchase of ships like the *Massachusetts* gave the department more flexibility since quartermaasters did not have to deal with new charters every few months, it also meant a greater material resource burden for the agency with the need to provide for the crew in addition to any soldiers on board.[27]

Additionally, by October 28, Stanton made the decision that ships sent to the Gulf Coast should not draw more than six and a half feet of water due to the shallow harbors found there. This restriction excluded some of the larger ships in the fleet, such as the sidewheel steamboat *Alabama* that had a 676 gross ton capacity, because of "her great draught of water." It simply sat too deeply in the water to be able to safely maneuver the shoals and sand bars that were common along the Gulf Coast. Rather, such ships had to remain a distance from the shore and lighter, smaller, flat-bottomed row boats, carried supplies from ship to shore. Thus, the process of loading or unloading ships at ports like Brazos Santiago or Point Isabel was slow and painstaking. With the significance of these ports, the department deemed it best to simply limit the type of ship that carried goods there to ones that had a far shallower draw and navigated harbors more easily.[28]

On October 20, 1846, Stanton forwarded a circular from the War Department to all quartermasters commanding a depot. The circular detailed an act passed by Congress in January 1823 that dealt with the handling of public monies. The circular instructed each depot to keep track of all vouchers and receipts and to report this information quarterly to the Quartermaster's Department, which would then report to the War Department. Up to this point in the war, the quartermasters had been less than accurate when submitting their quarterly account reports on time. Furthermore, the circular directed the commanders to appoint an agent or clerk to specifically keep the books so as to not find themselves in a situation where their books were late and could not be submitted at the predetermined time. Such instructions, though coming from Stanton and the War Department, echo what Jesup had been training the quartermasters to do all along. Regular reports were a key activity that Jesup tried to impress upon all of his quartermasters. Without regular, accurate information, it was impossible to tell how much money or supplies went to the armed forces. Without effective accounting of resources, the risk of corruption dramatically increased because no one could hold the officers accountable for their expenditures. Though Jesup had made some headway with his department and most of the quartermasters proved honorable, this circular added an extra layer of security and oversight for the department.[29]

Accounting and resource management were not unknown to the quartermasters when the war started. Throughout the early 1800s, the US Army oversaw several resource management tasks, including leasing of public lands, overseeing developments by the Army Corps of Engineers, and conducting national geographic explorations. During the 1830s and 1840s, the Springfield Armory exhibited one of the most sophisticated methods of accounting and control procedures. Officers trained at West Point brought their knowledge of efficient management, which allowed Springfield Armory to "enforce norms of output, to attain disciplinary power over labor, and to yield significant productivity gains." Colonel Sylvanus Thayer served as superintendent of West Point and oversaw a massive revision of the coursework and methodologies taught at the military academy. These measures included numerical grading on exams and an emphasis on engineering, scientific, and mathematical principles. The methods employed by the West Point officers during the 1840s reduced material waste, set production norms, and increased accountability for loss or waste. The net result was an efficient factory setting that established the level of quality and amount of production an average worker could be expected to produce. This information allowed the Quartermaster's Department to have a benchmark for the cost of goods and labor when contracting out production to civilian firms during the war. The armory additionally worked to improve the uniformity and interchangeability of small-arms parts for easier repair and refitting during wartime.[30]

In mid-October 1846, a terrible hurricane hit the Gulf Coast. It ranked as a what would now be considered a Category 5 tropical cyclone that wreaked destruction across the southeastern United States and much of the Caribbean, hitting Cuba particularly hard.[31] Its devastation earned it the name "The Great Gale of 1846." Such a violent storm dramatically interrupted Quartermaster's Department transportation. It wiped out the coaling station at Key West as well as Fort Zachary Taylor in the southern Florida Keys. By November 1, Stanton began rebuilding and resupplying of the Key West depot. The Gulf of Mexico by the mid-1800s earned a reputation for hazardous travel due to "northers," strong gusting winds that regularly delayed or damaged ships. This storm disrupted shipments and travel between Mexico and the United States. Without the coaling station at Key West, department steamers had to take larger loads of coal to travel the extra distance to Mobile or New Orleans, meaning less room for men and supplies. Despite the loss of the depot, Stanton and the department quickly reacted and rebuilt the location to allow support for the armies in the field to continue without too much disruption.[32]

As the Key West depot was being rebuilt, Stanton shipped more coal at Jesup's request to Brazos Santiago. The shipment contained some two thousand tons of "best-anthracite" coal. Stanton explained that "anthracite coal is regarded as the best for all northern steamers in the Government employ in the Gulf for the burning of which they are fitted." Much of this coal arrived aboard two of the department's newer river steamers, the *Gopher* and the *Dragon*. The coal depot at Brazos Santiago not only supplied the steamers that carried goods from the United States to the depot but also to the steamers that navigated the Rio Grande. Without sufficient coal reserves at Brazos Santiago, supplies flowing upriver would be delayed. By this point, Taylor's capture of Monterrey and the subsequent two-month Monterrey Armistice was ending. Hostilities could therefore resume at any time, and Taylor's army needed to be resupplied regularly to continue the campaign.[33]

The capture of Tampico, a coastal Mexican town halfway between Brazos Santiago and Veracruz, opened new logistical possibilities for the department. A town of about seven thousand inhabitants, it resided some five or six miles upriver from the mouth of the Pánuco River. The city fell to the navy's Home Squadron under the command of Commodore David Conner on November 14, 1846. His force captured Tampico with hardly a fight due to the help of Ann Chase, the wife of the United States consul at Tampico. One newspaper lauded her actions, saying, "The annals of modern times exhibit few instances of female patriotism more noble, chivalrous, and brilliant than that of Mrs. Franklin Chase, at the recent taking of Tampico." She certainly showed bravery relaying information to Conner on the position, number, and strength of the Mexican soldiers and their fortifications. She also publicly declared that Conner would land immediately with thirty thousand troops, creating a sense of fear in the Tampico citizenry and leaving the city ready to comply with Conner's request for surrender. On November 28, 1846, news reached Washington that Tampico had been captured. Tampico became a supply depot. With the fall of Tampico, not only did the department gain a new port for transporting men and supplies, but also the United States took control of the customs office and established a tariff on trade going in and out of the city. This arrangement brought revenue into the war effort, though much of it remained in the hands of the Tampico City Council.[34]

Taylor's Army Faces Santa Anna at Buena Vista

As General Taylor resumed operations, a new assistant quartermaster replaced Whiting at Camargo. Captain Benjamin F. Graham assumed support duties at the Camargo depot, which had renewed importance because of Taylor's proposed operations. Being new to his post, Graham did not fully understand all the department regulations, and that left him in a bit of a predicament. In traveling to his new post at Camargo, he incurred costs from his transportation and that of his baggage. He failed to submit his routes and distances in his claim for reimbursement. Therefore the department denied his initial request and sent him a copy of the regulations of the Quartermaster's Department. Section 983 clearly stated that transportation for baggage would only be paid for on subsequent journeys, not the initial one to a post of duty. Such were the intricacies of the department. While the growing bureaucracy provided many benefits in efficiency, effectiveness, and elimination of corruption, it did often penalize those who lacked extensive knowledge of the regulation maze.[35]

General Taylor knew that marching from Monterrey to Mexico City was logistically unfeasible due to the combination of long, strained supply lines susceptible to attack and the lack of water and forage on the way. Instead, he decided to capture Saltillo, an undefended but important city. It sat on the southern road approaching Monterrey and provided access to the rich farming center of Parras. Saltillo provided Taylor with an appetizing target that gave his army a better defensive position and access to foodstuffs. The Americans entered the city unopposed on November 16, 1846.[36]

Despite the successes of the American armies in the field, Mexico did not seem willing to capitulate. Therefore, President James K. Polk called for more volunteer recruits from nine states: Massachusetts, New York, Pennsylvania, Virginia, North Carolina, South Carolina, Mississippi, Louisiana, and Texas, with the last state providing several mounted units. It fell to Stanton, still acting in Jesup's stead, to "meet the exigency involved by this call for additional forces." Stanton wrote that he should be able to provide all the camp and garrison equipage within the requested timeline. Jesup and Stanton divided the task for outfitting these new volunteers. Jesup oversaw Mississippi, Louisiana, and Texas, while Stanton handled Massachusetts, New York, Pennsylvania, Virginia, and the Carolinas. The department shipped some of the cargo destined for Brazos Santiago on the newly chartered *Eudora*, a steamer that had a respectable 430 gross ton capacity but, uniquely, had a shallow enough draft to navigate the sand bars near Brazos Santiago. The shallow draft allowed the ship to be unloaded without lighters.[37] This call for new volunteers not only placed new pressures on the department but also meant that the war would not be as short as many had hoped. The longer the war lasted, the more expensive it became. An extended war fought thousands of miles from the United States heartland would only continue to add costs.[38]

As the war continued, Captain Vinton stationed at New York received orders from Stanton on November 19, 1846, to "purchase and ship monthly Gunny Bags 25,000 bushels of oat to the depot at Brazos San Iago." The department began establishing protocols for a drawn-out conflict lasting an indeterminant time. Setting up monthly shipments versus shipping on demand not only allowed for regular access to supplies in the campaign theaters, but it also automated some of the routine army requests, allowing quartermasters to focus on other aspects of procurement and transport. A small step, but each component that was streamlined allowed for greater focus elsewhere. Stanton chose Vinton's New York depot because light-draft vessels could be more easily obtained in that port. In a separate letter to Captain Dusenbury, Stanton made it clear that "none of their vessels be allowed under any pretext whatever to load beyond 6ft of water." Stanton wanted to be sure that all ships could navigate Brazos Santiago without the use of lighters.[39]

To meet the renewed and expanded demands for transportation, Stanton procured the screw (propeller) driven steam ship *Washington* with a 224 gross ton capacity. He ordered it immediately brought up to perfect repair, loaded, and dispatched to Brazos Santiago with cargo. Screw driven steamships navigated shallow waters better than sidewheel steamships. With the common sand bars along Brazos Santiago, such ships represented an added value. The expanding fleet of steamships again meant larger coal reserves at the coaling stations. By November 24, Stanton focused on furnishing coal to Brazos Santiago and Key West to keep the steamships operating. He told Captain Dusenbury to purchase and ship to Galveston, Texas, "two thousand tons of Cumberland coal as soon as it can be obtained in your market at $5 or less per ton." Stanton elaborated on obtaining a good price for coal stating that "if the mining and transporting companies connected with the Cumberland coal business think that the interest of the Government is to be made the sport of combinations and monopolies, they may, perhaps, find out their mistake in a way little calculated to promote their own." Stanton held any company trying to profit off the war in contempt. He would not suffer anyone gouging the department to make an excess profit during wartime.[40]

By December 1846, the department began to run into wagon shortages despite waiving certain specifications and increasing payments. The main factor limiting production fell outside of quartermaster control. Wagons needed to be constructed of seasoned timber, but due to the demand for wagons early in the war, not enough timber had been prepared for seasoning. At this point there were few reliable methods for speeding up the seasoning process, so wagon builders simply had to wait until the wood dried enough to be worked. In addition, a workman shortage arose as many of the workers had joined volunteer companies, decreasing the number of available craftsmen. The rise of the railroads in the northeastern United States also had hampered wagon production in the years immediately preceding the war. These factors combined to reduce the number of wagons readily available, and the department had to get creative in its procurement methods to meet the demands of the army.[41]

As the war neared its second year, the Quartermaster's Department required more funds to maintain the necessary levels of supplies and transportation for the expanding theaters of war. The treasurer of the United States provided the department with a large amount of specie to be used by the New Orleans depot. Stanton assigned Captain Clark to transport these funds from New York to New Orleans. Clark was allowed to choose his method of travel, either by land or by sea. The treasury in New York provided him with $503,500 for delivery. Stanton ordered that the money should be transported only by the "best, safest, and most expeditious route from New York to New Orleans." He also added one consideration for Clark: if he used seaborne routes, then he should "effect an insurance on the money confided to you." This is a reasonable suggestion because specie that sank with the ship would simply be gone. At this point in United States history, the country still operated on the gold standard. A loss of this amount of physical currency would deal a significant blow to the war effort. This mission demonstrates the hazards of transferring money between one location and another during this era. While in transit, any number of obstacles threatened the money, the most prominent always remained the weather while traveling at sea. Clark and the specie arrived safely.[42]

The Battle of Buena Vista, also known as the Battle of La Angostura, began on February 22, 1847, when General Taylor's outnumbered Army of Occupation met Antonio López de Santa Anna's rapidly gathered army about seven miles south of Saltillo, Mexico. The first day of the battle proved a bloody collision for both sides, who had to fight across the gulches that crossed the plains beneath the mountains. Taylor's forces barely held their lines during the most intense fighting. By the end of the first day of the battle, many of Taylor's subordinate officers thought the battle was lost and the retreat should begin. Taylor stood fast. The next morning the opposing field was empty, Santa Anna had retreated from Buena Vista. News of political issues in Mexico City had reached Santa Anna and necessitated his return to the capital. Taylor won a tactical victory over Santa Anna because he still held the field while the Mexicans retreated. Nevertheless, it proved to be a strategic defeat because Santa Anna had crippled Taylor's forces to the point that the Americans would be unable to continue hostile operations until reinforcement and resupply. Further limiting Taylor, President Polk reassigned half of Taylor's army to General Scott's new army, preventing Taylor from making another significant military gain during the remainder of the war. While Santa Anna may have lost the battle, it effectively ended any American action in northern Mexico beyond occupation. Equally as debilitating, Winfield Scott's campaign in central Mexico began to draw some of Taylor's most experienced regulars from his army, leaving him even less able to make any significant advances. The Americans had secured control over much of northern Mexico, but that control did not impel the Mexican government to surrender. Scott prepared his new campaign to capture Mexico City, and it proved to be an even greater logistical feat than that of supporting Taylor's army in northern Mexico. [43]

~

The supply networks utilized and established by the Quartermaster's Department during the northern Mexico campaign, such as the Rio Grande Line, allowed Taylor's army to achieve victory there. Many of the wealthier merchants in South Texas used these new trade routes, overland and by river, to expand their trade into Mexico and along the Rio Grande. In addition, new towns established by merchants, such as Rio Grande City and Brownsville, grew to be major trade hubs after the war. Merchants such as Henry Clay Davis and Charles Stillman not only profited from selling land in the new towns, but they also benefited from securing US Army contracts transporting goods or renting land for military bases. These business dealings laid the foundation for a future power shift in the region as Anglo-Americans encroached on Mexican or Tejano control due to the Anglos' connections to the army. Relationships between army officers and civilian contractors persisted in the years after the war, allowing for the flow of American dollars into the Rio Grande Valley via these men. The economic advantages translated into a political advantage. None of these changes would have occurred, however, without the efforts of the Quartermaster's Department along the Rio Grande during the first phase of the war between the United States and Mexico.

Taylor's army managed to capture the urban center of Monterrey and confirm its occupation of northern Mexico against Santa Anna at the Battle of Buena Vista. Although these battles left Taylor's forces weakened, they undeniably controlled northern Mexico. During the roughly one year of occupation of both sides of the Rio Grande Valley, the Quartermaster's Department spent significant funds establishing depots and maintaining the occupying forces. The American soldiers received their pay and then spent it on both sides of the river; merchants received contracts to transport goods; and teamsters of both nations worked for the quartermasters. This period changed South Texas in dramatic ways. It demonstrated that wealth could be made and fortunes improved even for the average laborer. While only the savviest or most well-positioned merchants fully capitalized on the opportunities, many common Mexicans still migrated north of the river seeking work from the army or American and European merchants.

Although the war in northern Mexico represented an undeniable victory for the United States, the Mexican government did not concede. Furthermore, President Polk set his sights not just on the Nueces Strip but New Mexico and California as well. This meant the war continued. South Texas, however, experienced unique postwar results not seen to the same degree in the Western Territories or in central Mexico.

CHAPTER 4

The Western Campaigns in New Mexico and California

1846–1848

T he campaigns in the far west by the US Army during the Mexican-American War sought to seize two of the most economically desirable territories in western North America: New Mexico and California. Santa Fe, New Mexico, lay within a huge economic trade network that stretched from Mexico to Missouri. The distance from Mexico City left Santa Fe isolated from that national center, and so Santa Fe established strong economic ties to the United States via the Santa Fe Trail during the decades preceding the war against Mexico. California, if taken, would provide the United States with much-desired trade routes with Asia. If the Americans could gain control of this Mexican province, they would complete what Christopher Columbus had promised to do in 1492. The United States would have ports on both the Atlantic and the Pacific Oceans, allowing the country to trade with virtually every nation-state in the world. Also, given time, these ports would have the ability to project United States power and influence around the globe. While the Western Campaign is not the most militarily significant operation of the war, the territory it gained made it one of the most important for the future of the United States.

Controlling the Santa Fe Trail was the most immediate goal of the Western Campaign. The trail initially developed during the late 1700s as an informal trade route connecting the Spanish, French, Osage, and other American Indian groups. Sporadic trade grew up between the United States and Spanish Mexico by the early 1800s, trade that dramatically increased after the Louisiana Purchase. Much of this cross-border trade consisted of manufactured goods from the United States and Europe transported to Santa Fe and Chihuahua, Mexico, in exchange for silver mined in central and northern Mexico. Although travel remained risky along the roughly eight-hundred-mile trail due to hostile environments and the presence of Native Americans, the opportunity for large profits by the 1820s continued to draw merchants willing to take the risk. Eventually, Senator Thomas Hart Benton persuaded President James Monroe to authorize a survey of a road stretching from Fort Osage—just west of present-day Kansas City—to Santa Fe. This action effectively formalized the trail that already existed and ensured that it would be maintained and protected. Independence, Missouri, grew quickly into a short-lived hub of trade for the United States, Santa Fe, independent fur trappers, merchants, and American Indians. This overland trade continued to grow during the next few decades until it produced a substantial amount of annual income. The trade between the United States and Mexico along this route by 1860 consisted of 5,948 men, 22,170 wagons, 464 horses, 5,933 mules, and 17,836 oxen. By the late 1870s, annual trade amounted to a conservative estimate of about $5 million. When the war began in 1846, the Santa Fe Trail was well established, making it an appetizing target to pursue on the way to California. President Polk saw the opportunity Santa Fe, New Mexico, and California presented in economic terms and sought to add them to the United States. Because the long-standing trade network had served to tie Santa Fe more closely to the United States than to Mexico City, the idea of capturing the territory was considered even more desirable and feasible.[1]

The land itself became the army's greatest enemy in the West. The vast distances, arid conditions, and oppressive heat often served as a more daunting enemy than Mexican forces. Most of the western portion of North America was unsettled by any significant non-Indian population. The future American territories of New Mexico, California, and Utah were the primary settled areas, and New Mexico was the only one of these that contained long-term settlements populated by those of European descent. Although Utah never formally became a Mexican territory or state like New Mexico or California at this time, Mormons had settled around the Great Salt Lake in their effort to escape religious persecution in the United States. The hostile landscape of the American West necessitated a monumental effort of supply and preparation by the Quartermaster's Department to ensure that the armies in the far west had the supplies necessary to carry out their tasks in the war. The department prepared resources and equipment for the overland supply trains prior to departing from the westernmost military bases and outposts in Kansas. Steam vessels transported supplies to California to support the army when it arrived from the overland march. These efforts aided the conquest of Mexico's far northern frontera, including the Rio Grande Valley, transforming it into the American Southwest.

Preparation for the Western Campaigns began during the summer of 1846 just as General Zachary Taylor began to push into northern Mexico. The department faced a daunting task of not only supplying the most expansive theater of the war but also three separate campaigns within the distant Western Theater. This arena stretched from San Antonio, Texas, all the way to the Pacific coast of California. The theater's northern boundary bumped against the formerly disputed Oregon Territory. This vast tract of land made up between one third and one half of the entirety of Mexico. General Stephen W. Kearny led the New Mexico Campaign to take Santa Fe, hoping to avoid much of a fight. Captain John Charles Frémont—son-in-law to Senator Thomas Hart Benton—led American troops to seize control of California, although the *Californios*, Hispanic Californians, sought to establish their own "Bear Flag" Republic during the turmoil of the Mexican-American War. Unlike Kearney, Frémont went beyond what the US government formally authorized and caused much consternation among officers in California. Due to the great distance between California and Mexico City, the Californios had grown more autonomous and saw the war as a chance to secure their independence from Mexico. While General Kearny marched his forces westward, Captain Frémont slowly began taking actions of his own in California. Simultaneously, the US Navy operated against Mexico's Pacific coast including California.[2]

Kearny Marches to Santa Fe

The War Department placed General Kearny in command of the California Expedition troops, which included three hundred regulars of the First United States Dragoons, eight hundred sixty Missouri mounted volunteers under Colonel Alexander W. Doniphan, two hundred fifty volunteers in a pair of light artillery companies, a St. Louis company of one hundred mounted volunteers called the Laclede Rangers, and two small companies of infantry. Kearny headed first to Santa Fe, then onto California. The expedition was also accompanied by fifty Indian scouts, a party of topographical engineers, and an interpreter. In all, the complement of troops numbered just under seventeen hundred men. The main force under Kearny departed on June 27, 1846, including the troops under Colonel Doniphan. Reinforcement of the expedition followed in mid-August under the command of Colonel Sterling Price, who had twelve hundred men, mostly mounted volunteers. These troops included one full mounted regiment, one mounted extra battalion, and one extra battalion of Mormon infantry, all of which were volunteers. They also included a few regulars in charge of heavy artillery. This secondary expedition followed the Santa Fe Trail and eventually joined Kearny. The final addition to the western forces came in the form of the Mormon Battalion, which included only Mormon volunteers from Council Bluffs, Missouri.[3]

The relationship between the United States and the Mormons—the Church of Jesus Christ of Latter-day Saints as it was also known—was tumultuous. Many states had passed shoot-on-sight orders for followers of the Mormon faith. As a result, the Mormons became one of the most heavily armed nongovernmental factions in North America. Given the potential of the Mormons siding with Mexico after fleeing United States territory to escape persecution, the army decided to offer a deal to them: service for a promise of security. On Friday June 26, Captain James Allen of the First Dragoons met with Mormon leaders at Mt. Pisgah, Iowa, to secure an agreement with the religious sect. Eventually Mormon leadership agreed, and Captain Allen traveled to Council Bluffs, where Brigham Young, the foremost leader of the Mormons, announced that a battalion made up of Mormons was joining the army in the war against Mexico. Allen promised that although it served in the army, it could still choose its own leadership from its ranks. By July 16, about four hundred and fifty men had gathered in the square at Council Bluffs. These men signed up to serve for one year of military service. The new Mormon Battalion began its journey to Fort Leavenworth on July 20. Accompanying the newly mustered soldiers were some Mormon women and children. They arrived at Fort Leavenworth on August 1, 1846.[4]

The Mormon Battalion made up a small portion of the volunteers in Kearny's Army of the West. Frank Edwards, a volunteer joining the Kearny expedition, noted that many new volunteers came from St. Louis since it was one of the largest population centers in the area as well as a trade hub for the region. Many of the young men in St. Louis jumped at the possibility for glory they thought the war would bring. Men like Alexander Doniphan volunteered alongside other Missourians who answered the 1846 call to arms by Missouri's governor, John Edwards. These eager volunteers formed the First Regiment of Missouri Mounted Volunteers. According to Edwards, "each soldier was to furnish himself with a good horse, saddle, clothing—in short, everything except arms." This reliance on volunteers to provide their own mounts and saddles greatly relieved the Quartermaster's Department of the supply burden for these mounted riflemen.

While the department sent what resources it could afford to support Kearny's operations, the overland distance limited what the expedition could receive in a timely manner from the eastern depots.[5]

Captain William M. D. McKissack and First Lieutenant Abraham R. Johnston served as the quartermasters preparing and supplying soldiers in the western theater. McKissack received assignment as assistant quartermaster at Fort Leavenworth and helped prepare the western soldiers for their long march. The California Expedition, including the Mormon Battalion, camped at Fort Leavenworth and received the standard equipage for soldiers, which included a .69 caliber flintlock musket (a smooth-bore 1816 model), a cartridge box, bayonet, and a knapsack with a blanket. Soldiers also received a small cotton haversack with a few days' worth of rations and a canteen that held three pints of water. For the Mormons, the only standardized piece of uniform was a white leather waist belt.[6]

On June 16, 1846, Kearny appointed Johnston as regimental adjutant to help organize supplies. Johnston quickly recruited every teamster and supply wagon in the region. The Quartermaster's Department reported that it required 1,556 wagons, 459 horses, 3,658 draught mules, and 516 pack mules to support the Army of the West. Cattle and oxen beef on the hoof totaled 14,904. Supply for Kearny's army as it crossed a continent was thus no small accomplishment, though supply difficulties plagued every facet of the western campaigns.[7]

Kearny parsed out his army, staggering the departure times due to the limited availability of water and grass. The first units left the fort on June 22, made up of companies A and D of the First Regiment of Missouri Mounted Volunteers. The main expedition force set out on June 26, 1846, with Kearny and the rear troops leaving a few days later on June 29. The small army was accompanied by fifty mounted Shawnee and Delaware Indians to serve as scouts and interpreters as well as countless civilians working as teamsters and merchants. The California Expedition left when the annual merchant train departed from Independence, Missouri, on June 26. The final unit lined the road for miles with its 414 wagons heavily laden with dry goods for sale in Santa Fe and Chihuahua. The Mormon Battalion and the other reinforcements left Fort Leavenworth on August 11. The Quartermaster's Department sent supplies to Fort Bent, west of Fort Leavenworth, for the reinforcements to restock their supplies before taking the Santa Fe Trail to join Kearny. The expedition's cattle served as a mobile food source since there would be little access to steady supplies between Fort Bent and Santa Fe. All told, Kearny's Army of the West marched with roughly three thousand men and twenty thousand animals.[8]

Kearny received orders from President Polk via the War Department to take one of his contingents and invade Mexico to capture Santa Fe. The task fell to Kearny and his Army of the West, with Doniphan as his second in command. While Kearny marched southwest toward Santa Fe, the California Expedition under Captain John C. Frémont began operations on the Pacific coast. Frémont and his roughly sixty troops arrived in California in 1845 as part of a surveying expedition. It is unclear if Frémont operated under US Army orders or on his own initiative. Nonetheless, he sided with Anglo settlers at the start of hostilities against Mexican forces. Polk's bold plan resulted in the United States seizing control of vast portions of northwest Mexico, particularly the sparsely populated regions of New Mexico and California.[9]

Charles and William Bent established Fort Bent, also known as Bent's Fort or Bent's Old Fort, as their first trading post at the mouth of the Fountain River in southwestern Colorado. The brothers built a second fort and operated it downstream by until William tore it down and constructed a third fort even farther downriver. Kearny and his army used this latter fort on their march to Santa Fe. The US Army set Bent's Fort as the first point of general rendezvous for all the detachments and government supply trains. Subsequently, the Quartermaster's Department converted it to a provision depot for army use. Kearny later appointed Charles Bent as governor of New Mexico once Santa Fe surrendered to the US Army, but he was later murdered during the Taos Rebellion in 1847. This fort represented the last bastion of United States influence before entering Mexican territory.[10]

Kearny's advance with the Army of the West began by June 30, 1846, marching with such speed that it precluded receiving the initial shipments from Philadelphia to supply this vanguard force. The reinforcements brought some of these supplies with them, while others were shipped via steamboat and other vessels to California. The quartermasters at Leavenworth managed to obtain the needed camp and other equipage for the initial expedition from Missouri and other surrounding states and territories. Quartermasters moved many of the supplies from St. Louis to Fort Leavenworth by river steamer. General Jesup appointed Major Thomas Swords, whom he declared "one of the ablest officers of the Department," to accompany General Kearny on the Santa Fe Expedition as well as to continue with him to San Francisco. The New York–born Swords graduated from the United States Military Academy at West Point and quickly found himself in the Quartermaster's Department where he served through the Mexican-American and Civil Wars. Swords supervised the preparations and then traveled with Kearny's army to California. On the initial leg of the journey to Santa Fe, Swords was delayed until mid-August, when he joined Kearny and presented him with his formal notice of appointment as brigadier general. Captain Robert E. Clary relieved Captain McKissack in July so McKissack could travel with Captain Robert Allen to assume quartermaster duties at Santa Fe.[11]

McKissack and Swords worked diligently at Fort Leavenworth to prepare the overland expedition. The first leg of the journey to Santa Fe stretched roughly eight hundred miles, which was followed by an additional eight-hundred-mile march to San Diego. Jesup ordered several hundred wagons sent west, with two hundred to be kept in deposit at Fort Leavenworth and a similar number at Jefferson Barracks. Kearny took many of these wagons with him along the Santa Fe Trail or replaced ones he requisitioned form Fort Leavenworth. The quartermaster teams prepared wagons laden with provisions to be sent ahead to Council Grove and Fort Bent for resupply along the first two-thirds of the march. The wagons left Fort Leavenworth in groups of twenty-five to thirty at regular intervals, regardless of when the troops left on their march. The army broke up the supply trains to provide adequate forage for the animals along the route. The result of this distribution left some portions of the army destitute for supplies for short amounts of time. Each of the wagon trains included a superintendent-general, or wagon-master, and the wagoneers, all of whom traveled armed, thus eliminating the need for an armed guard to escort each caravan. This march proved to be less hazardous than later marches because of the established nature of the Santa Fe Trail.[12]

The bison herds that roamed the plains Kearny's army crossed provided an occasional boon of fresh meat and supplemented the expedition's sizeable herd of cattle and oxen. Frank Edwards noted that at Pawnee Forks several of the army's hunters killed three buffalo, and he tasted bison for the first time. This herd consisted of three to four thousand bison. A secondary benefit of the roaming herds came in the form of buffalo chips, or dried manure patties that could be burned for fuel, as many future western settlers would discover. This source of fuel proved to be invaluable because the plains lacked enough wood to support an army. By July 21, most of buffalo country lay behind the army, and rations were running short, a problem that became common in the marches across this inhospitable land. Half or quarter rations paired with scarce water made the last leg of the march to Bent's Fort uncomfortable to say the least. At least the soldiers had resources ahead and behind; such assurances did not persist throughout the western campaigns.[13]

From Bent's Fort to Santa Fe

By July 29, Kearny's vanguard reached the rendezvous for the Army of the West at Bent's Fort. Susan Magoffin, wife of a merchant who traded on the Santa Fe Trail, was at the fort when the army arrived. She described what the soldiers saw as they approached the fort, stating, "The outside exactly fills my idea of an ancient castle. It is built of adobes, unburnt brick, and Mexican style so far. The walls are very high and very thick with rounding corners. There is but one entrance, this is to the East rather. Inside is a large space some ninety or a hundred feet square, all around this and next the wall are rooms, some twenty-five in number." This place also offered the last chance to rest before pressing on to Santa Fe. The army faced another problem on the next 330 miles to Santa Fe; the plains that stretched between the two points lacked access to water and had very little grass for the horses. Kearny decided to put his men on reduced rations, leaving them "only half a pound of flour and 3/8ths of a pound of pork per day [for] each man." The restrictions deprived the soldiers of coffee, sugar, salt, rice, and any other foodstuff that was not considered essential weight on the march. A new meal, slapjacks, resulted from this rationing. This meal consisted of flour and water fried in fat; while not appetizing, it did keep the troops fed and marching. At this point in the march, the Army of the West consisted of about 1,750 men, though reinforcements followed several weeks behind. In addition, the expedition found draught mules at the fort to replace the ones "we had billed by fatigue on the march," from pulling the heavy artillery. Of the one hundred fine cannon horses that the expedition started with, not more than ten made it to Santa Fe. While at Fort Bent, Kearny sent scouts toward Taos and Santa Fe to report on the intentions and disposition of the New Mexicans.[14]

Inexperience of the teamsters and a lack of Quartermaster's Department regulations for executing such an expedition compounded the hardships of the trip to Bent's Fort. The quartermasters procured wagons, draught animals, and teamsters from across the western United States for the support of Kearny's army. The western United States extended just past the Mississippi River. Illinois, Missouri, Arkansas, and Louisiana made up the furthest edge of the American West prior to the Mexican-American War. The annexation of Texas increased that reach, but much of the land to the north of Texas remained unoccupied by Anglo-American settlers. The US Army marched into unfriendly lands far distant from the line of settlement in the United States, so it struggled to support its troops in the field. Due to the rush to supply Kearny and get his troops under way, the department purchased equipment regardless of condition and recruited teamsters who were inexperienced on the hard, inhospitable Santa Fe Trail. Many wagons broke down, and draught animals died of exhaustion along the trail. According to Kearny, $5 million worth of government supplies, equipment, and animal remains littered the trail, and the loss greatly jeopardized his expedition. Kearny as well as other commanders often requested additional supplies as the stores they brought regularly ran out. This leg of their journey was only the first of many.[15]

The geography between Fort Bent and Santa Fe meant the Army of the West needed to cross arid, desert-like terrain before finding a more hospitable environment nearer to Santa Fe. According to John Hughes, a volunteer in the First Regiment of Missouri Mounted Volunteers, "the American desert, is perhaps, no less sterile, sandy, parched, and destitute of water and every green herb and living thing than the African Sahara." Furthermore, it makes clear the logistical hardship the army faced as it marched, because it needed to obtain and transport enough water for the men and draught animals to survive. Kearny supplemented the dwindling rations by purchasing additional foodstuffs from passing American merchants; in particular, he bought flour from a merchant from Taos. Not only was the flour welcomed, but the merchant also provided news of Governor Manuel Armijo's actions. Hughes concluded that, "the Roman army under Metelus, on its march through the deserts of Africa, never encountered more serious opposition from the elements than did our army in its passage over the American Sahara." While his hardship is most likely exaggerated for the dramatic effect it would have on the readers of his memoirs, it is a vivid representation of what the soldiers faced on their long march.[16]

The expedition reached Santa Fe on August 18 and marched into the city without meeting any resistance. There was an alleged Mexican army that planned to confront Kearny's forces, but command disputes led to the supposed army's dissolution.[17] Not a shot was fired other than a thirteen-gun salute signifying United States occupation of the city. The city and effectively the larger territory of New Mexico put up little resistance to the army extending American control into the region. Due to the ever-growing trade connection with the United States, Santa Fe had increasingly allied itself with American merchants. Many residents did not resist the replacement of the weak Mexican government with a force seemingly more able to project military and political power. Once in Santa Fe, the soldiers erected a pole in the middle of the plaza to fly the American flag. The soldiers also found a few pieces of artillery, some hidden, including a six-pounder cannon that bore a lone star of Texas and the name "M. B. Lamar," the former president of Texas.[18]

Edwards, like many of the soldiers, found the food in Santa Fe as intriguing as its people. The first night in Santa Fe left the occupying army sadly bedraggled as soldiers set up tents in no formal order and men staked famished animals in the sand; soldier and animal alike spent a supperless night. The army, however, would not lack for food there in the coming days, and many soldiers received their first introduction to Mexican culture and food, including tortillas. Eventually, the soldiers who remained after Kearny's departure erected Fort Marcy overlooking the city.[19]

With Santa Fe captured, Kearny's forces needed to procure forage for their animals. Santa Fe lacked any immediate access to such forage, so grazing animals outside of the city became the best alternative. Kearny and his forces were left with a limited number of animals while most grazed. They also took the animals to Galisteo Creek, which was abundant in water and grass, and the grazing detachment set up a camp there to oversee the animals. After several days of rest, grass, and water, the horses and draught animals recovered from the exhausted state in which the march to Santa Fe had left them. The difficulty in obtaining enough forage continued to plague the expedition, especially once it set out for California. The Quartermaster's Department had little ability to help with this problem, since the expedition operated so far from regular supply lines.[20]

The occupation of Sante Fe differed from that of the Rio Grande Valley primarily in that the merchants who accompanied the army along the Santa Fe Trail already had existing ties and networks in the city. While in South Texas, merchants sought additional advantages during the occupation, the same did not occur in New Mexico. Because of the territory's isolation from Mexico City, the change in governments did not disturb the society nearly as much as it did along the Rio Grande. Trade continued as usual in Santa Fe; the new leadership took command of the city; and life went on relatively unaltered despite the presence of the US Army. The primary exception came with the short-lived Taos Revolt that claimed the newly appointed Governor Bent's life. The revolt of Hispanic New Mexicans and Puebloans in Toas against the occupying US forces caused almost all of the casualties in New Mexico. The US Army quickly crushed the rebellion.

NAVAL RESUPPLY AND OVERLAND REINFORCEMENTS

Back on the East Coast, Assistant Quartermaster General Colonel Henry Stanton received orders from Jesup to "control the loading of the vessels of the

California Expedition." This maritime expedition sailed from New York around South America and into the Pacific Ocean. Stanton organized the voluminous stores, baggage, camp equipage, and subsistence for the voyage, but he also chartered any additional ships needed to make the journey. He worked with expedition commander Colonel Jonathan D. Stevenson and the acting assistant quartermaster, Lieutenant Joseph L. Folsom, to obtain the requisitions. This operation presented an important component of a multipronged attack to seize sparsely populated California, one of the territories President Polk most wanted from Mexico, before the war concluded. [21]

At the behest of President Polk, the seaborne portion of the California Expedition made ready to depart by the second week of September 1846. Jesup, in a note on September 5, 1846, ordered Colonel Stanton to "double, or quadruple if necessary, the stevedores . . . employed in such occasion. They must all be gotten off next week, or at least you must have them ready to go. If Colo. Stevenson should not be ready, that is his affair, not ours." The department, as far as Jesup was concerned, would not be the weak link in the army's chain that held up the expedition to California. Ships were chartered, and wagons were procured until only loading remained. In a follow-up letter on September 11, Jesup ordered Stanton, Captain David H. Vinton, and Captain Michael M. Clark to focus their efforts on getting the ships loaded as rapidly as possible. He impressed upon his trio of quartermasters that "the occasion is an extraordinary one, and if necessary extraordinary means must be adopted." Jesup was determined to get the California expedition out to sea before the end of September 1846.[22]

The expedition planned to set sail from New York, travel to New Orleans, then on to Río de Janeiro to resupply during the trip to California. Once in the Pacific, the army ships planned to contact an American merchant in Mazatlán, a city in the state of Sinaloa on Mexico's west coast, to further resupply. US Navy forces captured Mazatlán later in the war. Jesup proposed that this merchant also be used to secure supplies for the American forces arriving in the Pacific. Stanton received orders to charter this merchant's vessel and put him in the employ of the department for transporting supplies. Merchants such as this offered dual benefits for the overtaxed quartermasters: they provided a ship for transporting goods, and they also used their contacts in the foreign trade networks unfamiliar to Jesup and his men.[23]

Since the California Expedition sailed to the furthest reaches of the Mexican frontier, Jesup approved requisitions for some interesting equipment to help in such a remote territory. He ordered Lieutenant Folsom and Captain S. B.

Dusenbury to obtain a portable sawmill. This tool allowed the troops destined for California to establish their position more quickly because they could produce some of their own lumber for construction. Clothing also presented an interesting problem for the California Expedition. Since a large portion of the men planned to march from Fort Leavenworth to the west, the trip would be hard on clothing and shoes. As a result, Jesup ordered Colonel Stanton to procure uniforms from department contractors and make them available to Lieutenant Folsom as he prepared his ships destined for San Francisco. Secretary of War William Marcy originally ordered this purchase, but he later amended it, instructing that the ships should leave immediately and not wait for the clothing if it would hold up the expedition.[24]

Jesup and his quartermasters also busily prepared supplies for the detachment of Second United States Dragoons that would accompany Kearny. For that primary purpose, Captain Vinton, another assistant quartermaster stationed in New York, was assigned to assist Lieutenant Folsom in his preparations. On September 14, 1846, Folsom, who had recently been promoted to captain, received notice from Jesup that Congress had appointed him as an assistant quartermaster for Kearny's expedition to Santa Fe. Folsom reported to Colonel Stevenson for orders until Kearny arrived to take command of the troops. Jesup also noted that "one if the greatest difficulties attending the expedition will be the ready supply of funds," for the Treasury Department lacked any regular system to supply funds for distant operations. A large enough sum to meet payroll and other marching expenses could not be approved by the time Folsom and Kearny would leave. Jesup overcame this obstacle by planning to "dispatch an officer of the Department across the Isthmus to meet or join you with funds as soon as an appropriation be made at the next session of Congress." Jesup also petitioned Congress for an additional vessel for the department's use in the Pacific.[25]

By the time the Quartermaster's Department began mobilizing transports and supplies for the California Expedition, it had achieved a surplus of resources. This abundance did not stop American entrepreneurs from trying to take advantage of the wartime demands by selling their merchandise to the army at premium prices. By September 1846, American businessmen regularly wrote Jesup, offering ships to charter or supplies for purchase. On occasion, if the offer met the needs of the department and the cost proved acceptable, Jesup approved the expense. More often, Jesup thanked the businessmen for their offers and referred them to an appropriate assistant quartermaster, with instructions to him to keep the offers in mind for current or future operations. Once the department had achieved a surplus of resources, it could be more discerning about the prices of goods and chartering ships, further increasing the quartermasters' economic efficiency.[26]

Once the ships carrying the California Expedition sailed in late September 1846, some men and supplies remained at New York that were destined for California. Vinton got orders on October 8, 1846, to take the ship *Brutus* to transport "such supplies as we may have to ship and the officers and men of the California Regiment left behind on the sailing of the transports." The *Brutus* was to be prepared for the "voyage without loss of time" and was directed to the Bay of San Francisco. Stanton ordered Vinton to fill the ship with army supplies and men and allow the remaining space to be occupied by the Navy Department. This arrangement was unique because the branches of the military traditionally did not work well together. During the Mexican War, however, there were several examples of army-navy cooperation. While each service branch kept careful track of its supplies and kept materials separate, cooperation was nevertheless important for the war effort.[27]

During September 1846 in Santa Fe, Kearny set to work preparing for the California Expedition to leave from the recently captured city. The distance from supply depots and department price limits on the purchasing of animals and supplies left Kearny with subpar animals in many cases despite the availability of finer stock in Santa Fe. Pending completed preparations, he planned to depart around September 25. Further complicating the expedition, the Paymaster Department had not provided any pay to the soldiers since departure from Fort Leavenworth. Soldiers therefore could not supplement their rations and gear with purchases from Santa Fe merchants. Obtaining funds for soldiers became increasingly difficult the further west the army went. Industrious soldiers even began cutting their brass buttons from their uniforms to sell for around twenty-five cents each, carving wooden buttons to use in their place.[28]

Sterling Price sent word to Kearny on September 20 that the reinforcement expedition needed to be supplied. Kearny quickly sent provisions back on the road to aid Price and his men. The department hired private contractors to procure and drive fourteen hundred head of cattle to follow the reinforcements, but they had lagged too far behind to relieve Price's troops. Only Kearny's actions allowed Price to resume normal marching speed in his advance toward Santa Fe. The field armies experienced much hardship during the long march west because the department simply had no means of delivering supplies west of Santa Fe. The armies, once they eventually departed for California, marched with only their supplies until they could meet up with the transport vessels the Quartermaster's Department sent to meet them in California.[29]

The reinforcements for Kearny, including the Mormon Battalion, arrived in Santa Fe on October 9, 1846. On the outskirts of town, the soldiers prepared themselves to march into the town square by fixing bayonets and marching in rank for inspection. Colonel Doniphan welcomed the reinforcements at Santa Fe. The army occupied the city with two regiments of about sixteen hundred men, one under Colonel Doniphan and a second under Colonel Price. The journey left the troops disheveled with worn-out attire. The Mormons, already lacking uniforms, looked especially unkempt and endured contempt from some of the other soldiers. Once in Santa Fe, Colonel Philip St. George Cooke took over command of the Mormon Battalion. Cooke concluded that the battalion was in poor shape, but a lack of Quartermaster's Department funds and resources left little to be done. Even the mules, he concluded, were utterly broken down. As part of the planned reorganization of the battalion, he appointed First Lieutenant Andrew J. Smith as quartermaster and Second Lieutenant George Stoneman as assistant quartermaster. Most of the women who had accompanied the Mormons were sent back, but five were allowed to stay with the army.[30]

DESTINED FOR CALIFORNIA

With Santa Fe secured, the next phase of the campaign could begin. Kearny and three hundred dragoons set out from Santa Fe for California, leaving first for San Diego. Colonel Doniphan led a secondary expedition made up of his 856 cavalrymen from Santa Fe to Chihuahua, Mexico, via El Paso, Texas, then down the Rio Grande to embark for New Orleans. This latter journey covered approximately thirty-six hundred miles by its conclusion. Doniphan planned to rendezvous with General John E. Wool, moving southward from San Antonio to join with General Taylor's Army of Occupation at Monterrey. A portion of the troops under the command of Colonel Price remained in Santa Fe. Doniphan became involved with the Navajo Indians, however, before he could leave Santa Fe. This mission derailed his portion of the expedition for a few months.[31]

The remainder of Kearny's army, with the Mormon Battalion following later, set out from Santa Fe on October 19 with a supply train to support them. It included twenty-five government wagons, fifteen mule wagons (three mule wagons for each company, each one pulled by eight mules), six ox wagons for heavy equipment, four mule wagons for the battalion command (field and staff, quartermaster, hospital department, and paymaster), five company wagons (purchased by the troops to haul their equipment to ease the burdens of marching long distances), and twelve family wagons. The Quartermaster's Department provided rations for sixty days, with full rations of only flour, sugar, coffee, and salt. Troops received enough salted pork for thirty days and enough soap for twenty days. The department also provided pack saddles to carry more goods on the draft animals, a fortunate decision since Kearny quickly realized that the rough terrain his force needed to traverse could not be crossed with wagons. Pack saddles proved to be the only way to move the supplies.[32]

New Mexico provided enough towns for the army to purchase corn, wood, and fodder each night, especially for small groups of soldiers operating in tandem with the army or patrolling as part of the occupation of New Mexico. Indian corn was available in large quantities because it served as the primary currency by which tithes were paid to the former Mexican government in the region. Furthermore, grass and good spring water were available in sufficient quantities for the expedition's use each night. Access to a ready food supply alleviated some of the pressures on the Quartermaster's Department in providing food to soldiers in this far-flung region.[33]

On October 7, Kearny turned west from the Chihuahua road towards Alta California. By October 9, the terrain again was too difficult to manage with wagons, and they were abandoned in favor of pack saddles so that travel would not be impeded. The army headed to California, following four young Apache as guides across the southwestern territories. On October 19, Kearny and his men crossed the Continental Divide in western New Mexico, and they welcomed the fresh mountain air that night. By November 8, the army reached Pima-controlled territory in what is today southern Arizona near Tucson. The trip from the Pima lands to the Gila River turned out to be a dry, trying time for both man and animal as mules subsisted on the bark and leaves of willow or cottonwood trees.[34]

The first excitement on the march came from finding the remains of a camp with the markings of several hundred horses. Kearny feared that Mexican forces had returned, but his scouts returned with several caballeros who were transporting a herd of about five hundred horses. This event took a day to sort out, giving men and mules a chance to rest. On December 5, Kearny's vanguard saw an approaching group of horsemen flying the stars and stripes. The leader of this band was Captain Archibald Gillespie of the Marine Corps. He was carrying correspondence for Kearny from Commodore Robert F. Stockton, which was dispatched after receiving word of Kearny's approach. Both forces

THE LAST DAY WITH THE WAGONS

The terrain on the march westward from Santa Fe proved too difficult for the traditional wagons. The army under Kearny abandoned its wagons and shifted to mules to carry the bulk of their supplies to California. Image courtesy of the University of Texas at Arlington.

camped for the night and planned to set off for the final march into California the following morning. The next day presented the first combat for Kearny's small army at the Battle of San Pasqual near San Diego. Kearny's men and the few supporting Marines managed to resist the Californio lancers, Mexican Californian mounted troops with lances, long enough for American reinforcements to arrive on December 7. With this new support, Kearny marched into San Diego. Despite a serious wound, he recovered quickly once in the city and by December 20 resumed regular activity.[35]

Once the inconclusive Navajo Campaign ended, Doniphan resumed the march to Chihuahua. Adding to the pressure to depart, three to four hundred traders with 315 wagons waited for the Missouri Regiment under Doniphan to march so they could follow the army to Chihuahua. The impatience on the merchants' part came not from political or military concerns but from the understanding that each delay cut into their profits. The lure of the army's protection kept the merchants waiting until Doniphan was prepared to march. It took until December 14, 1846, for the first group of Doniphan's soldiers to depart from Santa Fe under Major William Gilpin. Their first major objective was El Paso del Norte along the Rio Grande; it was another town of about ten thousand inhabitants roughly two hundred miles from Santa Fe. Doniphan continued the piecemeal approach of disbursing his men when marching in this inhospitable terrain. Several smaller forces interspersed with supply trains worked better than trying to move and supply a single, large force in the desert-like conditions through which Doniphan and his men marched.[36]

The march into the Mexican heartland meant that Doniphan's army passed through the *Jornada de Muerto*—Dead Man's Journey or Route of the Dead Man—an exceptionally tough stretch of arid land between Fray Cristóbal and Robledo. The path began about nine miles south of Valverde and crossed the Rio Grande. Like some previous travelers, Doniphan chose to avoid following the river because it flowed through steep mountain passes and made the army susceptible to Indian attack. This stretch of land rightfully earned a reputation for being waterless, with only one watering hole before reaching El Paso. For Doniphan, the march was even more difficult than usual because winter had set in, making an already deadly journey even more hazardous. There was little to burn along this path, so the soldiers braved the stinging cold with little access to fire to provide escape from the frigid monotony. By December 22, the final column of soldiers reached Doña Ana, a small outpost ten miles below the Journada where water, forage, and food were available, although the army still had another forty miles to go before reaching El Paso.[37]

About twenty-five miles outside of El Paso, Doniphan faced his first battle as an independent regimental commander. The Battle of Brazito along the "Brazito" or "little arm," a channel off the Rio Grande, occurred on December 25, 1846. Doniphan's regiment faced Mexican defenders led by Lieutenant Colonel Antonio Ponce de León. Doniphan chose to wait for the Mexican attack after seeing their well-established defenses. The American soldiers managed to turn back charges by both de León's lancers and dragoons. Their victory in this small engagement earned Doniphan and his men great fame in newspapers across the United States.[38]

As the army neared El Paso, a volunteer named Frank Edwards recalled a "Señor Ponce, an old Mexican gentleman, and the richest man in the valley of El Paso, for assistance in getting corn and other necessaries for the soldiers. He supplied us, as far as possible, from his own store-houses, and, where these failed, he bought for us." Edwards elaborated, saying that the "valley here is the best calculated for the cultivation of the vine in any part of Mexico." The bounty of the Rio Grande area served as a respite to the soldiers. Whether Señor Ponce freely gave of his supplies as Edwards implied is unclear, but the incident does illustrate that supplies could be obtained from the locals. For the duration, Colonel Doniphan housed his men in two big buildings in the plaza. After a short period in El Paso, his army's supplies began to run short, necessitating the purchase of additional resources from local Mexicans, including limited wheat and rather abundant cattle. On January 31, messengers arrived at El Paso to alert Doniphan that his requested artillery was just seven miles north, but the gunners had run out of food. Doniphan immediately sent a wagon to resupply the detachment.[39]

It took until December 1846 for Kearny to reach San Diego, California. With the arrival of Kearny, a new conflict erupted between the various American commanders in California. Before the war began, Frémont already found himself in Mexican California as the head of a US Army survey of the Rockies and Great Salt Lake region. Frémont's force numbered about sixty-five men, making it a formidable militia force in sparsely populated California. The Mexican officials in California grew suspicious of him and ordered him out of the territory. Frémont did not go far, however, sensing war would break out soon. At the start of hostilities with Mexico, Frémont allegedly proposed a scheme encouraging settlers to revolt against the Mexican government. Frémont never wrote about such an idea, but as tension grew, eventually Anglo settlers began a revolt to establish the Bear Flag Republic. Frémont also organized his topographical engineers into the "California Battalion." He eventually assumed command of the Anglo forces in California until a US Navy ship arrived in Monterrey Bay under the command of Commodore John D. Sloat. Frémont admitted to Sloat that he operated without any authorization from the US government. Stockton, Frémont, and Kearny bickered with each other over supreme American command of the newly conquered territory. Distance from US Army command left room for such debate over leadership since letters could take weeks or months to travel across the western region. For the remainder of the war the three commanders vied for political and military control, with Kearny finally seizing both the governorship and leadership of the new military district in California. Eventually, Frémont's actions resulted in him being court-martialed after Kearny's arrival on the West Coast.[40]

Due to a scarcity of resources in San Diego for the army to purchase, Kearny sent Major Swords to Hawaii (then often called the Sandwich Islands) to buy foodstuffs, clothing, and medical supplies.[41] With supplies procured, despite the infighting between American commanders, the war for California pressed on. In late March 1847, four companies of the Mormon Battalion left San Diego for Los Angeles. Los Angeles also housed the regular army, which included the First Dragoons. California had its own supply network between the cities in that territory. Between San Diego and Los Angeles wagons carried coffee, sugar, soap, candles, and other needed supplies. While some of the supplies came from the local area, most came in by ships sent from the eastern coast of the United States. The goods were then transported to the various army encampments by wagon. The soldiers stationed in Los Angeles built a new military outpost there, Fort Monroe. Several battles occurred in the occupation of California between United States forces and either the Californios or Bear Republic forces. With the successful Battles of Río San Gabriel and La Mesa, United States forces entered Los Angeles with no resistance from the city. The Treaty of Cahuenga, signed by Frémont and two of General Andres Pico's officers, marked the end of armed resistance in California.[42]

Doniphan and the US Navy in the West

Doniphan and his army left El Paso on February 11, 1847, having chosen to proceed to Chihuahua to rendezvous with General Wool rather than to return to Santa Fe. The merchants traveling with the American forces received instructions from Doniphan to organize into two brigades in case of an engagement with the Mexicans. At this point during the long march from Fort Leavenworth, Doniphan began to consider the merchant wagons as hasty breastworks and the supplies they held as potential emergency resources. He marched toward Chihuahua but confronted confident Mexican forces several miles outside of the city.[43]

The Battle of Sacramento River took place on February 28, 1847, between the American forces led by Doniphan and a substantial Mexican force. The battle took place about fifteen miles north of Chihuahua, Mexico, at the crossing of the Sacramento River. Once in Chihuahua, the army quartered at the Plaza de Toros, a large amphitheater in the city used for bull fights. Many of the soldiers felt relieved to be in Chihuahua after a long march, particularly with access to the markets allowing them to purchase foods such as "light bread and sweet cakes" as well as butter to accompany them. Once in Chihuahua, Doniphan and his officers were to meet Wool, but the general had not arrived, so there was much discussion on the course of action. Finally, a dispatch of a dozen men traveled to General Taylor's position and returned with instructions to join him at Monterrey via Parras and Saltillo. The march was doubly difficult due to the lack of forage for animals south of Chihuahua. According to US Army volunteer Frank S. Edwards, the army needed to purchase "standing wheat as fodder for our horses. . . . Our poor animals had to live on the maize along, which sadly heated them with fever."[44]

After the capture of Chihuahua, Doniphan and his men marched to Parras. By March 25, Edwards noted that they had encamped some twenty-five miles from the "Bishop's Palace, near Monterrey." He also remarked on the destruction wrought by United States artillery throughout the city as they passed through it. Doniphan's army rendezvoused with Taylor's forces three miles from Monterrey at Taylor's camp at Walnut Springs, where the soldiers caught a glimpse of "Old Rough and Ready" for the first time. The travel-weary force received orders to continue to Camargo and then down the Rio Grande. Upon entering Camargo on March 31, the American soldiers realized that the river town had "become a place of some importance, for, although there are but few substantial dwellings, yet there is quite a large number of canvas houses used for the protection of pro-visions and other stores landed from the steamboats, when the river is high, and sent hence in wagons to the army. These canvas houses are of immense extent, and stand in a cluster, surrounded by a trench and embankment." With the Rio Grande too low for steamboat travel, Doniphan's force marched parallel to the river toward "Reinosa."[45] When they reached that town, they found several steam-boats along with fellow soldiers discharged by Taylor awaiting transportation to Brazos Santiago. After passing by Fort Brown and Matamoros, Doniphan's army encamped at Brazos Santiago until June 9, when they embarked on two steamers, the *Republic* and *Murillo*, destined for New Orleans and the mustering out of the far-traveled force.[46]

While Doniphan and his men marched and fought across northern Mexico, the US Navy focused on seizing ports in Baja California. After a blockade of the port of Mazatlán by Commander Samuel F. Du Pont of the Navy in the *Cyane*, it was occupied by American forces on November 11, 1847. Commodore Stockton of the Navy's Pacific Squadron had decided to capture the port town and eventually try to seize Acapulco. This plan was not feasible, however, and subsequent commodores and army commanders decided to pull back from Baja California. They lacked the necessary troops and ships to protect allies and subjugate enemies. This retreat resulted in the relinquishment of Baja California solely to Mexico; American leadership seemed satisfied with Alta California. Baja California was the last major attempt to annex any more territory in the far western theater of the war.[47]

The Western Campaign included severe obstacles testing the durability of United States soldiers as well as the Quartermaster's Department that provided goods to support them. Through careful planning and commander ingenuity while marching, American armies managed to cross the vast distances of the west and secured a piece of land that represented about half of Mexico's entire territory, which would add about a third of what is today the continental United States. The adventures in the West included mostly marching with limited fighting. The first and only religiously organized unit, the Mormon Battalion, grew out of these efforts to secure Mexico's far northern frontera. Although the alliance between Mormons and the United States would not last, it does represent the great lengths that the federal government would go to acquire land.

The conquest of Santa Fe concluded several decades of shifting loyalties from Mexico City to the United States. For years, the Santa Fe Trail connected the Mexican city more closely to Missouri than the Mexican capital. The Quartermaster's Department capitalized on the existing Santa Fe Trail and used it to supplement their supply efforts. With the city securely in the hands of the army, American forces were able to push south and west, continuing the conquest of the West. The southern push led to Chihuahua and eventually to Doniphan joining with Taylor and his forces in northern Mexico. Other detachments of the western army marched for California.

California was the most contested area of the western theater. Much of the contest was between Californians seeking independence or among the American officers attempting to conquer the territory. Once the hostilities ceased, the United States found itself in control of a great portion of the West Coast of North America, granting good ports and access to trade with Asian markets. One of the bitterest results of the loss of California for Mexico was the discovery of gold in 1849. The gold rush could have provided Mexico with valuable capital for the war effort, but it was the United States that reaped the tremendous economic and political rewards of the California gold fields.

The postwar results for New Mexico and California differed from the wave of colonization that occurred in South Texas. New Mexico's relative isolation made it an ideal intersection between Mexican and American trade, but it limited the number of settlers that might have flocked to it if located with easier travel access. California is an anomaly in its own right with the almost immediate discovery of gold in the territory and the subsequent flood of speculators from around the world. The territory's population skyrocketed even more so than in South Texas, rapidly making California a state. The primary difference between postwar California and South Texas is that along the Rio Grande the population remained predominantly Hispanic while in much of California the new Anglo, European, and Asian settlers quickly dwarfed the Hispanic population of the new state. Despite these differences, the Quartermaster's Department played an essential role in mobilizing, supplying, and transporting the armies that conquered these western territories. The end of the war saw these territories annexed and the new land greatly expanded the size of the United States. This land also rekindled the debate over the expansion of slavery, further complicating the meaning of these new territories.

Despite a similar occupying presence to that of South Texas, the same social and economic changes did not occur. South Texas and the border along the Rio Grande represented a unique mixture of accessibility and profitability that drew in settlers in greater numbers and from both sides of the border in ways not seen in Sante Fe in the decade after the war. California followed its own path with the 1849 gold rush rapidly increasing the territories population and pushing it towards statehood. Given that most of the population was Anglo or foreign the state's status as free or slave rekindled the tensions over the westward expansion of slavery. Laying the groundwork for the coming American Civil War in 1860, just twelve years after the end of the Mexican War.

Ultimately, the actions of the Quartermaster's Department allowed United States forces to reach across a continent and take control of Santa Fe, New Mexico, and California. The supplies, manpower, and logistical prowess facilitated the occupation of a vast portion of the West, which would serve as an important political tool in the treaty to end the Mexican War. Without these campaigns and the subsequent occupations of these regions, the United States may not have had the political bargaining chips to push Mexico to give up such robust land concessions at the end of the war.

CHAPTER 5

Central Mexico—Logistics of Conquest

Once it seemed apparent to President James Polk and Secretary of War William L. Marcy that General Zachary Taylor's campaign would not force the capitulation of the Mexican government, they looked for other options. Polk hoped a few quick battles would coerce Mexico into being more willing to sell California. Mexico and its people turned out to be far more resilient than expected, however, in the face of continued American success. If the battles in northern Mexico and the occupation of New Mexico and California by United States forces did not break the Mexican will to fight, the president concluded that Mexico City must be the new goal. If the capital was captured, he and his advisors concluded that Mexico would come to terms favorable to the United States.[1]

General Winfield Scott received the appointment to lead the new Army of Invasion at Veracruz and was tasked with capturing Mexico City. Polk and the American leadership hoped that the capture of the enemy capital would bring the war to a close. Most harbored notions that the Mexican government would yield before their capital ever fell. Nonetheless, the Quartermaster's Department received the task to mobilize a new army for Scott. The central Mexico campaign presented the greatest logistical hurdle of the war. The Quartermaster's Department transported supplies and soldiers from across the northeastern United States to New Orleans then on to Mexico. The campaign overcame the temperamental weather of the Gulf of Mexico as well as the dangers of springtime diseases like yellow fever. With the utmost preparation, the department helped coordinate the largest amphibious invasion of the war. Scott's campaign would end the war, forcing Mexico to cede claims to all of Texas including the Nueces Strip and the Southwest Provinces.

The American invasion and occupation of central Mexico and Mexico City left a lasting mark on the Mexican psyche. The occupation of a capital city by an enemy army is undeniably traumatic for the national identity of a people. Despite the occupation of Mexico City, the central Mexico campaign did not cause the same economic and demographic shifts seen in the Rio Grande borderlands. The population density of central Mexico insulated it from many of the foreign influences of merchants and postwar settlers that migrated to South Texas. Even though central Mexico did not change due to economic inroads by Anglo and European merchants or due to an influx of foreign settlers, the war left its mark on Mexico. The postwar years saw great changes for South Texas and the Rio Grande Valley, but Mexico experienced greater upheaval during the following decades.

Preparing for Invasion

General Scott submitted a memorandum on October 27, 1846, detailing an invasion of the Mexican coast, titled "Vera Cruz and Its Castle." He outlined the requirements to capture the port city of Veracruz and its defending castle, San Juan de Ulúa. President Polk, Secretary Marcy, and the rest of the cabinet debated the best course to bring the war to a close. Ultimately, they concluded the capture of Mexico City would force peace talks. Early in the war, it became clear that it was not feasible for Taylor to march his army to Mexico City from Monterrey. A hostile desert, a lack of roads, and the prohibitive distance of overland supply lines precluded that option. Former Consul to Mexico Francis M. Dimond briefed the cabinet on Veracruz and his experiences there during his time in Mexico. His discussion of Veracruz supported Scott's assessment of the city. Marcy and the commandant of the US Marine Corps, Brevet Brigadier General Archibald Henderson, supported Scott's proposed campaign. They already had their eyes on a possible expedition to capture Veracruz, and a campaign for Mexico City offered a chance to force Mexican capitulation and perhaps also to acquire California and New Mexico in the peace negotiations.[2]

In his memorandum, Scott argued that any effort to capture Veracruz without an advance inland would represent a waste of resources. He asserted that capturing Mexico City would be "a step towards compelling Mexico to sue for peace." The memorandum also outlined the forces he deemed necessary for such an operation: ten thousand men including two thousand cavalry and six hundred artillerists. Half the cavalry and all the artillery should be regulars, and they would need custom-built boats (see below) to land twenty-five hundred men.

This memorandum established the preliminary expectations Scott had regarding the forces needed to land in the face of what he expected would be staunch opposition. Scott, as noted in his memoir, "did not doubt meeting at [the] landing the most formidable struggle of the war. No precaution was therefore neglected." Such a landing, Scott concluded, posed too great a threat for the enemy at its most vulnerable to allow it to be uncontested. Logistical and temporal obstacles deprived him of much he desired, but the army and navy mustered enough forces to execute a successful landing.[3]

Sixteen days after Scott's proposal went before the president and his cabinet, Scott submitted a supplement expanding some of his requests for men and supplies. He also detailed the defensive positions Taylor and Wool would hold in northern Mexico after the transfer of some of their forces to Scott's expedition. Scott wrote that "The *minimum* force (10,000 men) then proposed, I still deem indispensable." He believed he could capture Veracruz with this number of troops, but he cautioned Polk and Marcy that it would be ill-advised to proceed without twelve to fifteen thousand men. Scott proposed reducing the force in northern Mexico to about eleven thousand after reinforcements arrived to expedite the expedition. By reassigning these troops from Taylor's defensive line in the north, Scott believed he could have four thousand regulars and five thousand volunteers, with an additional twelve hundred men drawn from the naval blockading force to supplement the invasion. The more detailed proposal outlining not only what he felt was necessary but also the sources for drawing these men received the approval and initiated the transfer of Brigadier General William J. Worth's brigade from Taylor's army.[4]

On November 16, 1846, Scott submitted an expanded memorandum detailing the recommended manpower, logistical support, and vessels for the operation, and handed it to Secretary of War Marcy. He modified the total number of men to fourteen thousand, requested fifty ships from five hundred to seven hundred and fifty tons, and one hundred forty surfboats to put ashore five thousand men in a single landing. The Quartermaster's Department's workload already stressed the logistical bureaucracy, but the new memorandum expected even more out of the department. In addition to its production, procurement, and transportation of current forces, Scott required resources to support a third army in the field. Complicating the request, Scott, Polk, and Marcy all wanted the campaign to begin as soon as possible. Implementing the measures necessary to support Scott's inconsistent estimates for the men and material needed for the attack on

Veracruz and the subsequent march to Mexico City would be the Quartermaster's Department's finest military achievement of the war.[5]

As the Quartermaster's Department transported the men and material, the US Navy prepared to coordinate the landing with the army. Commodore David Conner also reported to Marcy that there were two possible landing points near Veracruz, but he did not comment on what size of force or how many supplies would be needed to take the beach. He only reported a lack of beef in the area. Conner's Home Squadron also received support once the decision for the invasion was made. Secretary of the Navy John Young Mason diverted the *Ohio*, a powerful ship-of-the-line, and three sloops-of-war to the Gulf. Four coastal brigs or schooners were purchased and outfitted as bomb vessels for use in the bombardment of the San Juan de Ulúa fortress. Bureaucratic inefficiencies seemed to be the chief reason that these ships did not arrive until after the landing. Polk even noted a lack of coordination between services, such as Secretary Mason's ignorance of the projected landing date.[6]

On November 23, 1846, Scott received his orders from Marcy, "Sir: The President of the United States desires you to repair to the lower Rio Grande, in order to take upon yourself the general direction of the war against Mexico from this side of the Continent, and more particularly to organize and conduct an expedition (with the co-operation of the navy) against the harbor of Vera Cruz." With this order Scott began his journey from Washington, DC, to Veracruz, where he and Commodore Conner would become the first soldiers to successfully invade the heart of Mexico since Hernán Cortés.[7]

Scott's Surfboats

This invasion marked the first time in United States history that a military commander requested custom-built boats for an invasion. Furthermore, Scott requested enough boats to put ashore five thousand men, including light batteries, in the first wave of landings. By the time of the invasion, he only had received half the surfboats requested, but Scott still managed to put ashore 2,595 men under Worth's command, equaling the number that his first memorandum called for in the first wave of the invasion. Once receiving the orders from Marcy to construct the surfboats, Assistant Quartermaster General Henry Stanton wrote, "The Department has been recently required to provide, at an embarrassingly short notice, one hundred and fifty boats or barges, of the description indicated in the drawings and specifications handed you yesterday, by the 1st of January!!"

Stanton's success at delivering the surfboats proved to be one of his greatest wartime achievements and an example of the Quartermaster's Department's growing proficiency.[8]

Lieutenant George M. Totten, a navy officer, designed the surfboats outlined by Scott and built near Philadelphia. The boats were double-ended, broad-beamed, and flat-bottomed, with frames built of well-seasoned white oak. The boats came in three sizes to nest together for transport: forty feet holding forty-five plus men, thirty-seven feet holding forty plus men, and thirty-five feet holding a maximum of forty men. All of these were quite heavy: large with oars weighed 6,522 pounds, medium with oars weighed 5,343 pounds, and small with oars weighed 3,942 pounds. Each surfboat carried a crew of six oarsmen, one coxswain, and a skipper. The boats nesting feature meant they could fit into ships with oversized hatches and be stored in their holds.[9]

To construct these landing craft in a timely and secretive manner, Stanton engaged the services of Captain Richard Fanning Loper on November 29, 1846. Loper was a sail and steamship builder in Philadelphia. He registered several patents for steamship engines and other ship designs. He seems to have earned the respect of the department in the area of creating technologically new vessels. In addition, his rank of captain is likely an honorific referring to the captain of a ship and ascribed to him for his service as an agent of the Quartermaster's Department or in reference to his shipbuilding expertise. Stanton employed Loper as an agent because of his "well known intelligence, judgement, & practical experience . . . with the construction, purchase, or charter of vessels, boats, and other objects required in the prosecution of military marine operations." He received a per diem allowance of three dollars as a special agent. Stanton requested the boats be built in the northeastern United States, particularly Baltimore, New York, Boston, and like places where quality shipwrights worked. The builders were required to make each boat strictly conform to the drawings and specifications on the plans provided to Loper. Shipwrights constructed the boats to land with heavy ordnance. To hasten completion, Stanton informed Loper that "as to the price, it is not deemed expedient to limit you," effectively giving Loper a wide berth to complete the jobs in the allotted time. The department provided an estimate of what the navy had calculated would be a reasonable price even including the rushed production. It concluded that the cost should be around $400 per boat. If Loper was unable to secure contracts for all one hundred fifty boats as Stanton feared, he was then instructed to contract the building of as many as could be constructed in the time frame.[10]

Loper received the drawings on or just after December 5 and proceeded to have copies drawn up by a skilled artist to distribute to the contractors building the landing craft. By December 7, Loper informed Stanton that contracts had been obtained successfully for all one hundred forty boats. Stanton impressed upon Loper to "urge all concerned to the utmost diligence. Let there be no failure if attention to the subject can prevent it." Furthermore, Stanton contacted John Lenthall at Loper's suggestion to construct a nest of three boats on the patterns provided by the department. John Lenthall was a shipbuilder and naval architect for the US Naval Yards at Philadelphia. The crafts that Lenthall produced were intended to "make up for the deficiencies of some of the contractors." Stanton had no intention of failing in completing the order for these landing crafts, even doubling up on some of the construction contracts to ensure the expected number of boats was ready to ship by the new year.[11]

Amazingly, the boats were completed in the thirty days as Scott had requested, though according to Assistant Quartermaster General Stanton it was, "One of the most difficult orders which has ever been imposed on me, the construction, equipment, and shipment for the Brazos of the 140 barges . . . are all off for their destination." Prompt delivery of the surfboats equaled the difficulty of their manufacturing. Scott estimated each boat would cost about $400, but the department negotiated the final contract for between $795 and $950 per boat. The 141 boats in forty-seven stacks were shipped partly in army vessels, whose decks had been cut to admit them into the hold, and partly on the decks of vessels chartered by the Quartermaster's Department. Only sixty-five of the finished boats arrived at Veracruz in time for the landing, however. Despite not meeting Scott's request, enough surfboats arrived to land the originally planned twenty-five-hundred-man first wave.[12]

Transporting the New Army

Problems plagued the acquisition of transports. The War Department had planned to contribute forty-one additional transports, but due to a series of misunderstandings, countermanded orders, and other unforeseen developments, this plan was not successful. Mistakenly canceled vessels, delays due to lack of materials and understaffed crews, and bad weather caused many of the problems. Of the vessels gathered for the effort of moving supplies and men for Scott's expedition, fifty-three came from Atlantic ports and one hundred sixty-three from Gulf ports, all various tonnage. As a result, Stanton struggled to meet the requested one hundred forty boats weighing about twenty tons for General

Scott's "Grand Expedition" and the several transports for the heavy supplies of ordnance and engineer stores. Bad weather at New Orleans further delayed the loading of cargo on chartered ships and delayed their voyage to Brazos Santiago.[13]

The transports carried many of the new regiments of volunteers mustered into service for Scott's expedition as well as transferred regulars from Taylor's Army of Occupation. On December 3, 1846, Captain Benjamin Alvord received an assignment to obtain transportation for the new regiment of Massachusetts volunteers. He furnished them with supplies and transportation from Boston to New Orleans. From there, they traveled to either Brazos Santiago or Tampico before moving on to the gathering point near Veracruz. On the same day, Captain J. L. Goolrick received orders to outfit and transport a battalion of Virginia volunteers. Lieutenant R. M. Johnston stationed in Charleston, South Carolina, did the same for the new regiment from that state. General Jesup, while operating out of New Orleans, directed the new volunteer regiments from Alabama and Louisiana to be put on transports once they were outfitted. A continual flow of soldiers traveled to Mexico as the war persisted. By December 10, Stanton sent out a circular stating, "Instructions have been given to muster the Volunteers into service, by *companies*, as they report themselves ready without waiting for the enrolment of the entire Regiments." These units departed for Mexico as soon as they received supplies and training instead of waiting for a full complement.[14]

Stanton, at Jesup's instruction, also purchased two iron-propeller boats for $17,000 each. The *Ocean* had a gross tonnage of 191 and the *Ashland* came in at 182 tons of cargo space. He had the vessels fitted out, loaded with coal, and dispatched for Tampico to rendezvous with Scott's expedition by December 4. Stanton reported the purchase of the *Washington* screw steamship with a 224 gross tonnage for $17,000. Stanton proposed purchasing the *Eudora* that the department already had chartered for $20,000. Most of these later purchased ships were driven by screw propellers because Stanton concluded that "no sidewheel and side-guarded vessels can be safe vessels at sea." Jesup also had Stanton contact Loper about constructing or purchasing some slip-keel vessels for use in shallow waters. Stanton purchased a fixed-keel ship, the *John Potter* with a capacity of 163 gross tons, from Loper that was initially offered to Major Eastland who inspected the ship for Stanton. Loper additionally agreed to construct six slip-keel vessels, two of which were propellers or screw-driven steamships that would be ready to sail by February 10, 1847. Loper agreed to build four additional slip-keel ships beyond the first six at Stanton's insistence. Jesup and Stanton desired the slip-keel ships because the slip-keel, more commonly referred to today as a daggerboard, was a centerboard that could be retracted from the hull of the ship when coming into shallow water allowing easier navigation. The centerboard provides stability for the ship and prevents it from being pushed sideways, but with a slip-keel, it can be pulled up to avoid getting caught on a sand bar or lakebed. Such slip-keel ships had been used on the Great Lakes for at least a decade before the Mexican-American War. This invention could be well used along the Rio Grande and other shallow-water ports.[15]

The *John Potter* set sail from New York in early December headed for Tampa Bay to pick up two companies of artillery and then proceeded to Tampico. As Captain Vinton prepared the *John Potter* to depart for Tampa Bay, he received orders from Stanton to purchase the steamship *Virginia*[16] with a gross tonnage of four hundred tons for $18,500. Shortly after his orders to Vinton, Stanton informed Alexander Gordon, a Quartermaster's Department agent in Pittsburgh, to furnish transportation and supplies for the regiment of Pennsylvania volunteers. As always, the department continued to ship coal, oats, and forage to the depots along the Gulf Coast in conjunction with the new troop movements. Ordnance and engineering supplies were also being shipped with the new volunteers. Vinton received orders on December 13 to charter three more ships to carry ordnance and engineering supplies on the decks between where the volunteers were being housed. These latter supplies were headed to Pensacola to await orders from Scott on whether to rendezvous in Texas or Mexico. The engineering supplies would be crucial for sieging Veracruz.[17]

With more ships being purchased and more volunteers arriving at New Orleans to support Scott's invasion or to replace the troops in northern Mexico that went with Scott, the financial reserves for the department dwindled. On December 7, 1846, Stanton informed M. Morgan, the agent for the New Orleans Canal and Banking Company in New York, that Captain Vinton would be coming to them to handle a transfer of funds. The company would be handing a draft of one million three hundred thousand dollars ($1,300,000) from the treasurer or assistant treasurer of the United States. Morgan would furnish "a joint-receipt signed by yourself as agent for the 'New Orleans Canal and Banking Company' and the 'State Bank of New York' together with an acknowledgement therein of your obligation to transport or transfer the amount specified to the city of New Orleans." Vinton also received a basic form of receipt from Stanton that he could use or modify as he saw fit. The cost of the war continued to climb. The department incurred such debts with the hope that the new campaign targeting Mexico City would hasten Mexico's capitulation.[18]

At Brazos Santiago, Scott's Army of Invasion gathered awaiting troops from New Orleans and regulars from Taylor's army to supplement the planned force landing on Collado Beach, south of Veracruz. As early as October 22, 1846, Secretary of War Marcy had considered Brazos Santiago as a potential gathering and embarkation point for any military expedition against Veracruz. As army and navy vessels traveled to Tampico and Veracruz, the Brazos Santiago Depot served as one of the main coaling stations. Thousands of tons of coal were delivered there over the course of the war. While loading coal, ships often took on fresh water and provisions while they had the opportunity. In late 1846, Jesup moved his headquarters to Brazos Santiago to help coordinate Scott's landing at Veracruz. The growing port became the key forward logistical center for the entire war. The expansion of trade along the Rio Grande to meet the new needs of the army eventually led to economic growth in the Valley.[19]

As late as December 15, 1846, Scott still called for the forty-one more transports originally promised by the War Department to bring supplies, ordnance, volunteers, and surfboats. Bad weather delayed most of these vessels by twenty-five to thirty days, and through a misunderstanding, ten were countermanded by the War Department. Meanwhile, Worth's men needed transport to Isla de Lobos (Wolf Island) as promptly as possible. Isla de Lobos lay some fifty to sixty miles beyond Tampico and served as a midway point between Tampico and Veracruz. In response, Scott told Captain Abner Riviere Hetzel of the Brazos Santiago Quartermaster Depot to quickly charter five vessels capable of holding eight hundred men and supplies each.[20]

FINAL PREPARATIONS TO LAND AT VERACRUZ

While Scott moved his men into position near Veracruz, the department continued working on getting ordnance from New York to the Gulf of Mexico. Stanton reiterated his orders to Vinton to prepare two to three ships to carry the ordnance and volunteers from New York. Originally ordered on December 5, the ships still had not departed by December 15. Stanton wanted those boats embarked and headed to Mexico to support Scott's expedition. Stanton had also moved the rendezvous location for the South Carolina regiment of volunteers from Charleston to Hamburg. He ordered quartermasters Samuel P. Heintzelman and Johnston to coordinate and prepare the transports and supplies for the new gathering spot. Vinton sent the chartered vessel *Tamaro* and found a second vessel to carry the second lot of ordnance being gathered at Fort Columbus. Additional ordnance was sent from Fort Monroe as well. Vinton divided the volunteers between the two ships with two officers accompanying each set of soldiers.[21]

In a letter to Captain Dusenbury on December 15, Stanton gave instructions for outfitting ships to carry the regiment of Virginia volunteers. He included items such as an ample powder magazine, troop accommodations, and monthly charters that could be renewed. In addition, Dusenbury's transports also received some of the ordnance from Fort Monroe to ferry to Mexico. This example is just one illustration of how important civilian contractors were to the Quartermaster's Department. The department purchased numerous ships during the war, and most of those remained in steady service except when damage or fatigue called for repairs. To make up for the lack of government-owned transports, the quartermasters chartered vessels of adequate size and design to carry both men and supplies to the desired theater. Delays began to extend, and by December 26, Dusenbury had yet to obtain transportation. This holdup pushed Stanton to have Dusenbury aid Lieutenant Peter Valentine Hagner of the Ordnance Corps to secure transportation in Norfolk if that proved more expedient. On December 27, however, Dusenbury was able to send the charted ship *Charles* to transport the ordnance from Fort Monroe.[22]

By December 20, Loper completed the slip-keel schooners he was building for the department. Stanton instructed him "to call upon the purchasing branch of the service in your city for a suit of colors for each [ship] as soon as they are ready to display them." These new schooners not only expanded the carrying capability of the department, but they also provided improved access to the shallow ports used by the US Army along the Gulf of Mexico. Stanton additionally requested that Loper "take early and efficient measures for collecting and shipping, for such point on the coast of Mexico, as may be designated, the 140 boats . . . as fast as they are finished and inspected." Loper received approval to charter or purchase vessels on behalf of the department to ship the nesting surfboats. Lieutenant Totten of the Navy Department was loaned to the Quartermaster's Department to inspect the construction of the boats before accepting them into service and to oversee the final purchase of the completed crafts. Stanton had great trust in Totten's "professional skill and judgement" concluding that they "will be found highly advantageous." Totten's inclusion added a layer of oversight to the purchasing process, which, in Stanton's words, furthered the "combined operation of the Navy and Army on the coast of Mexico." He also requested that Totten go to the boatbuilding contractors and urge them forward to guarantee the boat be completed and ready to ship by January 1. The cooperation between the army and navy began months before the impressive, combined operation of landing some ten thousand American soldiers on the coast of Mexico.[23]

During early January 1847, the department equipped the new volunteers and transported them to Mexico. The new recruits replenished Taylor's reduced force or traveled directly to join Scott's invasion. Most of the veteran troops from Taylor's army transferred to Scott's control for the Mexico City campaign. The new recruits easily filled the gaps in the ranks for the armies remaining in northern Mexico. As fighting was moved to central Mexico, green, inexperienced volunteer recruits represented less of a liability in the north than in active combat further south.[24]

A week after reaching Brazos Santiago, on December 27, 1846, Scott officially called for the detachment of a portion of General Zachary Taylor's troops—one thousand cavalry, four thousand regulars, and four thousand volunteers, less those already headed to Tampico—for departure from that port. Although Scott traveled to Camargo for a meeting, Taylor did not show up to discuss the movement of troops. On January 4, Secretary Marcy noted that their intelligence had reported no large covering army being assembled at Veracruz and expressed hope that Scott would be able to take the city and castle before such a force could be assembled. On the same day, Stanton wrote to Loper about the shipping of the surfboats. These boats represented the key component to the upcoming amphibious landing.[25]

On January 5, Stanton ordered Vinton to charter several new vessels to transport five thousand troops. Stanton suggested that six ships capable of carrying four hundred men each over short distances, eight barges or brigs, and six schooners be obtained. Vinton used the normal chartering and outfitting standards to prepare the ships. Each would be chartered for three months and equipped with at least one month of water in combination with other supplies. Stanton also offered to carry supplies that the Commissary Department had ready to ship if room allowed on the newly chartered vessels. Even with much of Scott's force in transit to or already having arrived in Mexico, the department needed to prepare for further operations against Mexico. The hope for a short war, by January of 1847, had long passed. Jesup and his quartermasters chose to continue troop movement and operations as if the war would persist for the foreseeable future.[26]

The Financial Bureaucracy of War

The beginning of the new year marked the end of a financial quarter for the Quartermaster's Department. As per the federal law requiring quarterly reports from all government officials handling public money, the commanding quartermasters of each depot sent the department a report of all their finances. Some of the quartermasters sent their reports in on time, but many received prompting letters from Stanton requesting that the reports be sent in and citing the law that required it. Stanton reported each of the officers that failed to submit reports, although in each letter he expected that each officer would provide satisfactory reasons for the delay with the eventual submission of their quarterly reports. While the department appeared flexible, giving some temporal allowances during wartime for reporting, the quartermasters still had a duty to report on the use of all public funds. The department made note of any delay that could be amended later should the reports come in. Jesup and Stanton were careful in applying the law so there could be no accusation of corruption or inaccurate accounting on behalf of the Quartermaster's Department. Despite the department's best efforts, even the quartermaster general found that accurately accounting for all wartime spending by the US Army was near impossible.[27]

By January 1847, a common and somewhat embarrassing habit had formed among the department quartermasters. When the officers lacked the immediate funds to pay for a necessary purchase, they made the payment out of their personal funds. While it was not unheard of during the nineteenth century for army and navy officers to bear some costs personally during their service, the amount of debt that some of the quartermasters incurred while waiting for funds was extraordinary in some cases and less than ideal for the department's bookkeeping. In one letter, Stanton wrote to Colonel Thomas Hunt authorizing him "to draw on me at such times for funds for the service of the Quartermaster's Department at New Orleans, this will obviate, to some extent, the difficulties and embarrassment under which we labor in making direct remittances to you." In particular, the periodic purchases of steamships by Hunt required the department to reimburse him for sums of around $18,000 in each instance. While the department struggled to keep balanced books that upheld the legal guidelines, continually sending large remittances to quartermasters within the department might appear as less than reputable. Streamlining the process and giving Hunt the ability to draft bonds directly against the Quartermaster's Department eliminated some of the potential accusations or appearances of corruption. If there were no major payments to reimburse quartermasters, the better the department looked.[28]

Stanton was proud to inform Jesup on January 14, 1847, that the department completed the surfboats and that the vessels carrying them were en route to

Brazos Santiago. Stanton added that "the difficulty of transporting them to this destination has been little inferior to that of their rapid and hurried construction." The department purchased new vessels to carry the landing craft to promote expeditious shipping. Six experienced boat builders and ship carpenters accompanied the boats to Mexico in case any damage occurred to the landing craft before the amphibious assault took place. Other vessels carrying troops and ordnance were under way, and any remaining transports received direction to Isla de Lobos rather than Brazos Santiago. Undoubtedly stressful, managing the production and transportation of troops, supplies, and surfboats for the new campaign while maintaining support for the occupying armies in northern Mexico was a logistical feat that surpassed any previously undertaken at this point in United States history.[29]

On January 19, Congress passed a revised estimate of funds necessary for the additional ten thousand regular troops and an auxiliary force of volunteers called into service to continue the war. The funds allotted for the additional forces included fuel, forage, bedding, and armaments, as well as the costs of transportation and any expenses for specialty troops such as cavalry. In all, Congress allotted $12,314,800 for the Quartermaster's Department to use in service of putting these new recruits into the field. A separate estimate for clothing and camp/garrison equipage came in at $1,340,000. These two quoted costs were for the ten thousand regular troops. An additional $12 million was set aside for the volunteer troops to be equipped and transported. This sum spent to maintain and continue the war, in addition to what the war already cost, added up to a significant expense. Nevertheless, it was an expense the government was willing to pay to secure its territorial goals.[30]

On January 22, Stanton sent a circular letter to all quartermasters with instructions from the former secretary of the treasury, Levi Woodbury, explaining how to use treasury notes. The Quartermaster's Department could issue these notes in payment for goods and services in lieu of specie or a local bank note. Furthermore, treasury notes would earn interest until repaid by the US government. The earning of interest on treasury notes soon became a problem for the department. To gain as much interest as possible before the government repaid the debt, recipients of the notes wanted the earliest date possible on the note. The secretary of the treasury concluded that, "Treasury Notes, made under the act of the 12th of October last, and placed in the hand of the disbursing officers to meet public liabilities, have no legal existence or validity whilst in the possession or under the control of such officers; that for all legal purposes they are to be considered as issued *when they are delivered in payment by such officers, and not until then;* and consequently that no interest should be added to the sum expressed in the body of the note, when it is so delivered in payment." Quartermasters were to mark the notes clearly with the date issued to the recipient to avoid costing the government any extra payments in interest.[31]

The problem of the interest on treasury notes stemmed from a larger issue during the war involving debt. Because paying for everything in specie was not feasible, incurring debt was a necessity. The government, primarily through the distribution of treasury bonds via the Quartermaster's Department, began spending money it did not have readily available to continue with the war. The issuance of treasury notes allowed the government more flexibility to pay for the war, but at the penalty of increasing the national debt. The Treasury Department and the Quartermaster's Department had the same interest in frugality in ensuring that each task was completed effectively. Both departments approved of spending just enough money to execute the war and to avoid spending a cent extra.[32]

The new volunteers continued their progress towards embarkation points across the country, and the department worked diligently to outfit and transport these troops. Even with much of Scott's force on its way south to rendezvous at one of the chosen points off the coast of Mexico, volunteers continued to be mustered into service. On February 5, Lieutenant H. D. Grafton, acting assistant quartermaster at Pensacola, received orders from Stanton to prepare supplies and transports for the new Florida Volunteers who were headed to Pensacola. Grafton's instructions from Stanton gave him leeway to purchase any of the camp equipage not on hand to be able to send the troops off as rapidly as possible. The next day, the quartermaster at Fort Moultrie prepared to send Major Made with his company and all enlisted men at the fort to Tampico.[33]

The Amphibious Invasion at Veracruz

General Scott's departure from Brazos Santiago was delayed until February 15, 1847, when he set sail towards Tampico aboard the steamer *Massachusetts*. He ordered Captain Hetzel—a Brazos Santiago quartermaster—to continue chartering vessels to get as many troops en route by February 10 as possible. Upon his departure, Scott left orders for any remaining ships to take on water and head for the barrier island of Isla de Lobos. The invasion force finally crossed south of the Rio Grande's mouth and into Mexican waters. The final campaign of the war prepared to launch the largest amphibious invasion in United States history.[34]

On February 16, Stanton replied to Jesup's inquiry about the delay of the supply ships carrying ordnance for the expedition. The supply ships sent by Captain Vinton had orders to head to Isla de Lobos to rendezvous with the invasion force and to stop at Brazos Santiago and Tampico to receive any modified orders. Stanton argued that the transports were not late but rather had moved too swiftly and were "in advance of the troops destined for the expedition." The ships had orders not to delay long at Brazos Santiago because it lacked a protected harbor. Jesup, however, suspected that the ships were delayed at the Chandeleur Islands off the mouth of the Mississippi River. Stanton found this supposition unlikely. Oddly enough, in this exchange Stanton sounded more indignant than in any other letter to Jesup. Stanton always maintained a reserved voice in any disagreement with Jesup. The claim that Stanton had any part in delaying the expedition appeared to push him too far, and he wrote back with a vehement reply arguing that Jesup was incorrect and that the ships had overtaken the expedition and already reached Isla de Lobos. In a later letter, Stanton explained that an officer of the Ordnance Department gave orders to one of the transports to stop at the Chandeleur Islands to await orders. So at least one ship had not preceded the arrival of the rest of the expedition troops. Whether this tension between Jesup and Stanton extended beyond this incident is unclear, but the episode demonstrates the stress that the Quartermaster's Department officers were under.[35]

Isla de Lobos is located about sixty miles south of Tampico, roughly eight miles east of Laguna de Tamiahua. General Scott arrived on February 21, 1847, followed by Patterson and his volunteers on March 2. The day after his arrival, Scott informed Commodore David Conner that he was sending two vessels with ordnance supplies, two with surfboats, and some transports ahead to Antón Lizardo. After breakfast on March 2, the *Massachusetts* signaled each transport to send an officer aboard. There they received their sailing orders for Antón Lizardo. The *Massachusetts* got under way during the afternoon, with Scott's red and blue pennant on the main-truck, and the transports fell in behind her.[36] As the fleet sailed, the soldiers sang with gusto. As the landing was beginning, Stanton found himself, yet again, sending letters to the quartermasters requesting their quarterly reports. Despite their admirable conduct transporting and supplying Scott's expedition, the quartermasters still struggled to submit their paperwork on time.[37]

Commodore Conner, in anticipation of the landing, positioned the *Potomac* under Captain John H. Aulick near Isla Verde to help direct the incoming transports between Isla Salmedina and Antón Lizardo. Isla Verde is due east of Veracruz about three miles and Isla Salmedina is just off Antón Lizardo. The transports and naval vessels took up positions in the anchorage some ten to twelve miles between Isla Salmedina and Point Antón Lizardo east of Veracruz. Later, the *Albany* and the *John Adams* arrived to assist in that service. Aulick was instructed to put an officer aboard each transport to act as a pilot and to give the masters of the transport the information needed to pass safely inside Blanquilla Reef to Antón Lizardo. At least one transport ran aground and had to be pulled free by the *Princeton*. As the vessels moved to Antón Lizardo, midshipman William H. Parker recalled that "the first thing that excited our astonishment was the great amount of sail carried by the transports, and the next the skillful manner in which their captains threaded their way between the reef!"[38]

On March 5, Stanton began issuing orders on behalf of Jesup stating, "The Quarter Master General has recently made heavy orders for forage from the North for Mexico. I will thank you to purchase and ship in suitable vessels chartered by the month *one thousand* bales of hay and *thirty thousand* bushels of oats in sacks for Vera Cruz." Similar orders went to quartermasters in charge of major northern cities such as Philadelphia and New York. The requirement for forage increased as Scott prepared for the landing. Jesup anticipated what Scott needed after landing and presumably capturing Veracruz. The new port allowed Scott to unload supplies easily including the forage for draught animals on the march inland. Unfortunately, Stanton informed the quartermaster general that "the drain which has been made on the North for vessels for the service has been such as to create a great scarcity of them." Lacking transports, Stanton requested that Jesup send orders for any ships not needed in the landing to be sent back to the northeastern United States to receive new cargo.[39]

While at Antón Lizardo, Scott issued General Order No. 45, assigning the three landing waves to their respective transports and specifying which units would be in each line. The first line was under the command of General Worth. The second line was under the command of General Patterson, and the third line included the reserves placed under General Twiggs, which were made up of the Second Brigade of regulars. Ensuring that each line of battle included several different units further complicated organization.[40]

Conner and Scott met aboard the steamer *Petrita* to reconnoiter the beaches between Antón Lizardo and Veracruz for locations to land the surfboats. Accompanying them were Worth, Twiggs, Patterson, and Pillow, as well as Scott's staff, including Captains Robert E. Lee and Joseph E. Johnston and Lieutenants Pierre G. T. Beauregard and George G. Meade. They chose Collado Beach, "a gently curving strip of sand paralleled by a line of sand hills about 150 yards inland," two and one-half miles southeast of Veracruz. This sandy stretch of shore beyond the range of the castle guns proved to be a sound choice for the men making the landing.[41]

The *Massachusetts* fired a shot at 5:30 p.m. on March 9, 1847, signaling the beginning of the landing. The sailors rowed with gusto as the surfboats advanced on the Mexican coast. Not a single enemy fired a shot. General Worth and his men landed on the beach and quickly advanced up the first dune. J. Jacob Oswandel watched from his ship and remembered: "As soon as the surf boats struck the beach the soldiers instantly jumped on shore, some in the water. We are now looking for the Mexicans to attack our men, but on they rushed in double quick time until they came to a sand hill. Here they planted the flag of our country with three hearty cheers, responded to with great enthusiasm by every soldier on board the ships." Following Worth's 2,595 men, the surfboats ferried the remaining troops, supplies, and artillery to shore. In less than five hours, more than ten thousand men landed at Collado Beach without a single loss of life.[42]

On March 22, 1847, Scott called for the formal surrender of Veracruz, which Brigadier General Juan Morales—the Mexican commander at Veracruz—rejected. Bombardment from ashore and afloat continued to strike the city. After more losses, on March 29, the defenders of the city surrendered to Scott. He paroled the garrison and allowed civilians to move freely around the occupied city, in a similar fashion to the occupation of Tampico. General Worth assumed charge of Veracruz as military governor.[43]

With Veracruz in control, Scott quickly began ordering troops to secure the roads and bridges his army needed to begin the march to Mexico City. Private Theodore Ebbert, a volunteer soldier, recalled his unit being detailed to guard a captured bridge, writing that it was "ordered out to this place on Sunday with only one days provisions in our haversacks, but we did not starve as we had some brought to us the next day." Early on in Scott's campaign, the Quartermaster's Department continued to be taxed in suppling troops along an ever-lengthening route. Providing rations to Theodore Ebbert and the Second Pennsylvania Volunteers on the outskirts of Veracruz paled in comparison to shipping supplies the roughly two hundred fifty miles to Mexico City by the end of the campaign. Thankfully for the department, vittles could be purchased in Mexico, which cut down on the amount of food shipped from New Orleans, though food prices fluctuated greatly depending on circumstances. Right after the capture of Veracruz, Ebbert noted that vegetables and bread were quite expensive due to the Mexican army having taken much of the produce with them when they left the city. All of these financial and environmental difficulties would begin to compound during the Mexico City campaign.[44]

Scott Marches towards Mexico City

With the occupation of Veracruz, Scott pushed his army inland to escape the springtime yellow fever and continue the campaign to persuade Mexico to yield to American demands. Scott's forces followed the National Road, the old *camino real* (royal road) built by Spain, stretching between Veracruz and Mexico City. This route put the army squarely in the home state of Antonio López de Santa Anna, who sought to use his knowledge of the terrain to block and turn back the US forces at a narrow pass along the road called *Cerro Gordo* (fat hill). Santa Anna hoped to set up an ambush for Scott at this location because he knew that Scott's army needed to travel through this section of the road. Therefore, on April 2, 1847, the Battle of Cerro Gordo took place. Scott's officers, Captain Joseph E. Johnston and Lieutenant Pierre G. T. Beauregard leading the reconnaissance and engineer respectively, managed to reveal the Mexican positions over two days of investigation. Scott decided on a frontal assault paired with a surprise attack at the rear of the Mexican position over near-impassible terrain. The American surprise attack on the Mexican left flank caught the defenders off-guard as intended, and this outcome changed the course of the battle. After a few more hours of fighting, the Mexican forces fell back in chaos. The next day Scott's army took possession of Jalapa near the battlefield.[45]

After a pause in Jalapa, Scott sent General William Worth westward on the National Road with the goal of capturing the city of Puebla about eighty miles away. Before reaching the city, Worth came to Perote which was defined by its castle, originally built to defend trade along the camino real. The castle had served as a prison before it was deserted after the Battle of Cerro Gordo; within its walls the Americans found significant amounts of ordnance left behind. A lone Mexican colonel remained to surrender the town and more than sixty pieces of artillery, twenty-five thousand rounds of artillery ammunition, and hundreds of muskets. After meeting with some Puebla officials, Worth led his troops to occupy the city on May 15, 1847.[46]

Following his typical pattern, Scott paused in Puebla to allow for peace negotiations to occur. Scott hoped the capture of a major city so close to the capital would push the Mexicans to sue for peace. Mexican guerrilla fighters, both officially sanctioned and independent raiders, became an additional problem.

Supplies took extra time to travel between Veracruz and Puebla, then eventually on to Scott's army after it began to march towards the capital because the supply trains needed sufficient escort against guerrilla attacks. This problem persisted throughout the remainder of the war. Ebbert noted in a letter to his sister that "some of their Generals are in favor of the Gurilla [sic] warfare." Regular Mexican officers believed that regular operations would benefit from guerrilla activity. General Pedro María Anaya supported the efforts of government-sanctioned guerillas who raided Scott's supply lines in central Mexico. On April 28, 1847, he signed a decree that authorized light corps to function as part of the national guard if they received state approval, effectively this *reglamento* (rules/regulation) called for partisan warfare.[47]

Quickly Scott realized the problem of transporting supplies and men without adequate protection along the central Valley of Mexico. He detailed cavalry units to escort the supply trains to prevent having them cut, but this measure drained manpower and became an inglorious task that many soldiers loathed. Furthermore, the Mexican guerrillas proved so formidable that escorting a major general to his new unit was delayed because sufficient troops could not be mustered. The escorts for travel and supply grew initially from between twelve hundred to fifteen hundred men in April 1847; by July 1847 numbers increased up to twenty-five hundred troops, one hundred wagons, seven hundred mules, and $1 million in specie. This latter supply convoy came under attack by some fourteen hundred Mexicans killing thirty American soldiers and forcing General Franklin Pierce to return to Veracruz for additional troops. While guerrilla and Native American raids were a concern in northern Mexico, in central Mexico they became a dire problem that drained resources that otherwise could have been directed to Scott's aid.[48]

The final push to end the war began with a series of battles on the outskirts of Mexico City. Two of the most significant were the Battle of Contreras on August 19–20, 1847, and the Battle of Churubusco on August 20, 1847. These were some of the toughest battles of the war, though Mexican forces were challenged to present a united front against the US Army. Instead, infighting and jockeying for political advantage weakened some of the potential Mexican defenses.[49]

Once in Mexico City, the final bastion of defense for the city took the form of the castle or palace of Chapultepec, situated on a large, rocky outcropping. The imposing position of Chapultepec made it almost impossible to assault from three sides. Scott tried to force the capitulation of the castle by artillery barrage and through other means, but the defenders would not yield. Ultimately, the

Battle of Chapultepec on September 13, 1847, came down to a frontal assault that defined US Army tactics for a generation. With the castle captured, the remaining Mexican defenders across the city quickly began to capitulate to American forces. With this defeat, General Scott led his forces into the Zócalo, today called the Plaza de la Constitución, to officially take control of the city and began a tense, months-long occupation of the Mexican capital.[50]

The Treaty of Guadalupe Hidalgo marked the conclusion of the war on February 2, 1848, in a small suburb of Mexico City. Portions of the Mexican government relocated to Guadalupe Hidalgo during the attack on the city. The United States representative Nicholas Trist oversaw the negotiations with Mexican leadership. The treaty settled many of the territorial issues between the United States and Mexico. Most important, the border of Texas along the Rio Grande became the official boundary line between the two counties. The border, therefore, legally encompassed many residents who had never planned on becoming American citizens. The war created a new borderland in the Rio Grande Valley that altered their way of life for decades to come.[51]

~

The Mexico City campaign across central Mexico represents the most extensive logistical effort by the Quartermaster's Department. The quartermasters acquired ships, transports troops, and supplies and established an extensive network of supply depots across North and Central America. The supply system capitalized on existing trade networks across the Gulf of Mexico and the National Road to support the armies in the field. The success of this campaign provided the United States with its largest territorial acquisition since the Louisiana Purchase. A land gain that, according to Ralph Waldo Emerson, meant that the United States would "conquer Mexico, but it will be as the man who swallows the arsenic which will bring him down in turn. Mexico will poison us." Emerson's expectations proved quite true because after the annexation of land the fight over the expansion of slavery renewed in the United States, adding fuel to the glowing embers of civil war.[52]

Despite being the most significant occupation of the war, changes seen in the Rio Grande Valley, Santa Fe, and California did not occur in Mexico City or the Valley of Mexico. The Mexican population density prevented United States economic and social influence from penetrating into the country's center as it did along the borderland. Some discussion in the United States and Mexico considered the annexation of Mexico in its totality or perhaps becoming a protectorate of the United States until the Mexican government could stabilize. These proposals never came to fruition. A majority of Mexican officials harbored no desire to become part of or subservient to the nation that just defeated them militarily. In addition, American political discussion did not favor adding a large population of Hispanic, Mestizo, and Native American citizens to the United States, further complicating the growing racial tensions in the country.

The Quartermaster's Department was essential to the successful outcome for the United States. Furthermore, the Treaty of Guadalupe-Hidalgo granted Texas its southern border as the Rio Grande, allowing for the continuation of the inroads made during the war along the valley borderlands. The operations in this theater secured the claims of Texas and President Polk that the Nueces Strip belonged to the United States. Despite the majority of the population remaining of Mexican heritage, the presence of the army along the border, especially the Quartermaster's Department that controlled contract allocation, backed the new Anglo-American settlers that established new towns near the wartime and postwar military posts. The borderland occupation by the army, and the settlements made by Anglo-Americans, served as a catalyst for change in the region for decades to come.

Social and Demographic Changes after the Mexican-American War

1848–1860

The economic changes that occurred in South Texas in the twelve years following the war caused a shift in the demographics and societies of the region. The presence of new US Army installations supported by the Quartermaster's Department drew people to the Rio Grande Valley looking for work and opportunity. Anglo and European merchants who settled in the region before, during, and after the war took every advantage to maximize their profits and secure their place in the Rio Grande borderland. Average laborers— Anglo, Mexican, and Tejano—migrated to the area seeking work with the US Army and merchants as teamsters, muleteers, and numerous other ancillary jobs. This influx of new settlers altered the social dynamic despite Hispanic residents still outnumbering the new Anglo and European settlers. Earlier immigrants integrated into Mexican and Tejano society, often through marriage, but later arrivals retained more of the cultures from their countries of origin. Ultimately, a new hybrid society developed mixing the historically traditional social norms of Mexican and Tejano families with the influence of those with Anglo-American and European heritages.

Between 1850 and 1860 the population of Texas grew from 212,295 to 604,215, a 325 percent increase. Cameron, Hidalgo, Starr, and Webb counties grew by 75 percent from 8,541 to 11,623 residents, including 18 slaves and 104 free blacks. The census lumped most of the population, including Tejanos and recent Mexican immigrants, into the white category. Surnames are the only way to differentiate national and ethnic identity, but by 1860 many families included parents from both sides of the border. The growth Texas experienced in the north and east outpaced South Texas and the Lower Rio Grande Valley, but the borderlands growth rate was still impressive. The influx of new settlers from Europe, the United States, and Mexico created a new paradigm by 1860 for what a typical family and town looked like. New cultural norms developed in the region, reflecting the mixing of American business practices with Mexican and Tejano family traditions. South Texas counties underwent societal shifts from this new population of settlers. Along the Rio Grande counties Cameron, Hidalgo, Starr, Zapata, Webb, and Maverick all felt the influence of new quartermaster depots and army forts. Other counties more inland from the river also experienced these changes such as La Salle, Nueces, and Bexar Counties, but aside from Bexar and San Antonio, the population along the Rio Grande was far greater than that of the other interior counties of South Texas.[1]

With the growth of the quartermaster shipping infrastructure, labor demands grew drastically for everything from skilled steamboat pilots to muleteers. For skilled labor such as pilots, the men who had connections to the department received preference over those who did not. As for unskilled labor such as teamsters and muleteers, these jobs often fell to recent Anglo immigrants or Mexicans

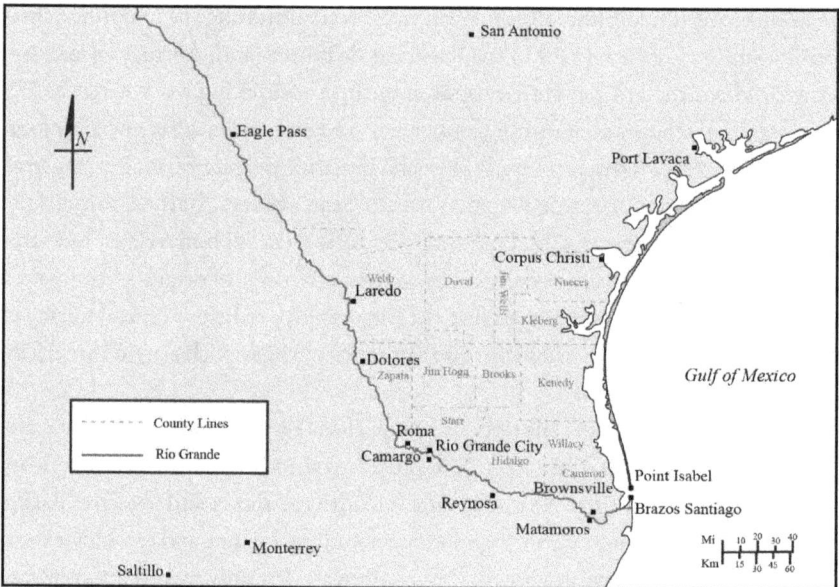

Postwar South Texas Counties

willing to cross north of the river for a more reliable source of income. This massive wave of new immigrants from Mexico allowed the region to maintain an ethic-Mexican majority that was heavily relegated to manual labor jobs. While several Tejanos maintained and even expanded their holdings and position in South Texas in the postwar period, only those who could adapt to the new Anglo-American governmental system succeeded. Such adaptation included learning English, participating in the new county governments, and being willing to work with the dominant military presence in the region. Historian Miguel Ángel González-Quiroga aptly noted that, "irrespective of racial differences, men on the frontier were valued for their worth." Whether Tejano, Mexican, or Anglo, only the residents who possessed the skills necessary to succeed rose to prominence in South Texas.[2]

Even more telling about the extent of the growth that occurred is that all of these counties came into existence after the war. The necessity to oversee the economic and demographic growth along the Rio Grande led to the formation of the county governments. Administrators, government officials, and customs officers were all needed to manage the new border region and the ever-growing population. The presence of the Quartermaster's Department and government investment in the region required that these local governments quickly develop, often under Anglo control, to manage the borderlands.

Political conflict in northern Mexico pushed some Mexicans to seek a more stable environment in South Texas as well as the nominal protection provided by the US Army camps. Troubles in northern Mexico regularly drove Mexicans north of the border seeking refuge from the frequent conflicts between the Federalists and Centralist factions as they vied for control of the future of Mexico. Such events ranged from the establishment of the Republic of the Rio Grande to the significant influence of Juan Cortina's mix of raiding and cult of personality. The frontera either in the far northern or southern reaches of Mexico fostered dissent and resentment of the federal government in Mexico City. These far-flung regions allowed dissidents to build their resistance efforts and continually destabilized the country. Although instability often resulted from their actions, the efforts of some of these actors were justified. Such a discussion lies beyond the scope of this project, but the effects of their actions continually pushed emigrants out of Mexico through the borderlands into South Texas.[3]

The Rio Grande Valley shared attributes of Mexico and the United States. The combination of instability pushing Mexicans out of their country, army dollars and jobs pulling them to the borderlands, and Anglo-American businessmen beginning to exert political hegemony in the region led to a unique society and culture developing along the Lower Rio Grande Valley. The cultural influence of Mexico is undeniable in the region. Richard King's ranch is a clear example of the hybridization of the Anglo and Mexican models of ranching. The rest of South Texas followed in this pattern, creating something similar to both the United States and Mexico but not fully resembling either country. This hybrid quality represents the true nature of borderlands. Historian Andrés Reséndez perfectly describes the experience of how these borderland citizens characterized themselves in the ever-changing cultural landscape. For Reséndez, "Identity choices almost always follow situational logic." The peoples living in South Texas were not Indian or Mexican or Tejano or Anglo, but they reflected a multifaceted identity that allowed them to present the most advantageous version of themselves in diverse situations. All people can identify themselves in any number of ways, and in the borderlands, a flexible identity served the vital purpose of survival.[4]

Historian Omar Valerio-Jiménez characterized the experience of the Lower Rio Grande Valley as a "binational contest over territory." The US-Mexican War brought in Anglo-Americans as agents of US national expansion, using municipal and county governments to begin exerting more political control over the region during and after the war. The creation of Brownsville is one of the best examples of this effort. During the war, the US Army and its supporting private contractors moved into Matamoros to occupy and capitalize on the city. Not only did the city provide a launching point for further invasions of Mexico, but it served as entrepot to the trade in northern Mexico. The establishment of a town opposite Matamoros drew much of the wealth out of the city during the postwar period. The governmental body that controlled Brownsville, and the larger Cameron County wherein it resided, allowed for a shift not only in the economic power to the northern bank but also a power displacement of the Mexican and Tejano citizens in favor of Anglo-Americans.[5]

Demographic Shifts in South Texas

Immediately after the occupation of Matamoros, the US Army began establishing methods of control over the civil government of the city. These measures formed the basis for postwar municipal and county governments in South Texas that favored minority Anglo-American leadership. While Mexican officials remained in nominal control of Matamoros, they were supervised by army officers. Effectively, Mexican officials could govern Mexican citizens without having any control over American soldiers who, at the height of the occupation, outnumbered the Mexican population of Matamoros about three to one. The quartermaster William Chapman even controlled the collection of taxes and directed the provisional police force. Chapman and the Quartermaster's Department are critical to understanding how the postwar period played out. What happened in Matamoros served as a blueprint for municipal and county government in South Texas after the war. The US Army utilized similar policies in the occupation of other captured cities, including Mexico City.[6]

The power shift in favor of Anglo-Americans due to the presence of the army was evident throughout the Valley, but the demographic shift in Texas presented a more complex situation that varied by region and county. In the center of Texas, there was a clear shift to Anglo dominance in demographics; in South Texas, however, the Tejano population remained an overwhelming majority. While Tejanos lost the demographic advantage in Central and East Texas, they maintained a strong majority in the South Texas along the Rio Grande, largely due to the ease of Mexican immigration. Despite this ethnic majority, the type of labor most Tejanos engaged in shifted away from occupations such as ranch and farm owners to heavily manual labor due to the changing power dynamic. Within Béxar and the Lower Rio Grande counties, the percentage of Mexican-Americans who owned their own farms or ranches in 1850 numbered 32.9 precent. By 1900, that percentage had fallen to 1.8 percent.[7]

Immigration numbers illustrate the unique process of demographic change across Texas during the second half of the nineteenth century. In 1850, about eighty-seven thousand immigrants entered Texas from across the United States, with roughly seventy-seven thousand being from the southern states. In the same year, Mexican immigrants numbered about forty-five hundred, most settling in the Lower Rio Grande Valley. This settlement pattern created a Mexican settlement region extending from San Antonio south, with the majority being below the Nueces River. By 1900, US immigration grew to about eight hundred forty thousand, and Mexican immigrants numbered seventy-one thousand. Although Anglos greatly outnumbered Tejanos and Mexican immigrants, Mexican-Americans generally confined their settlement to South Texas, creating a Mexican cultural zone within Texas. Even within this region, Anglos managed to dominate municipal governments despite often being the ethnic minority.[8]

After the war, about one hundred thousand Mexicans found themselves within the United States due to the Treaty of Guadalupe-Hidalgo. This shift created uncertainty for many Mexicans because it meant they needed to choose to become US citizens or move to Mexican territory south of the Rio Grande.

The deciding factor for many became "On which side of the river did you own the majority of your land?" Whichever side held most of one's land holdings typically determined where residents moved to secure claims. Many communities split as a result. The best example is Laredo, which lost a portion of its population to Nuevo Laredo, the new town established on the Rio Grande's south bank so the residents could remain Mexican citizens. The movement of the border created new political concerns for many of the longtime residents of the Lower Rio Grande Valley. The issues around land ownership and citizenship in a country that many fought against just a few months earlier muddied concepts of Mexican identity. While business could still be conducted across the border, laws, language, and ethnic prejudices changed significantly after the war. Similarly, Tejanos along the border had to decide which of the military conflicts to participate in throughout the nineteenth century. Some had chosen to participate in the Texas Revolution in support of Texas, while others remained neutral. During the Mexican-American War, most Tejanos chose neutrality rather than join American forces invading Mexico. Most border communities tended to focus on themselves and their own self-sufficiency rather than choose a side in the various conflicts.[9]

RIO GRANDE VALLEY POPULATION AND SOCIETAL SHIFTS

Significant postwar population growth from about nine thousand residents in 1850 to around fifteen thousand in 1860 took place in the greater South Texas region. Cameron County, the southernmost county of Texas, represents these demographic and social shifts well due to its large population. Just after the war, in 1850, Cameron County possessed the largest population of South Texas counties with 8,451 inhabitants. By comparison, Nueces County with the burgeoning town of Corpus Christi boasted only 689 people. Brownsville and Brazos Santiago are in Cameron County, explaining the rapid growth of this county in the decade after the war. In 1860, Cameron County had a population of 6,028 and by 1880 it was 14,959. The total population of Texas grew from 212,592 in 1847 to 604,215 in 1860, an increase of almost 300 percent in less than fifteen years. In 1850, eighty percent of the population in Cameron County was Mexican-American; by 1870, Anglos reached their percentage peak at 16 percent. Anglo-Americans never possessed a numerical advantage, yet they managed to dominate the region economically and politically. South, Central, and West Texas population increased from 20,859 to 75,153 people. South Texas also saw a significant number of Mexicans immigrating north to the American bank of the Rio Grande. By 1870, 65.3 percent of Tejanos in South Texas were nonnative born. Despite favorable numbers regarding ethnic majorities, Tejanos remained unable to stop the expansion of Anglo-American economic and political power.[10]

In Hidalgo County, the power dynamic related directly to the ownership of land, which provided legitimacy to both Anglos and Tejanos and defined who held sway in county and municipal governments. In 1852, Hidalgo County had thirty-nine Mexican or Tejano landholders and thirteen Anglo or European (83.5 percent Tejano, 6.1 percent Anglo, and 10.4 percent European). By 1865 these numbers had significantly changed: 48.7 percent Tejano, 26.8 percent Anglo, and 24.5 percent European. These numbers clearly illustrate the shift in land holding and thus power. In mid-nineteenth-century South Texas, land equated to power. While Tejanos regained some percentage of land ownership over the subsequent decades, the general trend that played out by 1900 was a region dominated by Anglo landowners with only about one third of all landowners in Hidalgo County being Tejano.[11]

Property ownership in the Rio Grande Valley changed after the US-Mexican War. While Tejanos and recent Mexicans represented the numerical majority of the landowners in Cameron, Hidalgo, and Starr counties, they no longer held the majority of the land or wealth. Residents in these counties with Hispanic surnames outnumbered Anglo and European surname settlers.

Despite more people with Hispanic surnames owning property, the largest landowners were all of Anglo or European decent, such as Henry Clay Davis, Mifflin Kenedy, Charles Stillman, and Richard King. Two of these men, Davis and Kenedy, married into Mexican or Tejano families, which muddies the waters of who is truly rising to dominance in the region. Despite the relatively common practice of intermarrying, enough Anglo/European only families existed to destabilize the traditional ruling class of South Texas.[12]

Historian Valerio-Jiménez analyzed a potential reason that contributed to this change in the power dynamic in South Texas. He proposed that Anglos became the dominant political force in the region because of a postwar arrangement with Tejano elites. By granting Anglos the ability to maintain order without

Table 1. Lower Rio Grande Valley Surnames

Year	Hispanic Surname	Anglo/European Surname	Percentage Hispanic
1852	137	105	57%
1855	200	124	54%
1860	181	98	57%

the constant need for force, local Tejano elites managed to keep some of their regional power. This relationship, according to sociologist and historian David Montejano, first arose during the wartime occupation of Mexican territory. The US Army controlled the territory but allowed Mexican elites to administer their residents as they had done before the war. Montejano calls this a "peace structure" that resulted from an accommodation between Mexican elites and governing Anglo-Americans backed by the strength of the US military. Since this arrangement allowed them to continue controlling their lands, Tejanos, almost to a man, accepted it. If Tejano elites wanted to gain access to the more lucrative markets of Anglo-Americans and particularly US Army contracts via the Quartermaster's Department, they needed to ally themselves with prominent Anglos. Furthermore, such alliances increased Tejanos' chances of securing their land claims as the newly arrived Anglos often became the lawyers and judges that decided such cases. Again, this power dynamic could not have shifted without the US Army backing Anglo American interests in the region.[13]

Tejanos wanting to retain control of their hereditary land in South Texas struggled during the early 1850s to have their land titles recognized by Texas and the United States. The primary attempt to settle the land disputes became the Bourland and Miller Commission, named for commissioners William H. Bourland and James B. Miller. As they began their work, the commissioners reviewed three types of claims: porciones along the Rio Grande that began in 1767, large grants for pasturage by Spain, and Mexican grants post-1824. The commission faced some initial resistance to the government stepping in to confirm titles and mediate title disputes. Of the claims reviewed, the commission recommended confirmation of 76 percent of them. The commission failed to address all title disputes, however, and a second commission called the Rio Grande Commission led by Charles S. Taylor and Robert H. Lane was organized to continue this work. Little is known about the activities of this commission beyond its final reports. The government ultimately upheld many Spanish and Mexican land claims. This validation did not prevent predatory land purchases from Mexicans and Tejanos in South Texas.[14]

GROWING DEMAND FOR LABOR

The founding and expansion of numerous towns north of the Rio Grande meant a new demand for labor. As the Quartermaster's Department used these towns to supply the installations along the river, and laborers from the United States, Europe, and, most numerously, Mexico arrived to settle in these towns. The political upheaval in Mexico that continued in the decades after the Mexican-American War pushed many out of the northern states into Texas. Add the pull of working for ranchers, merchants, and the US Army as teamsters or muleteers, and the South Texas borderlands became a true land of opportunity for the Mexican citizen. Working for the US Army and the Texas Rangers as scouts and in other auxiliary roles also drew Mexicans to Texas. Uniquely, debt peons from Mexico escaped their debt by crossing the border much as Texas slaves fled to Mexico to gain their own freedom. The unstable political and economic situation in Mexico during the end of the 1850s pushed as many Mexicans out of the country as were pulled by the lure of work north of the river.[15]

The way new entrepreneurs began to capitalize on the existing economic wealth of the region altered its social hierarchy. Before the war, northern Mexico's chief exports included hides, wool, and silver coin. These exports represented a huge amount of wealth that was further bolstered by the economic growth that the US Army was already instigating. The American occupation of the Rio Grande Valley began an economic renaissance for this borderland during and after the war. While soldiers remained stationed in the area, the demand for vittles of all kinds expanded regional markets. These men wanted fresh meats and vegetables as well as milk and all kinds of breads and cakes. This pressure caused a continual flow of United States currency into the Valley and northern Mexico via the soldiers, and of course the Quartermaster's Department, spending freely for these goods.[16]

The labor force demographics clearly denote the change occurring in South Texas after the war between the United States and Mexico. According to Tejano historian Arnoldo DeLeón, between 1850 and 1900 the percentages for the three major types of labor changed as shown in Table 2.

These numbers clearly show the shift in economic dominance along the lower Rio Grande. Charles Stillman, Richard King, and Mifflin Kenedy were prominent examples of Anglos obtaining large amounts of land, often supplanting the traditional Tejano owners. The immigration of Mexicans into South Texas accounts for the shift in some of these numbers, as many new arrivals took manual labor jobs that paid better than labor in Mexico. Nonelite Tejanos often found themselves unable to directly oppose Anglo-American expansion because of language and cultural barriers that separated them from Anglo society in addition to a lack of knowledge of American law. Despite the shift in land ownership and regional power, South Texas remained a Tejano cultural zone. It provided an important sense of security for Tejano residents, and many ranchos testified to the cultural vitality that held its own against the influx of Anglo settlers.[17]

Chapter 6

Table 2. Post-Mexican War Labor Changes

Labor Category	Tejanos		Anglos	
	1850	1900	1850	1900
Manual Labor	34.3%	67%	1.1%	29.7%
Skilled Labor	47.5%	12.7%	50.5%	23%
Ranch/Farm Owners	51%	15%	2.2%	12.2%

The shift in types of labor done by each group began primarily because of the economic distribution of US currency into the region. Anglos tended to receive preference over Tejanos, giving them an economic advantage. The sheer amount of money flowing into Texas brought both Anglos and Mexicans into the region in far greater numbers than ever before. Historian Thomas T. Smith illustrates this with his analysis of the army financial reports of the mid-to-late 1800s. The US Army's operating costs in Texas amounted to $11.3 million between 1849 and 1860, which represents roughly 6.2 percent of all army spending throughout the United States. These figures demonstrate that a significant amount of money flowed from government coffers into Texas, including the counties along the Rio Grande. This money pulled new people to the state, with a portion of those coming into South Texas, a region that housed many of the newly established posts. Smith calculated the annual spending of the army in Texas during the same period as $966,046 for operation costs. The two sections of this budget were divided between the Quartermaster's Department expenditures of $306,600 and the average army pay of $659,446. The annual average quartermaster spending in Texas amounted to only 5.3 percent of the expenditures in all other states combined, again demonstrating the disproportional spending by the army in the Lone Star State.[18]

Between July 1, 1849, and June 30, 1851, the US Army Quartermaster's Department paid $171,624 for transportation costs from the Texas coast to the inland forts and depots. Excluding $42,678 of that which paid for travel to Fort Bliss in El Paso, the Rio Pecos crossing and nearby forts, and from Houston to the North Texas forts of Worth, Graham, and Gates, the rest remained in South Texas. This left about $128,946 to either travel up the Rio Grande or from Indianola to San Antonio then overland to the interior forts of South Texas (Forts Merrill, Ewell, Inge, Clark, Duncan, McIntosh, Brown, and Ringgold Barracks). The quartermasters spent roughly $113,000 transporting supplies across northern South Texas with $15,646 for transportation within the Rio Grande Valley.

Much of this latter money went to the Anglo and European merchants who operated along the Rio Grande, such as King and Kenedy, and overland routes using contract muleteers and teamsters such as Henry Kinney and Henry Clay Davis.[19]

Initially, the army faced a labor shortage in Texas starting with its arrival in 1845. Much of the logistical chain required civilian employees, such as wagon teamsters, carpenters, blacksmiths, herdsmen, clerks, and stevedores. The army imported laborers from other places in the United States and Texas to come to the Rio Grande to help meet the labor demands. By 1856, the army employed 356 civilian employees in Texas, and at its peak in 1851, it employed 488 civilians. Laborers of Tejano and Mexican decent found a niche in US Army employment as scouts and guides, making up about 47 percent of this work detail.[20]

The army explored Texas looking for the best routes to supply the new chain of forts and installations established during and after the war. Many of these paths became wagon routes and roads, having a lasting impact on the landscape of Texas. Due to the locations of the forts and depots, the main supply routes developed into well-traveled thoroughfares that directed the growth of towns and settlements. The army also ordered railroad surveys, producing volumes of scientific information that resulted in the first detailed map of the Trans-Mississippi West, although politics at the time prevented settling on a route for the rail line.[21]

The amount of money flowing into the state represents an influence, but the fact that much of this money went into the hands of private contractors and laborers changed the effect of this economic boon to the region. Smith's breakdown of the Quartermaster's Department expenses also illustrates just how much of the $11.3 million could have realistically gone into the hands of civilians in South Texas. The specific designation of quartermaster civilian employees represents a cost of $1,020,800 between 1849 and 1860, translating to 27.7 percent of all quartermaster spending that went directly into the hands of either private contractors or laborers. In addition, the department spent $1,169,000 on animal forage and $812,000 on transportation in Texas, being 32.5 percent and 22 percent of the total spending respectively. The army usually purchased both animal forage and hired transportation from civilians, allowing for an even greater amount of money to flow into the hands of businessmen in the region. Men like King, part owner of a steamboat company that operated up and down the Rio Grande, made quite the profit carrying goods for the army, thus propelling themselves to the forefront of South Texas economy in a disproportionate way compared to the longtime Tejano residents of the Lower Rio Grande Valley.[22]

TEJANOS ADAPT TO ANGLO AMERICAN AND EUROPEAN IMMIGRANTS

The growth of new towns along the established US Army trade routes brought many new settlers to Texas. The concentration of many new male arrivals to the region presented the most significant economic influence, aside from the Mexican Cession, on the economic development of the Rio Grande Valley. During this postwar period, the trend of growing US cities influenced the economy of Southwestern territories. Regions like the Lower Rio Grande Valley and Santa Fe had progressively reoriented towards the United States over Mexican markets and economic influence. This influx of men and the persistence of the US Army's presence in the region upset the power balance in the Valley. Mexicans who now found themselves on the wrong side of the border after the war, were forced to decide whether to remain or cross to the Mexican side. Several elite Tejanos chose to remain and become American citizens to retain their land holdings. The Tejanos who chose to stay adapted to a new power structure to thrive.[23]

Tejanos who maintained control of their land retained social status in South Texas. Marriage was the best way to secure land for new immigrants, Mexican, Anglo, and European alike. It is usually unclear if these marriages occurred due to love or practicality, but the union meant a firmer hold on their land. Mexican immigrants such as the Salvador Vela family of Reynosa migrated to the Rio Grande Valley in 1857. Vela's children either acquired ranches of their own or married into Tejano landholding families. Other Tejano families married a mix of foreign and local spouses, expanding their landholdings each time. Edward Dougherty was a New Yorker of Irish descent who met and stayed with María Marcela García during the Mexican-American War. Their daughter married first the sheriff of Hidalgo County, then, after he died, Mariano Treviño of a Tejano ranchero family. Tejano families such as these did not have a tidy lineage from one national background. Rather, much like the borderland that they inhabited, the families became a mélange of the numerous peoples that settled in the region during the years surrounding the war.[24]

Other prominent families interacted with Anglo and European settlers in different ways. Juan Cortina's family long owned the Espiritu Santo land grant encompassing 260,000 acres. Family members sold some of this land to Charles Stillman, sparking a dispute in court. Eventually, they deeded some of the disputed land to end the legal case and secure confirmation of their remaining lands in South Texas. Some Mexicans and Tejanos saw such actions as abuses by new Anglo immigrants. In some cases, men like Stillman took advantage of the situation along the border, but often they did nothing more devious than Tejano and Mexican businessmen engaged in during the same period. By contrast when Henry Clay Davis married Maria Hilaria de la Garza, the heir to the large estate of Carnestolendas, it propelled this landed Tejano family to greater heights and power in South Texas than ever before. The complicated relationship between Tejano families and newly arrived immigrants obscures the true motivations of Tejanos and the Anglo/European immigrants. It is not as simple as one taking advantage of another. Instead, each side benefited in some way from the arrangement either gaining power, security, land, or simply a more welcoming face to interact with the US government and army now ensconced along the Rio Grande.[25]

Francisco Yturria, a Matamoros native, began his career as a clerk for Charles Stillman and was involved with Mifflin Kenedy and Company. He married Felicitas Treviño, the daughter of an original Spanish land grantee in Cameron County. Yturria expanded their land holdings by purchasing lands adjoining those of his wife's inheritance. Through his dealings with Stillman, King, Kenedy, and other Matamoros and Brownsville businessmen, Yturria became one of the wealthiest and most influential men of this time in the region. He was one of the few Mexican merchants who worked his way up alongside the Anglo and European immigrants to South Texas. Men like Stillman and his compatriots were more interested in business competency than racial hierarchy. The Yturria Bank, established in 1853, represented one of the pillars of his wealth. Yturria capitalized on access to hereditary Tejano lands the same way many of the Anglo merchants did by marrying into the historical land-owning elite. While Yturria is more the exception than the rule, his story illustrates that social mobility did exist for those who could ingratiate themselves with the Anglo and European settlers rapidly rising to prominence during the decades following the Mexican-American War.[26]

New Anglo-American entrepreneurs began to supplant most of the earlier Mexican/Spanish suppliers. Though the Anglos began to gain preference in the region, entrepreneurs of all ethnicities launchrd many new economic activities in the postwar years. "The frontier made the transition from economic backwater to dynamic crossroad of exchange" due to the efforts of Tejanos and Anglos in only a few years. With this growth in business, the markets within the Lower Rio Grande Valley began to shift even more securely into the hands of the United States. Reséndez terms this shift "market persuasion" but qualifies the concept by stating that Mexican nationalists might have described the experience as a "market nightmare." The influence of these market changes forced Mexicans,

Anglos, and Tejanos of South Texas to choose their identity because of the borderlands environment. This is not simply American expansionism and conquest, but a complex interaction of peoples, ideas, and markets that created a unique borderland landscape.[27]

One of the most efficient methods that nonnative Texans used to work their way into South Texas and Mexican markets was marriage to Mexican women. Immigrants such as the Irishmen John McMullen, James Power, and James McGloin all obtained grants from the Mexican government to settle families as empresarios. Each married into high-born Hispanic families. Power is a good example; he married María Dolores Portilla, daughter of Felipe Roque de la Portilla, who helped Power settle families in Refugio and San Patricio. The marriage between Power and Portilla brought the knowledge of settling Texas and making a living ranching in the harsh environment. By marrying into prominent Mexican or Tejano families, these merchants obtained long-standing social and economic connections the markets throughout the Lower Rio Grande Valley. Mexican/Tejano women and their families also benefited from marriage as it opened up new connections within the United States or in other foreign countries. Such relationships further complicated how people described themselves. Children growing up in these borderlands could often choose the most beneficial aspect of their heritage in any given situation.[28]

Prior to the Mexican-American War, most European and Anglo settlers integrated into Mexican society. They learned Spanish, married into Mexican families, and some became Catholic, establishing generally amicable relations with their Mexican neighbors. Following the war, the flood of new Anglo Americans that did not assimilate as fully disrupted the prewar way of life in South Texas. The Hispanic landed aristocracy that did not adapt quickly became susceptible to encroachment by Anglo newcomers into their spheres of power. The historically landed elites often demanded and retained their privileges in the border towns along the river. The further away from the Rio Grande one got, the worse conditions got for Mexicans and Tejanos in South Texas. Conversely, Mexican and Tejano day laborers benefited greatly from the growing economy due to new American and European migrants. They found better wages and living conditions north of the border, especially compared to their peon status in Mexico. The Mexican-American War and the establishment of new towns and military outposts drew in new residents that caused a change in South Texas culture from one that followed traditional Mexican values to a hybridized culture that mixed American and Mexican ways of life.[29]

Several prominent Anglo-American and European settlers arrived just before or during the Mexican-American War. These men sought opportunity first in the Mexican northern frontier along the Rio Grande then after the war in the developing borderlands separating the two nations. New towns, businesses, and trade routes developed due to the actions of the new settlers that laid the blueprint for modern South Texas today.

Henry Clay Davis, the twenty-two-year-old Kentucky native, arrived in San Antonio on November 9, 1836, searching for adventure. After serving in the Texas First Cavalry Regiment for a year-long contract among other exploits, he arrived in Corpus Christi, eventually working for Kinney. Learning from the expert tradesman Kinney, Davis earned some wealth of his own trading between South Texas towns establishing new trade routes. Just prior to the Mexican-American War, Davis arrived in Camargo and caught the attention of Maria Hilaria de la Garza, the heir to the large estate of Carnestolendas, Porción 80. They married on April 21, 1846. Settling on the estate lands, Davis established Rancho Davis and Davis Landing along the Rio Grande. Davis Landing eventually became an important stop for steamers on the river carrying army supplies. The marriage to Maria Hilaria allowed the adventurous American soldier to create a town and trade center from the ground up.[30]

Rancho Davis grew into Rio Grande City, becoming one of the primary trade hubs between Texas and Mexico. The city was laid out by Davis and Captain Forbes Britton. Davis also established Ringgold Barracks near the town and landing, renting it to the US Army for $600 a year. His old mentor, Henry Kinney, attempted the same strategy in Corpus Christi, renting land to the US Army for $60 a month. He and partners also ran the sutler's store at the fort. The foresight Davis exhibited had turned a relatively undeveloped piece of land across the river from Camargo into an essential trade hub on the Rio Grande including overland wagon routes to Mier, Laredo, and Corpus Christi, eventually establishing regular trade with New Orleans. Mifflin Kenedy established a warehouse around 1854 to support the river steamboat company he ran with King. Davis's determination made him one of the most prominent men in the region, being elected as a state senator for Starr, Webb, and Cameron counties in 1849. The combination of acquiring land and status from Tejano elites and capitalizing on revenue from the US Army allowed Davis to acquire power and status in South Texas that prior to the war belonged almost exclusively to Tejanos.[31]

Italian-born Albert Champion migrated to Mobile, Alabama, in the early 1840s before settling in the village of Point Isabel, Texas. After expanding his wealth as a merchant and grocer, he established two ranches in Cameron County, La Gloria and La Florida. In 1850 he married Estéfana Solís, daughter of a founding family of Point Isabel. Albert, his two brothers Peter and Nicholas, as well as a cousin, George, all married the daughters of Lazaro Solís. Champion, aided by his brothers and cousin, used their knowledge of ranching and commerce to help grow the fledgling town of Brownsville in addition to their own coffers. The new army posts at Point Isabel, Brazos Santiago, and Brownsville all aided the family's success. Their financial success saw Champion become a large landholder in Cameron County and rise to social prominence. Between 1850 and 1876, he acquired over fifteen parcels of land in and around Brownsville worth a total of $4,434. His marriage into a Tejano family added legitimacy to his status in South Texas just as it had many other merchants.[32]

José San Román, a Spaniard, arrived in Matamoros in 1846 after learning the merchant trade from the Thorn M. Grath Company in New Orleans. He established a dry goods company that extended to both sides of the river, including the newly founded Brownsville. Román and business partner John Young operated several boats on the Rio Grande until they sold most of their interest to Mifflin Kenedy and Company in 1857. His success and connections outpaced every other merchant in Brownsville, including Charles Stillman. His trade routes stretched from New Orleans to Matamoros/Brownsville then established connections throughout northern Mexico with fellow merchants in Tamaulipas, Coahuila, San Luis Potosí, and Chihuahua.[33]

The new residents—Mexican, Anglo, and European—took advantage of every avenue they had to grow their wealth, influence, and land holdings. Most interpersonal communication between Anglos and Tejanos was fair and amiable. However, the more removed the two communities became the more conflict occurred, distorting their perceptions of each other. Property ownership united Tejanos and Anglos. If Tejanos held on to their prewar land, their postwar relations with newly arrived Americans seemed to be more equitable. Land provided a tangible and undeniable sense of worth for both groups, which created a foundation on which to build a biracial community. This land-based meritocracy did not translate to the lower classes of Anglos or Tejanos who lacked access to land ownership as in other parts of Texas, the United States, and Mexico.[34]

The US Army and South Texas Businessmen

Felix von Blücher is representative of the relationship between businessmen and the US Army in the Lower Rio Grande Valley as well. When von Blücher

CAMP RINGGOLD.   TEN. RG. CAVALRY, NEAR MATAMORAS.

Ringgold Barracks, established by Henry Clay Davis, served as a US Army base adjacent to Davis Landing. The barracks utilized the riverboat trade for supply and served as a transition point to supply army forts and depots further into Texas. Image courtesy of the University of Texas at Arlington.

first arrived in Texas he joined Prince Carl of Solms-Braunfels in Texas in the establishment of New Braunfels. During the Mexican-American War, he served as interpreter for General Scott throughout the invasion of central Mexico. After the war he settled in Corpus Christi during 1849, coinciding with Kinney and Davis as he established Rio Grande City. In 1853, von Blücher received a contract to survey the army road to Eagle Pass. His prewar experience and his wartime contacts translated into a survey contract. This contract allowed von Blücher to interact with the trade routes and benefit from the army dollar in Texas.[35]

The US Army lacked the infrastructure and manpower to meet all its needs effectively. Therefore, civilian contractors served as the primary source of labor. This arrangement, however, also provided some advantage to the civilian contractors who now had access to the US Army as support for their business endeavors. The US Army paid von Blücher "rather well" for his work and, as a part of his contract to dig wells for the army, he commanded "a column of some 30 wagons, conducting the work under his direction at his own pace." Civilian contractors gained experience and reputation working with the army, helping them establish themselves in the region. Furthermore, businessmen who worked with the army tended to know each other well and worked together to improve each other's standing. South Texas merchants and ranchers Richard King and Mifflin Kenedy at times offered Blücher valuable advice on where they invested their money. The ranching empires that King and Kenedy built are extreme examples of what an early connection to the army could help an individual to achieve, but even with less prominent cases, like Blücher, such relationships helped individuals become financially successful and more firmly established. Few Tejanos enjoyed the same social and economic mobility as Anglo immigrants to the Valley. Most often, Tejanos were relegated to peon labor, depriving them of the advantage of a positive relationship with the army.[36]

A Spanish missionary, Emmanuel Domenech, commented on the relationship between civilians and the US Army during his travels across Texas. He noted that "the American camps were rather a source of gain to the colonists, than a protection against the Indians." Although professedly there to protect against Native American or Mexican attacks, army forts served more as a tool for profit for colonists than true security. Domenech continued that "before the horses were saddled, provisions packed, and pistols loaded, the perpetrators were nowhere to be found." While he conceded that the US cavalry could sometimes overtake the Indians, the lack of roads and the terrain generally presented significant obstacles for the army to overcome when attempting to track down Indians. The US Army never managed to implement any successful major campaigns against the Plains Indians until the post-Civil War period. This Spaniard on a religious missionary trip noticed the clear disparity between what the army professed to do and the actual effects of its presence. The army served more as an economic stimulus and reinforcement of Anglo dominance than as an efficient defense against Indian and Mexican attacks.[37]

Numerous other settlers and merchants followed the same pattern as the men discussed. Henry L. Kinney and Charles Stillman founded Corpus Christi and Brownsville, respectively. Stephen Power served as lawyer and advisor for many of the wealthy men in South Texas whose business ventures he also invested in. The merchant and newspaperman Simon Mussina and businessman Humphry E. Woodhouse grew their wealth and rubbed shoulders with the most powerful men along the Rio Grande. Even the US Army quartermaster at Fort Brown, William Chapman, became involved with land speculation and investing in business ventures during his time near Brownsville. All of these men used their talents and connections to achieve success during the ever-changing social situation following the war.

While the US Army may have been ineffectual as a stalwart defense against Indian attacks, its presence encouraged and supported business and trade along the Rio Grande. Though the army's defense was imperfect, locals did sometimes exaggerate the size and scope of Indian attacks to persuade the government to send more troops to their region. The arrivals of troops, and even bases or depots, meant more money in the region and more funding for local volunteers. Because of the Native American raids, the border remained porous, particularly due to the Comanches and Lipan Apaches. Mexicans, at times, crossed north of the border to pursue Apaches who had seized horses and mules from their ranches. Furthermore, despite the US Army's claim of professional detachment in its "exercises of violence," soldiers often mirrored their civilian counterparts in engaging in violence against Indians. The continuous raids along the border and into Mexico plagued the Valley until after the American Civil War. Despite the risk, many Anglos, Europeans, and Mexicans migrated to the borderland in the Rio Grande Valley seeking their fortunes.[38]

Tejano-Anglo Tensions in South Texas

Tejanos maintained a clear ethnic majority in the Lower Rio Grande Valley, though they systematically lost economic and political power throughout the second half of the nineteenth century. Three factors contributed to the Anglo dominance. First, the presence of the US Army created a support structure that reinforced Anglo control of the growing economy based upon supplying the frontier forts. Second, many Texans superimposed the negative historical memory of Mexicans caused by the Texas Revolution and Mexican-American War upon Tejanos. This factor, however, was not as present in South Texas as it was in eastern and northern Texas. Finally, American laws favored Anglo-Texans over Tejanos. Whether the advantage stemmed from language or economic influence, more often than not, Anglos reaped the benefits when conflicts came before the courts.

One of the most significant legacies of the Mexican-American War in Texas is the biting and deeply rooted racism Anglo-American immigrants felt and exhibited toward Mexican Texans and Tejanos. The memory of the Alamo and San Jacinto paired with the resounding victory of the US Army during the war against Mexico shaped the Anglo mindset, relegating Tejanos to second-class citizens in what had been their own homeland prior to 1846. Helen Chapman, wife of an army officer, realized the racial disparities created with the influx of

Anglo immigrants, and, in a letter to the editor of the *Indiana Bulletin*, made a public defense of the rights of Tejanos. In her letter, she argued that crimes committed by one Mexican did not automatically become crimes of all Mexicans in Texas. Maria von Blücher, wife of Felix von Blücher and a Prussian immigrant to Corpus Christi, however, showed far less sympathy for Tejanos than Helen Chapman. When a young Tejano annoyed her and did not remove himself at her request, she took violent action. Maria wrote that the Tejano "was tied and 100 lashes were administered, and his knife was taken from his hand and broken, which is equivalent to removing an officer's sword." Maria's husband, Felix von Blücher, found work with the US military as an interpreter. The power his wife wielded not only demonstrated the racism of the period, but it also revealed how the family's relationship to the US Army may have allowed additional latitude to deal with Tejanos more harshly than another citizen without such connections could have. Emmanuel Domenech also commented on the harsh treatment of Tejanos by Anglo-Americans. A Tejano sweeper who accidentally knocked dust onto an American walking by received "seventeen severe wounds to the head and shoulders" from the American's knife. Furthermore, Domenech asserted that "such acts were of almost daily occurrence." He noted that the Texas Rangers were particularly harsh against the Mexican Texans.[39]

As citizens of both countries vied for power during wartime occupation, economic and political competition often manifested itself in outbursts of violence between Mexicans and American soldiers or merchants. Such issues continually arose regularly in both of Mexico's northern and central theaters of the war. A review of the General and Special Orders of Generals Zachary Taylor and Winfield Scott revealed a continual stream of court martial cases attempting to deal with the growing friction. These stresses during the war translated into a magnified resentment many Texans harbored for Mexican-Americans/Tejanos in South Texas. In the army, the division between the regulars and volunteers magnified some of these issues since many of the infractions resulted from the actions of volunteer troops who lacked discipline of the regulars. While some Anglo-Americans who came to the Valley from outside of Texas, such as Richard King, lacked the same level of prejudice against Mexicans, the average Texan certainly possessed some biases against people of Mexican descent because of the repeated conflicts between the two peoples.[40]

The Cart War (1857) and the so-called Cortina Wars (1859–1860, 1861) are the two most prominent manifestations of ethnic tensions between Anglos and Tejanos leading to negative historical memory on both sides during the interwar period. Across Texas, Anglo-controlled communities began passing resolutions prohibiting Mexican peons from entering the country and associating with blacks. Poisoned by bad memories, tensions between Tejanos and Anglo-Texans often became violent. The Cart War was the culmination of these tensions over labor competition in the land-borne shipping of goods across Texas. While Anglos managed to dominate many of the larger economic endeavors in the state, Tejano laborers still held the freight business between the coast and interior trade with San Antonio and its environs. This Tejano control led to resentment and exacerbated the long-standing racial animosity, which culminated in Anglos murdering and violently intimidating the Tejano drivers who had been guaranteed citizenship rights under the Treaty of Guadalupe-Hidalgo. Despite Anglo teamsters regularly trying to infiltrate the carrying trade, they could not undercut the rates set by Tejano cartmen. During the summer of 1857, a quasiwar of lawlessness, harassment, injury, and pillaging of Tejano carts sought to intimidate Tejano cartmen to relinquish control of the trade to Anglo merchants. Pressures from the Mexican government and the US secretary of state brought the conflict to an end. Though ultimately an unsuccessful effort for Anglos, many Tejano cartmen lost their lives during the fighting. The Cortina War stemmed from challenges to Tejano human rights. Juan Cortina, a well-known Tejano leader, injured a Texas lawman after intervening on the behalf of another Tejano. This confrontation sparked a decade-long conflict along the Rio Grande. These events reflect how "the general view of Tejanos, even those born in Texas, remained largely negative."[41]

Helen Chapman clearly saw the inequality of the legal system between Tejanos and Anglo-Texans, "The laws of Texas as I understand [them] would greatly restrain the privilege of voting among Mexicans. . . . But where perjury is a crime of daily and hourly occurrence . . . the meanest bribe of a glass of liquor can procure any number of votes." Without the ability to vote for legal changes that supported them effectively, Tejanos found themselves hindered in the court system. The Treaty of Guadalupe-Hidalgo promised equal citizenship, but in practice that rarely was the case. These legal obstacles contributed to the progressive loss of land experienced by Tejanos. Adverse court rulings and lawyers' fees paid in land were two of the dominate means of separating Tejanos from their land. Violence and economic sabotage, such as the killing of cattle, also became tools to drive Tejanos off their land. Many Tejanos recognized that Anglo law enforcement turned a blind eye when Tejanos suffered from crime. The period between 1821 and 1848 had created tensions between Mexicans and Texans. These tense feelings had hardened by the end of the Mexican-American War, leaving Texans far less sympathetic to the Tejanos and more willing to push them off their land. The violence described by historian William Carrigan rarely stemmed from strictly racial reasons, but the vigilante mobs were animated by their ethnic and cultural background. The historical memory of Texans created an environment that lent itself to such adverse relations, but there are examples of Anglo and European immigrants operating in a more synergistic kind of relationship. Intermarriage, business connections, and hereditary land ownership all factored into the more amicable relations present in South Texas than in other parts of the state. Even with the disproportionate power acquired by Anglo and European immigrants, Tejanos and Mexicans who lived on their land or worked for them often remained loyal to their Anglo hacendado or jefe.[42]

A decade after the Mexican-American War, a period of change and relative peace took place, despite the racial tensions that sometimes resulted in violence. To understand the role and influence of the US Army during the 1850s along the Rio Grande Valley, one must look carefully at the multiple relationships between civilians and the military. The roles the army played in reshaping the region cannot be overstated. The influx of specie from the army caused an economic expansion; its presence encouraged settlement not seen before; and thus the close relationship between Anglo settlers and the army resulted in a power shift away from Tejanos.

The Quartermaster's Department served as a catalyst of immigration and economic influence that created a dynamic shift in the social and demographic hierarchy in South Texas. Across all of Texas, ethnic tensions between Anglo-Americans and Mexican-Americans increased. In the borderlands of the Lower Rio Grande Valley, however, the competition for political and social control underwent a different process with a unique outcome. South Texas was not a region of zero-sum political gain, but a place where an amalgamation of US and Mexican political and social heritage created a unique zone that could only exist in a borderland. The competing influence of two national identities often created competition between the two dominant ethnic groups in the region, but it also created a unique environment in which identity proved far more flexible than elsewhere in the United States. Although many Anglos sought to maximize the various advantages gained by the presence of the US Army or an Anglo-controlled state and municipal government, opportunities for Mexican-Americans still existed. Industrious Tejanos across South Texas negotiated the changing political landscape after the US-Mexican War, maintaining a Mexican enclave within Texas.

Without the presence of army contracts via the Quartermaster's Department, American occupation and settlement of South Texas would have been far more difficult and less appetizing to entrepreneurs. The potential for economic gain and the demand for labor drew citizens from both the United States and Mexico to take advantage of opportunities in the Lower Rio Grande Valley. This catalyst shaped the relationship between Anglos and Mexican-Americans in this region for generations to come and served as the foundation for the region's demographic and geographic future.

CHAPTER 7

Economic and Geographic Changes in South Texas

1848–1860

The conclusion of the US-Mexican War created a new economic paradigm in the new southwestern United States. The Treaty of Guadalupe-Hidalgo dictated that the United States received what became known as the Mexican Cession, the penultimate major land acquisition to complete the contiguous United States before the Gadsden Purchase in 1854. The Mexican Cession finalized the Texas border and included complete or partial acquisitions of land in New Mexico, Colorado, Utah, Arizona, Nevada, and California. With the new lands came new responsibilities and burdens for the US government. These lands were not vacant; instead, various Native American groups dominated these areas, necessitating the development of a chain of forts to defend the settled frontiers. These new and expanded military outposts served as the conduit for the American dollar into the Lower Rio Grande Valley region, infusing it with hard currency like never before. This monetary surge altered the economic equilibrium of the borderlands, creating a new power hierarchy that favored the more recent Anglo migrants. The creation of new frontier forts alone does not explain the change. The efforts of the Quartermaster's Department to meet the expanding demands of frontier operations continued the flow of American money into the western territories of the settled United States.[1]

The forts and additional supply depots established for the army along the Rio Grande during and after the Mexican-American War had significant economic and social influence upon the Lower Río Grande Valley. These military installations acted as a catalyst for change that rapidly altered the American-Mexican borderlands. The region underwent major shifts during the nineteenth century because of several state-building processes resulting in a unique social and economic environment. The war against Mexico and the establishment of military installations by the US Army and its Quartermaster's Department initiated the most influential of these processes that altered and defined the region for decades.

The new, officially sanctioned border along the Rio Grande altered the traditional regional boundaries of Texas. For most of Spanish and Mexican history, the dividing line between Texas and other Mexican states followed the Nueces River with its mouth at Corpus Christi. Although the border between neighboring nation-states had moved south to the Rio Grande, the inhabitants of this new borderland did not necessarily accept the change. The historical ease of crossing the river coupled with the growing demand for labor fueled by the US Army and the specie it provided rendered the river merely a political stripe on a map that served as an occasional hindrance to commerce rather than an actual barrier.

The war between the United States and Mexico also served as a catalyst that shifted urban geography and transformed the society of the valley that lay on both sides of that river. Prior to the war, the center of economic power and commerce on the Rio Grande was Matamoros. The war with the United States brought unprecedented wealth to the region, and Brownsville now supplanted Matamoros as the entrepôt for northern Mexico because Americans controlled the primary harbor in the Lower Rio Grande Valley, Brazos Santiago. Spanish and Mexican efforts at colonization left South Texas only sparsely populated prior to the Mexican-American War, with fewer than nine thousand residents. After the war, settlements along the American bank of the Rio Grande began appearing rapidly, resulting in a population boom never experienced in the Valley. Mexicans and Anglo-Americans, as well as some Europeans, began moving into the region to take advantage of the new economic opportunities created after the war. The most significant source of these opportunities was the influx of the American dollar via the US Army's greatly expanded presence. The army paid almost exclusively in specie, particularly the new "Double-Eagle" twenty-dollar gold piece.[2]

Anglo and European merchants settled in South Texas before, during, and after the war. These entrepreneurial men brought their skills, contacts, and wartime history with the US Army Quartermaster's Department to establish themselves or expand their businesses during the postwar years. Some of the most well-known, such as Charles Stillman, Mifflin Kenedy, and Richard King, profited heavily from quartermaster issued contracts, which they propelled into profitable land speculation and acquisition. Eventually these Anglo men became dominate leaders of Cameron County despite the region remaining predominately Hispanic. Other merchants followed their pattern of success, if not in as resounding a fashion as King and his growing King Ranch empire.

THE US ARMY IN SOUTH TEXAS

On August 31, 1848, General Orders No. 49 established Texas as the Eighth Military District as part of the Western Division headquartered in New Orleans. Colonel Roger Jones, the adjutant general of the US Army, issued the order as directed by Secretary of War William Marcy. The troops stationed in Texas numbered 1,488, which represented 14 percent of the regular army. The force sent to Texas included two-and-one-half infantry regiments, six dragoon companies, and one light and one heavy artillery battery. Colonel William Jenkins Worth (Brevet Major General) commanded the Eighth District and reported to Major General Zachary Taylor, who commanded the Western Division. Brevet Major General Persifor Frazer Smith officially replaced Taylor in 1850 as commander of the Western District because of Taylor's election as president in 1848. The establishment of this military district formalized the newly established series of forts, depots, barracks, and other military outposts in Texas, with a number of these in South Texas along the Rio Grande.[3]

The War Department established the Eighth District headquarters in San Antonio, making the town the initial center of all army logistical activity. The Quartermaster's Department also rented the Alamo as a storehouse from the Catholic Church for $150 a month. This arrangement was made several decades before Texans again began remembering the Alamo and turning it into a worldwide landmark and example of a valiant defeat. The department also leased another stone building to house arms and munitions along the San Antonio River. Eventually, this complex expanded with new adobe buildings in 1857. The San Antonio Arsenal handled weapons and ammunition while the San Antonio Quartermaster Depot at the Alamo handled the majority of supplies stored and shipped. This group of buildings formed the nucleus of all army goods received, stored, and distributed in Texas, a situation that differed greatly from those in other states where the federal government owned the public lands. The army could choose unoccupied federal lands in other states for their bases, but in Texas all installations were leased or bought from either the state or private citizens. This necessity to lease or purchase space for facilities again allowed for a continued flow of US government specie into the hands of Texas citizens. Historian Mark

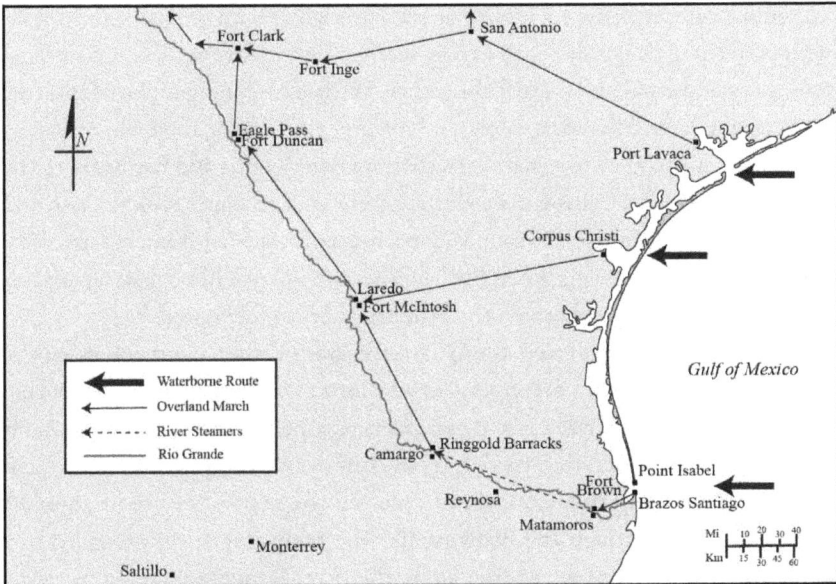

South Texas Forts and Supplies

Wilson calculated the annual expenditures of the Quartermaster's Department growing from $871,000 in fiscal 1844 to more than $4,295,000 in 1850.[4]

Shortly after the establishment of San Antonio as the central logistical hub, the Quartermaster's Department needed a supporting arsenal to supply the new posts on the Trinity, Brazos, and Colorado Rivers. The Austin Arsenal depot proved to be short-lived and quickly lost its significance as several of the forts in central and north Texas closed in favor of establishing more western positions. Although it had only started in 1848, by 1854 almost all logistical operations had ceased in Austin. The San Antonio Arsenal and Depot continued to operate until federal forces left in 1861. Indianola and Corpus Christi served as major ports of entry for supplies heading toward the San Antonio or Austin depots. These two ports received supplies that wagons and trains carried inland to the two hubs. From there the wagons and trains departed to the various forts supplied by each of the depots.[5]

While Matamoros served as the heart of the burgeoning American merchant wartime trade on the lower Rio Grande, the capture of Monterrey allowed businessmen there to delve even further into Mexican markets. Traders experienced some issues with the United States' Walker Tariff, temporarily causing a loss of economic protection from a higher tariff. Through careful business and a willingness to smuggle goods south across the Rio Grande from Brazos Santiago, however, many avoided the tariff altogether. With the opening of the Monterrey markets, goods such as hides, wools, and fruits began making their way to American merchants who were eager to sell their own dry goods and hardware to the Mexican merchants. During 1847, many American merchants took the risk and shipped goods to Monterrey from Matamoros until trade with interior markets began to slow. Discovering when the Mexican control would be reinstated after the ceasing of hostilities became the primary concern for traders.[6]

After the war with Mexico, the Quartermaster's Department enhanced the existing river trade system to support the new forts along the Rio Grande. During the war, the army expanded two major ports, Corpus Christi and Brazos Santiago/Point Isabel. Between the Mexican-American War and American Civil War, the forts along the Rio Grande received the majority of their supplies through Brazos Santiago and Brownsville. The army's logistical needs led to a larger amount of steam navigation along the river. Supplies traveled to Texas by sea because of the poor overland transportation network. They arrived from New Orleans at the Texas ports of Galveston, Indianola, Corpus Christi, and Brazos Santiago. From there, private contractors hauled the goods overland or up the Rio Grande to the frontier forts.[7]

The Quartermaster's Department expanded two new logistical systems to supply their frontier forts: the Santa Fe Trail and the Rio Grande Line. Although both existed informally, the army created a regulated system to ensure the frontier locations were regularly supplied. The Rio Grande Line was the supply system that developed along the lower river valley. It was more akin to upper Mississippi or Missouri river transport systems rather than the Santa Fe Trail into West Texas system because the Quartermaster's Department could take advantage of waterborne logistics. Steamers offloaded via lighter vessels at Brazos Santiago or cross-loaded to river steamers for the trip upriver to Fort Brown, then supplies could be moved farther upriver by contract steamers, such as the ones run by Kenedy and King, to Ringgold Barracks, near present day Rio Grande City. Brazos Santiago was integral to the Rio Grande Line because it still represented the best point to transfer goods.[8]

In the period following the war with Mexico, 1848–1860, the trade passing through the Rio Grande Valley remained remarkably similar to what existed prior to the war. The dominant export goods remained specie and bullion, beef hides, and used steamboat machinery left over from the war. Wool eventually returned to its prewar levels after a period of reduced production, and a new export, lead, began being exported from the mountains around Monterrey and Saltillo. Imports remained unchanged: dry goods, hardware, lumber, and furniture with the occasional piece of machinery on a ship's manifest. The Valley itself consumed little of these imports, most of which found their way to the markets in northern Mexico.[9]

THE URBAN GEOGRAPHY OF POSTWAR SOUTH TEXAS

The newly established US Army installations along the Rio Grande developed relationships with the towns that flourished alongside them. Tejanos dominated the general prewar population, and the Anglo newcomers settled mostly around the new towns. The movement of the international boundary to the Rio Grande not only encouraged a shift in population but also transformed the urban landscape of the region. After the war, the Mexican towns on the left bank found themselves paired with an American, specifically Anglo-dominated, counterpart on the opposite bank. US Army garrisons accompanied many of these new American towns due to forts or other military facilities being established nearby. The forts enforced United States jurisdiction and endeavored to repel any attack by Mexican or Indian forces, but they also served as de facto support and business opportunities for US citizens, primarily white businessmen, newly arrived in the Rio Grande Valley. Military leaders often had political and economic connections to civilian leadership, influencing the Anglo-American ability to enforce social and economic claims. The support of the military gave newly arrived Americans a distinct advantage over the Tejanos.[10]

The economic influence of United States military bases and the communities that formed around them to meet their needs has been the focus of several important studies. The army often created markets for traders, laborers, and other miscellaneous workers needed by the soldiers on post. The notable aspect of the new military stations along the Rio Grande was that almost every new a fort, barrack, or depot was positioned across from an existing Mexican town. This geography created an interesting economic dichotomy with the river as the dividing line. New jobs and markets arrived with the numerous bases established along the Rio Grande, but Anglo immigration, while booming, could not meet the greatly expanded labor needs. This need for labor required turning to Mexicans in these towns across the river who were more than willing to accept army dollars for their services. While this situation provided a boon to the average laborer, the benefit became skewed as Mexicans and Mexican-Americans became relegated to manual labor while Anglo-Americans more often obtained control of companies and land. In some instances, these new US citizens maintained control over their ancestral land. However, the general trend was one where Mexicans and Tejanos began to often find themselves doing manual labor while the middle- and upper-class jobs went to recent Anglo arrivals.[11]

The port of Brazos Santiago dominated the ship-to-shore leg of trade along the Rio Grande. While the little port received mixed evaluations by military officers as to its beauty and usefulness, General Thomas S. Jesup valued the port during the war. It played a crucial role in Taylor's invasion of Northern Mexico and contributed to Scott's invasion at Veracruz. In the postwar years the port continued its prominent role as a transfer point. The government contracts for the ferry trade drew steamboat pilots to the Rio Grande in hopes of making their fortune as the river economy boomed. Two of the most notable of these pilots were Mifflin Kenedy and Richard King. When King first arrived in May 1847 and came ashore at Brazos Santiago, the "place hummed with activity generated by commerce and its handmaiden, war." Almost every merchant along the Rio Grande made use of Brazos Santiago as they shipped goods to and from the United States, Europe, and elsewhere around the world. Quartermasters and entrepreneurs alike took advantage of the new depots and forts (Fort Polk, Fort Brown, Camargo, and Ringgold Barracks) built as part of wartime efforts to supply the army. Accompanying the new bases came other improvements: military roads, wagon roads, geographic surveys, boundary surveys, and even some agricultural experiments. The economic boom that started at Brazos Santiago with entrepreneurs like King and Kenedy left lasting results on the entire Rio Grande Valley.[12]

Ocean-going steamships could not navigate past the barrier islands where Point Isabel and Brazos Santiago were located. Instead, the Quartermaster's Department, then private shippers like King and Kennedy, used smaller more specialized vessels to complete the various stages of transportation. Ships arrived at Brazos Santiago, unloaded to shore or cross-loaded to small crafts, then loaded on shallow draft steam vessels that could navigate the lagoon en route to the river. Once on the river, the vessels either traveled up to Brownsville/Matamoros themselves or transferred the cargo to larger river steamer that could navigate upriver. These vessels then carried goods along the Rio Grande to the forts and depots at Rio Grande City, Roma, Eagle Pass, and Brownsville.[13]

Colonel Joseph K. F. Mansfield viewed Brazos Santiago as "a good one and accessible to vessels from all parts of the States, being at the entrance to the bay at

Point Isabell, and nine miles along shore from the mouth of the Río Grande. . . . This depot [was] indispensable and in [connection] with that at Indianola will answer all the demands of the Service." The port on Brazos Island facilitated the rapid growth of the new town of Brownsville, across the river from Matamoros and on the original site of Fort Brown, which the army moved a few miles north of the city. Fort Polk, established March 26, 1846, lay near the mouth of the Rio Grande across from Brazos Santiago at Point Isabel. Brownsville soon capitalized on its location north of the river, monopolizing access to Brazos Santiago. During the war, all goods traveled through the fledgling city of Brownsville before entering Matamoros and the rest of northern Mexico. By 1848, Helen Chapman, the wife of Lieutenant William Chapman, noted that even "Matamoras [was] getting very much the appearance of an American town. You meet at every turn men from the States with the fresh and energetic manner of those who have been born on a soil that yields its fruit only to those who earn it by the sweat of their brow." The location of Fort Brown and the supply depot at Brazos Santiago facilitated the establishment and growth of Brownsville. The settlement of this new town represented the three most significant trends facilitating the settlement of these new American towns: first, it was settled across the Rio Grande from a preexist-ing Mexican town, Matamoros; second, there was a fort and supply depot near the new town, Fort Brown; third, Anglos quickly dominated the socioeconomic landscape. These three factors describe almost every new town established during and after the Mexican-American War in the Rio Grande Valley.[14]

Major William Emory noted that in 1857 Brownsville, "contain[ed] about three thousand inhabitants. . . . The town has sprung up since the Mexican war, and owes its prosperity chiefly to the contraband trade with Mexico." Helen Chapman also wrote, "The new city of Brownsville is growing faster than I supposed any city could grow." She noted that the inhabitants of Brownsville included "some men of property and influence, but most of them are mere adventurers." The large influx of new men into the region often disrupted the established social, political, and economical balance that existed between Tejanos and Anglos. With the growth of the town, Fort Brown also prospered. Chapman commented, "Fort Brown is really becoming a very comfortable place to live." Colonel Mansfield, in his report on military installations in Texas, wrote that the fort was "directly opposite Mat-amoros, and the only military command near the coast of Texas, indispensable, and well placed, and contiguous to Brownsville." The interrelationship between the town and fort was not lost on him in 1856. This relationship could be found in each new American settlement along the Rio Grande. By 1859 Anglos petitioned the federal government to keep Fort Brown in Brownsville because it served as a vital part of the South Texas economy. The garrison at Fort Brown numbered 291 in 1860. Residents in the Rio Grande borderlands appreciated the military presence in the region and the economic benefits it brought.[15]

Edinburg grew up opposite Reynosa, a town of about fifteen hundred inhabitants. Although the town did not have a military installation in its immediate vicinity, it was situated halfway between Brownsville and Rio Grande City, a geographical position that allowed it to take advantage of the river trade that supplied the new military installations along the river. Meanwhile, Rio Grande City, established October 26, 1848, grew out of Davis's Landing, a small trading outpost, after the army established Ringgold Barracks nearby. The settlement was situated just below the mouth of the San Juan River, with Camargo located not far away on the Mexican bank. Supplies arrived by steamer at Ringgold Barracks year-round from Brazos Santiago, although the facility was 120 miles upriver from Fort Brown. Comanche and Lipan Apache raids often reached as far as the Ringgold Barracks–Camargo region, which posed a threat to army supply lines and led to frequent military operations in the region. During the war with Mexico, Taylor also concerned himself with securing the Camargo-Monterrey supply lines from Mexican attack. By 1860, the garrison numbered 141 soldiers. It also served as a preferred base for the survey of the Mexican-American border, which looked at geology and climate as well as topographical surveys including the small islands in the river. Rio Grande City followed the pattern of having both a Mexican town and US Army base nearby, which promoted growth of the town.[16]

Roma grew out of the river trade between the forts. It lay about sixteen miles north of Ringgold Barracks and was at the head of steamboat navigation. The town was "built upon a high bluff of yellowish sandstone." Trade along the Rio Grande sustained several fine residences and warehouses. Mifflin Kenedy, business partner to Richard King, worked hard to develop Roma to break the trade monopoly previously established at Davis's Landing or Rio Grande City. This early effort demonstrated the lengths Kenedy and his partners went to secure their economic advantage on the Rio Grande. Toward the end of the 1850s the estimated amount of trade in Starr County, primarily at Roma and Rio Grande City, was about half a million dollars a year. A majority of the goods fueling this trade went into Mexico, demonstrating that while there was a defined border, trade activity was not restricted to one side of the river. Additionally, while many trade goods followed the customs laws, just as much contraband crossed the border as did legal trade.[17]

Laredo was a unique case among the patterns of town development after the war with Mexico. It was one of the few towns already on what became the American side of the Rio Grande. As a result, many Mexican citizens crossed the river to establish Nuevo Laredo. Fort McIntosh, established March 3, 1847, was built near the city. According to Emory, "Laredo was once the residence of proprietors of countless horses and cattle, which have been run off by the Indians," but "it has [at] present fallen into decay, and derives its support principally from the United States garrison (Fort McIntosh), one mile above the town." In 1860, Fort McIntosh's garrison included sixty-three soldiers and ten laundresses. While Laredo did not follow the exact pattern of settlement, and Tejanos retained a greater degree of control there for longer than in other new communities along the river, the new border and the location of Fort McIntosh affected the socioeconomic landscape and local geography around the town.[18]

Eagle Pass, with a population of about five hundred citizens in 1857, grew near Fort Duncan, established on October 7, 1854. William L. Cazneau, a profitable businessman from Laredo, bought up over a thousand acres of land at a crossing called *Paso del Águila*. Cazneau planned to sell the land to settlers, but the Mexican silver mined at Santa Rosa, through the Piedras Negras, proved a greater interest. Having been granted a special permit, he began a silver bullion trade stretching from Eagle Pass to Indianola, then onto New Orleans and the United States Mint. Mansfield wrote that the fort was "the westernmost of the military posts placed at intervals along the lower Río Bravo. The town of Eagle Pass adjoins the fort, and is a place of some trade, having a few large warehouses, built of the bluestone obtained in the neighborhood." It resided "120 miles from McIntosh and 45 miles from Clark and like Fort McIntosh is well placed and indispensable for some time to come." Fort Duncan marked the outer edge of the military posts designed to serve as a barrier against both Mexican and Indian incursions. The garrison at the fort included ninety-nine soldiers, five servants, and seven laundresses with their sixteen children under the age of five. The families recruited to the area by German empresario Friedrich Groos mainly found employment in freighting for Fort Duncan and other army outposts. Eagle Pass, like the other new towns, grew out of the new economic opportunities that the army, often through the Quartermaster's Department, created in the Rio Grande Valley. The combination of a military outpost and a profitable silver trade route drew settlers to Eagle Pass.[19]

The army established two interior forts not along the coast or Rio Grande: Ewell (May 18, 1852) and Merrill (March 1, 1850) along the Nueces River. Merrill was positioned nearer to Corpus Christi while Ewell was closer to the Rio Grande. Fort Ewell was built of adobe with a less than optimal location according to Captain William Grigsby Freeman: "Indeed a less inviting spot for occupation by troops cannot well be conceived." These forts served as midway points for the supplies traveling from Corpus Christi and San Antonio to the western outposts. Due to the need to supply troops for the new western forts, Ewell and Merrill closed in 1855, and their contingent of troops moved to other bases. Military installations not located on the Rio Grande, and therefore not able to take advantage of that connection to Brownsville and Brazos Santiago, did not survive, underscoring the river's role in the army's changes in the area.[20]

The new urban centers along the lower Rio Grande served as focal points for Anglo settlement. Anglo-Americans favored founding towns close to their ranches, military forts, and to hubs of commercial activity. Despite growing Anglo influence, Tejano culture had a significant impact on the development of Anglo settlements. For instance, Richard King's Santa Gertrudis Ranch, at its inception, resembled a Mexican ranch more than one fashioned after methods imported from east of the Sabine. The same goes for many of the new towns established along the Rio Grande. Much of their population and labor force consisted of Mexican nationals who crossed the river in search of the economic opportunities the army provided so they had at least the initial appearance of older, Mexican-dominated settlements. Monterrey and San Antonio became the two urban centers of trade that facilitated the growth of the new and old Rio Grande villas. The new towns and military installations benefited from the overlapping spheres of influence between the two cities. They grew as a result, and the new settlers who capitalized on the potential wealth flowing across the border became economically and socially powerful in their own right. But the owners of many of those new buildings were Anglos, who benefited either directly or indirectly from military spending. Not only did army money go directly into the hands of soldiers, laborers, and other merchants, but the secondary use of the money was almost as influential. Soldiers, for example, neither simply drank away their money, nor hoarded it like misers. Instead, they spent their money in the local communities that grew up around these new military installations. This spending of money translated into economic growth for merchants, commercial investments, new businesses, and new real estate endeavors.[21]

The trend of towns growing adjacent to military bases was not unique to South Texas. Across the United States settlers followed the army as they established frontier outposts. Not only did the soldiers provide a measure of protection for the townsfolk, but they also represented a ready market to purchase any number of goods and services not available from the quartermaster or the commissary. For the Rio Grande Valley, this ready market began during the war with Mexico and continued in the postwar period. During the American occupation of Mexican territory, including the city of Matamoros, many American merchants avoided paying the high Mexican importation tariff because of the army's control of the region. While foreign goods, mainly European, continued to have the high tariff placed upon them, the occupation allowed American products to be treated as tariff-exempt domestic goods. In addition, the postwar years saw many Mexican businesses and merchants move north of the river due to the comparative absence of trade restrictions and state or municipal taxes that existed in Mexico. The primary effort to counteract these issues in Mexico took the form of the *Zona Libre*, or free trade zone, encompassing the border towns of Matamoros, Reynosa, Camargo, Mier, Guerrero, and Nuevo Laredo. This policy created a zone along the border exempt from trade duties. It caused a boom on both sides of the river, although that boost came from smuggling as much as from legitimate trade. Not only did Anglo-Americans have a dedicated market from the new military bases along the river, but during and after the war, they established many inroads into northern Mexican markets. This combination fueled a collective social and economic power shift in the region from Tejanos to Anglos.[22]

Anglo and European Merchants in South Texas

The merchants that settled in South Texas before and after the Mexican-American War benefited from the Quartermaster's Department presence, and their expanding wealth accelerated the rise of Anglo power in the region. During the two decades that preceded the war, many merchants along the Rio Grande chafed at the restriction placed on free trade imposed by the government in Mexico City. The postwar years saw new opportunities for trade along the new border. Most of these merchants were more than willing to work with and even marry into Mexican and Tejano families. The allure of profits, and perhaps love, overcame any racial misgivings these men might have had. Several Anglo and white European businessmen arrived prior to the war, such a Henry L. Kinney who founded Corpus Christi. Others arrived during or after the war as soldiers or contractors for the US Army and Quartermaster's Department. The connection between the rapid financial growth for these men and the presence of the US Army is clear. The new forts and installations needed to be supplied, and these merchants already had connections with the army or Tejanos in the region. By serving as middlemen they maximized their profits. The Anglo and European settlers used their business acumen, marital access to land, and their unique skillsets to take every advantage they could in the postwar years. Their mounting wealth made them prominent members of the society. As they founded towns and ranches of their own while often marrying into the Tejano elite, these Anglos became key powerbrokers in South Texas.[23]

The Connecticut-born Charles Stillman established a network of industrial and mercantile enterprises after he settled in Matamoros by way of New Orleans in 1828. He made his wealth as a cotton broker, in real estate, silver mines, merchandise outlets, and shipping along the Gulf Coast and up the Rio Grande. By the time the Mexican-American War broke out, Stillman held a position of wealth and prominence in Matamoros. During the war, he allied with other merchants and businessmen such as Mifflin Kenedy and Richard King to establish a riverboat trade that benefited from contracts to carry soldiers and supply for the US Army. As Brownsville came into existence under Stillman's guidance, his wealth only grew, though he eventually sold much of his land to his partner Kenedy. Some of the land acquired included that claimed by Doña Francisca Cavasos, which became contested by her heirs. Eventually, they settled for a portion of the land sold to Stillman via his lawyers in exchange for the confirmation of the land ownership for the remaining thirty-eight leagues of land. Juan Cortina, Cavasos' son, felt his mother and her heirs had been tricked out of their land. The founding of Brownsville left Stillman's mark on South Texas. The city grew, with the aid of Port Isabel and Brazos Santiago, into one of the wealthiest cities along the Rio Grande. The gateway town of Brownsville served as an import and export hub for the region. Many of the shipments passed through Brazos Santiago and Port Isabel and then onto Brownsville and Matamoros via oxcart and wagon before continuing into northern Mexico. Historian J. L. Allhands noted: "In 1859, imports valued at $4,000,000.00 passed through Port Isabel, about three-fourths of which was silver bullion."[24]

Mifflin Kenedy and Richard King quickly became two of the most prominent names in South Texas after their arrival during the Mexican-American War and their association with Charles Stillman. Kenedy hailed from Pennsylvania and King from New York, but both served as riverboat pilots in the northeast. When the war began Kenedy made his way to the Rio Grande and found work with the Quartermaster's Department piloting its riverboats. King followed within the year. During the war they became acquainted with Stillman, who eventually partnered with them on their postwar steamboat company M. Kenedy and

Company—later changed to King, Kenedy and Company. They maintained a virtual monopoly on the Rio Grande riverboat trade for about twenty-five years following the war. Kenedy married Petra Vela de Vidal, a wealthy Mexican woman from Mier, Mexico. She had inherited her first husband's wealth and paired it with what she inherited from her father, making her exceptionally wealthy for the period. When she married Kenedy, the union provided him with enormous amounts of additional capital as well as contacts throughout South Texas and northern Mexico.[25]

William Chapman graduated from West Point in 1833, eventually posted to General John E. Wool's army in San Antonio, Texas, as a staff assistant quartermaster. After fighting in the Battle of Buena Vista, February 22–23, 1847, he became the quartermaster of the army depot in Matamoros. He did much to improve the city streets, central plaza, and the schools during his tenure. Chapman helped selected the site for the new Fort Brown which geographically anchored Stillman's new city of Brownsville. He served as the fort's quartermaster from 1848 to 1852. During this time, he entered a business relationship with Richard King to acquire land that would become the King Ranch. Previously, he worked with Kenedy and King granting their shipping contracts to carry quartermaster supplies along the Rio Grande. This relationship gave Kenedy, King, and Stillman an advantage over competing shipping companies on the river. Ultimately, these contracts, in addition to their other mercantile enterprises, bankrolled the acquisition of massive tracts of land across South Texas, particularly in Cameron County.[26]

The cooperation and success of Stillman, King, Kenedy, and Chapman are the most well-known and documented examples of South Texas merchants who benefited from the US Army presence along the Rio Grande. Other merchants benefited from the army dollar and cooperation with these men as well. The following settlers arrived just before or during the Mexican-American War and took advantage of the sparsely populated borderlands to establish themselves as merchants and landowners. At times some of these merchants went head to head with Stillman and his cohort, but almost always the dominant merchants chose to cooperate, regardless of nationality, to drive out the smaller businesses and relegate the local economy into the hands of a few men.

Stephen Powers arrived in South Texas in 1847 when commissioned as a first lieutenant in the Tenth US Infantry as part of General Taylor's army of invasion. Previously he had already served as the US Consul to Basel, Switzerland, in 1839. At the end of the war, he settled in Brownsville in early 1849, reestablishing his law practice in the newly founded city. Some of his most well-known clients included Richard King, Charles Stillman, and Mifflin Kenedy. His firm focused on land titles in the disputed area between the Nueces River and Rio Grande. This skillset and knowledge of US law gave his clients a decided advantage in acquiring large tracts of land from Tejano landowners.[27]

Simon Mussina, a Jewish American merchant and newspaper editor, migrated from Philadelphia to Brownsville where he partnered with Stillman and Samuel A. Belden. Once in Brownsville Mussina acquired controlling interest in the *American Flag* newspaper, developing it into one of the most well-known newspapers of the time. The three partners laid out the city of Brownsville, and Mussina's newspaper helped popularize the city and the commercial efforts of the partners and their other business acquaintances. Many of the men that arrived in the South Texas borderlands following the war formed factions that aided each other's business endeavors. This synergy, aided by the US Army dollar, fueled their rise to power and social prominence during the 1850s. [28]

Humphrey E. Woodhouse arrived in Texas from New York when the wholesale and retail house he worked for sent him to Brazos Santiago in 1847 on a merchant vessel. He traveled and sold his merchandise in Matamoros, where he began working for Samuel A. Beldon before moving to Brownsville to start his own merchant business in 1848. By 1854 he partnered with Charles Stillman to extend their trade routes to the interior of Mexico. Woodhouse broke off the partnership with Stillman and refocused his efforts on the shipping trade between New Orleans and Padre Island, at its peak owning or invested in about fifty vessels. He also built a wharf in Point Isabel and ran a general store there although he called Brownsville home. Leading the opposition to the steamboat partnership of King and Kenedy, Woodhouse tried to find ways to avoid their high frate costs on the Rio Grande.[29]

Several other settlers and merchants capitalized on the opportunities presented during the twelve years following the war. Samuel A. Belden, a merchant and business partner of Charles Stillman, helped lay out the town of Brownsville in 1848. Belden, Stillman, and Simon Mussina sold lots for the town as the Brownsville Town Company. Jeremiah Galvan, an Irish immigrant, settled in Brownsville and capitalized on a relationship with the US Army and other merchants in South Texas. He specialized as a receiving agent for specie transports from Mexican and American customhouses. James G. Browne used his mercantile businesses and connections to acquire vast amounts of land. At his peak, he held 114,000 acres of land in Cameron County. When combined with the King and Kenedy families, they owned 97 percent of the county by 1890. Major Samuel P. Heintzelman, a mining engineer who graduated from West Point, served in the Mexican-American War, and by 1859 arrived in South Texas to lead the decisive battle against Juan Cortina near Rio Grande City. While on the border he invested $10,000 in mining the once-rich veins of Villaldama.[30]

These men—in addition to Henry Clay Davis, Francisco Yturria, Albert Champion, José San Román, and Felix von Blücher mentioned in the previous chapter—greatly benefited from the new social and economic order established during and after the war with Mexico. Some leveraged existing relationships with US Army and Quartermaster's Department, while others simply took advantage of the social and economic upheaval along the border left in the wake of the war. Whichever route taken, each man sought to gain advantage and position whenever possible.

THE STEAMBOATS OF KING, KENEDY, AND STILLMAN

Dominating the postwar Rio Grande Line was the steamboat company organized by Richard King, Mifflin Kenedy, and Charles Stillman. King and the King Ranch are iconic in Texas lore, so examining at the rise of King's empire and how it relates to the expanded role of the Quartermaster's Department during and after the war is illuminating as an example of the army's influence on the region. King first became involved with the army during the Second Seminole War in Florida. This experience put him in contact with General Zachary Taylor's forces, many of whom accompanied Taylor to Corpus Christi before the war with Mexico erupted, giving King many contacts to set up his joint steamboat operation along the Rio Grande. King's friend, Kenedy, invited him to join an economic venture on the river in 1847, which became their riverboat company. Arriving at the newly established Fort Brown, King secured work as one of three pilots on the steamboat *Colonel Cross*. Shortly after, before his twenty-fourth birthday, King was promoted to captain of the *Colonel Cross*. The Rio Grande was shallow and full of sand bars rather than deep and wide open like the Mississippi or Ohio Rivers, which many riverboat pilots were used to navigating. But the experience of King and Kenedy on other difficult rivers made them valuable resources to the army, propelling them toward success.[31]

By the end of the war, both Kenedy and King had become captains of steamboats ready to benefit from the continuing demand for transporting supplies upriver to the newly established army installations along the Rio Grande. One stroke of luck for these young captains came at the end of the war when the

Quartermaster's Department auctioned surplus river boats at a fraction of what the army had originally paid for them. On December 6, 1848, the department published in the *American Flag*, a Brownsville newspaper, a list of river steamboats for sale: *Colonel Hunt, Whiteville, Brownsville, General Jesup, Wm. R. McKee, Hatchee Eagle, Troy, Colonel Cross, Colonel J. Stephens, Dragon*, and *J. E. Roberts*. King managed to get his old steamboat, the *Colonel Cross* for $750, a bargain compared to the $14,000 that the department originally paid for it. The two friends began building their river freight empire, ferrying goods from Brazos Santiago to Matamoros, Rio Grande City, Roma, and other towns along the river. King proposed purchasing more ships to expand their business, and by 1852 the *Grampus* and *Comanche* were plying their trade along the river. The *Grampus* did the slower, heavier work along the coast, while the *Comanche* spryly navigated the river.[32]

Following the war, Brownsville became part of Cameron County. One of the first tasks that the new county government undertook was establish new ferry lines along and across the Rio Grande. Cameron County planned six new ferries to operate from Brazos Island (Brazos Santiago) to Rio Grande City and all the way to Laredo. Men like Stillman, King, and Kenedy took advantage of their prior experience with the army to capture as much of the ferry trade as possible. For a period, both Matamoros and Cameron County issued ferry licenses for operating on the river. Not all river crossings happened on licensed ferries, but enough regular ferry traffic occurred to make it more than profitable. In addition to the normal travel and trade, the California Gold Rush brought about 765 men into Brazos Santiago, and they eventually traveled upriver and then overland to California. Though short-lived, this influx provided a temporary boost to the ferry trade during its first few years. This postwar trade greatly expanded the Rio Grande Line and laid the financial groundwork for economic and political power shifts along the river.[33]

The true success for M. Kenedy and Company came from the deal they made with the United States government. This agreement's architect was Major William W. Chapman, who as previously mentioned served as the quartermaster at Fort Brown until mid-1852, when he received a promotion to serve as the quartermaster at the new army headquarters in Corpus Christi under General Persifor F. Smith. Chapman aided Kenedy and King in obtaining monopolistic contracts to supply the forts along the river. Chapman even argued in letters to superiors that M. Kenedy and Company had the only good boats along the river and represented the best persons with whom the army should contract. Becoming friends with Major Chapman proved to be one of the most fortunate turns of events for M. Kenedy and Company. This connection also clearly illustrated how the civilian and military relationships worked along Texas's southern frontier. In these newly burgeoning towns and military outposts, who you knew was as important as whether or not you were competent. Such blatant favoritism exhibited on behalf of King and Kenedy by Chapman over other riverboat captains represented only a portion of the potential discrimination. Anglo army officers showed a preference for men they knew from the war over other competitors and Mexican or Tejano alternatives. Obtaining government contracts was difficult for most newcomers, but it was virtually impossible for Mexicans and Tejanos, who represented a recent national enemy.[34]

Contracts issued to M. Kenedy & Company and Richard King in 1856 illustrate the profits available for these men who negotiated their wartime relations with the Quartermaster's Department into private contracts after the war. On October 31, 1856, M. Kenedy & Company received a contract to transport troops between Ringgold Barracks and Brazos Santiago or anywhere in between for $4,000. The quartermasters signed several contracts with King issued in November of the same year. These three contracts totaled an additional $4,150 for the riverboat company. Each contract specified baggage and units being carried. King and Kenedy eventually received a more monopolistic contract from Chapman after some political intrigue and economic competition between them and Captain James B. Armstrong, another riverboat proprietor. Ultimately, King and Kenedy relied on their relationship with Stillman and Chapman to secure a monopoly on riverboat transportation, both US Army contracted and civilian, until after the Civil War.[35]

Chapman's relationship with King did not end with the acquisition of the army contract. There were unproven rumors that Chapman was a silent partner of M. Kenedy and Comapny. The most clearly established connection, however, came through real estate investments and speculation. King's partner Stillman not only pushed for the establishment of Brownsville, but he also seized the opportunity to profit off the land purchases around the burgeoning town. He guided Chapman to delve into real estate and to establish himself physically and financially in the Rio Grande Valley. Not only did criticisms emerge of how Chapman handled the army shipping contracts with M. Kenedy and Coompany, but ties between Chapman, King, and Stillman became more apparent, demonstrating how closely linked economic and real estate power became on the northern bank of the Rio Grande. The presence of the army with its new bases along the river paired with the continual flow of government dollars into the region to create an almost impenetrable economic wall for anyone not in the inner circle. Without the constant flow of money into the area to support the Quartermaster's Department's shipping needs, men like the partners of M. Kenedy and Company would have lacked the capital necessary to propel themselves to higher economic and social standings. The fact that King built one of the largest ranches in Texas during this interwar period clearly illustrates the undeniable power shift that occurred as a result of the change in the economy. No longer did the Rio Grande Valley depend on exports from Saltillo, Monterrey, and Matamoros to make a profit; instead, the army became a major source of capital. This power shift created a ripple effect in South Texas, where the army and then those that profited from the army became the dominant employers of the region.[36]

King purchased land in an area called the Wild Horse Desert; in particular, he obtained part of the Rincón de Santa Gertrudis Grant. The Santa Gertrudis section served as the basis for a growing ranching endeavor that King thought would be even more profitable than the steamboat business. His thinking proved to be correct in many ways. Santa Gertrudis, in later years, would become a breed of cattle originally bred first on the King Ranch and the only true American breed. Having been raised outside of Texas, King lacked the long-standing disdain many Texans felt for Mexicans and Tejanos. This nonprejudicial outlook allowed him to benefit from the most knowledgeable men in South Texas, Anglo or Mexican, to establish his ranching empire. King set up the ranch in the pattern of a hacienda with himself at its head, the *hacendado*. His men usually called him *El Capitán* or *el patrón*. The most defining aspect of King's new Anglo-Mexican hybridized hacienda became how he established a permanent labor source for his ranch. Unlike many Anglo ranchers who hired cowboys, King transplanted the entire Mexican town of Cruillas to his ranch to live and work. The people of Cruillas took what they could carry and traveled to King's Santa Gertrudis Ranch to rebuild their town around his hacienda, becoming *Kineños*, or King's people. This singular event, probably more than any other, exemplifies the changing economic environment in South Texas. An Anglo newcomer, profiting from army contracts, acquired old Spanish and Mexican land grants to establish an Anglo version of a hacienda worked by people from a Mexican town relocated hundreds of miles to his ranch. King recreated a semifeudal system in South Texas, completely altering the economic and social dynamic of both Hispanics and Anglos in the region. The wealth gained from his riverboat monopoly enabled him to become a significant employer in the Rio Grande Valley, within about a decade of his arrival to work for the Quartermaster's Department.[37]

WEALTH AND LAND IN SOUTH TEXAS

Brownsville became known as a place of rich men by the end of the 1850s. Among the most prominent were José San Ramon, Charles Stillman, Samuel A. Beldon, Francisco Yturria, Humphrey E. Woodhouse, Jeremiah Galvan, Richard King, and Mifflin Kenedy. A vast amount of wealth in the form of trade goods flowed into Brazos Santiago; the annual tally of the goods that entered the Valley ranged from $10 million to $14 million. Shipments of specie leaving the Rio Grande reached New Orleans, where deposits of $200,000 were made every two weeks. The mercantile wealth achieved during this decade propelled these men—Anglo, Mexican, and Tejano alike—to new heights along the river. What is most defining about this period is that men like King, Kenedy, and Stillman arrived in South Texas during the Mexican War and by 1860 had established themselves as some of the most dominant, wealthy figures in the region. That most were Anglos or European indicates that not all shared equally in the new economic system spawned by military investments and operations.[38]

Tax records provide insight into the fortunes of the residents in the Rio Grande Valley, although it is unlikely that any of these wealthy men accurately reported their property holding to the tax collectors. What they did report illustrates a unique social dynamic within the region. Often by a significant margin, Anglo or European residents possessed the largest amounts of land and recorded wealth on the tax records. In Starr County, Henry Clay Davis's land made him the wealthiest resident by a wide margin with recorded assets of $19,700 in 1852. While his recorded wealth on the tax records declined to $15,000 by 1860, he remained the wealthiest person in the county. A parallel situation occurred in Cameron County with Stillman, Kenedy, and King. In 1852, the records show Stillman possessed $33,000 of assets and property. His two business partners, King and Kenedy, rapidly grew their own wealth over the 1850s. Kenedy in 1852 recorded zero assets, by 1856 he claimed $4,910, and in 1860 $19,115. King's wealth grew even more dramatically, starting in 1852 with $9,000 in assets, it decreased in 1856 to $5,100, then skyrocketed to $24,000 in 1860. Their company recorded a worth of $50,000 in 1860, making it one of the most valuable businesses in Cameron County.[39]

Land ownership had undergone significant changes since the end of the war. The census shows that new immigrants from Mexico, Europe, and the United

States made up roughly 64 percent of the population. These new arrivals also held about 95 percent of the assessed real estate in South Texas. While Tejano and Mexican landowners in the region remained the largest group in numbers, they tended to own less land per person. Total wealth paralleled the change in land ownership. American immigrant wealth accounted for about one third of all wealth in South Texas, even though most of these residents arrived only in the last ten to fifteen years. Newcomers such as Richard King rapidly became some of the wealthiest men and largest landowners in South Texas in just a little more than a decade following the war. [40]

Complicating the economic status these men achieved in the Rio Grande Valley is the traditional boss or hacendado/jefe culture in the region. Throughout Mexico, during Spanish and Mexican periods, the landowner, or boss, served as the center of everyday life. The residents of the land turned to the wealthy landowner for help, decisions, and any number of other aspects of life. This cultural tradition persisted with the rise of the new Anglo and European landowners that began to dominate South Texas after the Mexican-American War. More important, this culture gave these men the votes of those that lived and worked on their land. By the mid to late 1800s, Richard King and his descendants claimed influence over around five hundred thousand votes, according to South Texas politician James (Jim) B. Wells. Each of the men discussed controlled or influenced the political system by directing votes towards themselves or chosen candidates, which further enhanced their status. Some Hispanic families retained similar control such as the Guerra family of Starr County. Other counties, such as Cameron, shifted into the hands of Anglo and European merchants and ranchers.[41]

～

The presence of the army, particularly the Quartermaster's Department, during and after the war with Mexico laid the foundation for the economic growth that followed. It served as a catalyst for entrepreneurs, mostly Anglos, to enter the Rio Grande Valley seeking wealth. The borderlands that surround the river became a place of rapid change during the war, and afterwards that change became more pronounced. The forts and depots established along the Rio Grande by the United States demanded constant supplies to be maintained. The department, with the aid of private contractors met this demand during the 1850s, providing a constant flow of specie into the region. This influx of resources drew immigrants and migrants from both sides of the border to South Texas to seek opportunity in the new economic landscape that grew in the region after the war. With the growth in population, new towns grew up around the army bases, further driving the demand for goods but also ensuring that Anglos would become the dominant group.

Men like King, Kenedy, and Stillman took full advantage of their wartime connections to propel themselves to the forefront of South Texas society. Army contracts provided a launching point for larger ranching endeavors. They continued to seek influence in the markets of northern Mexico for both personal gain and in the interest of the United States. Controlling trade on the Rio Grande allowed for more political capital in the borderlands. Whichever person or group could garner favor with the army gained immense advantage over other competition, whether American or Mexican. The wartime benefits enjoyed by merchants allowed for deeper roots in the postwar period and increased efforts for control between these two nations and their agents. Whether consciously or not, the United States and Mexico, through their regional proxies vied for economic, and thus political, control over the borderlands even after the war between the two nations ended in 1848.

Ultimately, this struggle resulted in a major power shift along the Rio Grande as Anglo-Americans began to gain more and more influence and power in the area. Despite remaining a demographic minority as compared to Mexican-Americans or Tejanos, Anglos began to dominate the power structure of the region. This hegemony can only be explained by the economic changes that occurred during and after the war. Even after the end of the war and the establishment of the border, interaction did not stop, and certainly trade continued. The border existed only as an abstract idea for most people living on the United States' southern frontier or Mexico's northern frontera, though borderland power shifted in response to the evolving economy. Without the favorable contracts from the Quartermaster's Department, steamboat transporters and merchants would have lacked the financial capital to take advantage of wartime inroads into the northern Mexican markets. Furthermore, without the establishment of army bases and depots, many of the new towns in the Rio Grande Valley would not have existed, negating the opportunity for acquiring wealth north of the river. Thus, power would have remained firmly in the hands of Mexicans and their Tejano counterparts north of the river, albeit within a much smaller population and much more restricted markets.

Anglo-Americans, however, used all their advantages fully during and after the war. This acknowledgment is not meant to condemn Anglos, nor to victimize Mexicans or Tejanos. While there certainly were cases of victims and villains, all peoples in the borderlands were active players in their own stories. At the same time, the presence of the army in the Rio Grande Valley created a situation in which some longtime Mexican or Tejano residents became politically displaced due to the rapidly changing economic environment along the Rio Grande. Commerce proved the tie that bound Anglo-Americans, Europeans, and Tejanos together in South Texas, often overcoming the national and racial differences that plagued other parts of Texas.[42]

Conclusion

The economic, social, and political changes resulting from the US-Mexican War are inseparable from the presence of the US Army in the Lower Rio Grande Valley. The Quartermaster's Department's issuance of contracts and utilization of the trade networks along the river and overland served as a catalyst for this change. The army injected a significant amount of wealth into the region, particularly for the size of the population. Much of this money went into the hands of private Anglo and European contractors who carried supplies to the army posts on the Rio Grande and across South Texas. This change happened because of the war, but it was also due to a long process of expanding the role of the Quartermaster's Department within the US Army. The department's influence on the areas where it operated grew in proportion to its expansion.

When the war broke out, the Quartermaster's Department took advantage of trade networks such as the Rio Grande Line and the Santa Fe Trail during the war. The United States and its agents paid close attention to the evolving situation in Mexico during the early nineteenth century, particularly after Texas secured its independence. Decades of strife between Texas, Mexico, and Native Americans further shaped the region, making it attractive to American expansionistic desires during the mid-nineteenth century. The combined desire for territory and access to markets in northern Mexico began drawing American attention to the region. In addition, new Anglo and European settlers arrived on the Rio Grande before the war. This number only grew during and after the war. While the Republic of Texas never projected much power into the Lower Rio Grande Valley, once added to the United States as a state, Texas's claims of the Rio Grande as its southern border gave President James Polk the premise he needed to declare war.

The growth of the Quartermaster's Department during this same period created an organization that was primed to have a dramatic influence on the region. Acting as the financial agent of American expansion, the quartermasters introduced influential amounts of currency to the regions where they operated. During the war and the following decade until 1860, the United States spent between 10 and 14 percent on the military. Within the US Army about 10 to 14 percent was spent by the Quartermaster's Department, making roughly 1 to 2 percent of the United States total budget. Between 1847 and 1860, the Quartermaster's Department spent between $1 million and $1.8 million yearly across the nation. Departmental spending in South Texas exceeded $100,000 yearly with tens of thousands making it way to the Rio Grande Valley. The Quartermaster's Department expanded during the US-Mexican War to meet the needs of fielding multiple armies across three theaters: northern Mexico, the West, and central Mexico. As the department built more supply depots, it created a supply line stretching from New England to New Orleans and terminating at Brazos Santiago or by the end of the war at Mexico City. All the growing or new depots served as the vein in which military supplies and troops flowed between the two countries, a link that continued in many places after the war.[1]

The first theater of the war proved to be the most influential to postwar South Texas. As General Taylor's army advanced into Mexico, the Quartermaster's Department trailed behind, establishing depots along the path. The deeper the army advanced, the more developed the trade network became during the war. The department used the Rio Grande Line, a small ferry network along the river, to serve as a foundation for a more robust system. The growth of this network brought steamships, pilots, goods, and merchants into the region. Men like Richard King translated this wartime experience into postwar wealth from army contracts. Without the northern Mexican theater and the Quartermaster-instigated growth of the Rio Grande Line, the postwar years would not have progressed in the economic or social patterns that they did.

The western and central theaters of the war both represented unique logistical obstacles for the department. The campaigns faced harsh environments and vast distances for the army to cross, and the quartermasters often struggled to ensure that enough supplies traveled with the army's support trains. The central Mexico campaigns were defined by the logistical feat that the landing and siege of Veracruz represented. Furthermore, supporting General Scott's army along the National Road proved doubly complicated due to guerilla resistance. Ultimately, both of these theaters aided in the United States' goal of securing significant territorial gains from the Treaty of Guadalupe-Hidalgo. The western territories underwent their own versions of what occurred in South Texas, but the Rio Grande borderlands developed uniquely because of their location, population density, and distance from national centers. Central Mexico and Mexico City, although occupied in a similar fashion, were insulated from significant social changes seen on the periphery because of a much larger population and stronger social and cultural ties to the Mexican way of life. South Texas and the Rio Grande Valley became a perfect mix of ingredients to experience significant social and economic upheaval not experienced in Santa Fe or Mexico City.

The wartime experience of the Quartermaster's Department laid the foundation for a dramatic change in the Lower Rio Grande Valley. The growth of the shipping and ferry trade along the river allowed private contractors to make significant profits off army contracts after the war. The Anglo-American settlers who began to come in greater numbers built many of the new towns adjacent to the new military posts. The wealth gained by these men translated into political power in the region. With the support of the army, Anglos established municipal governments that favored Anglos over Tejanos or Mexicans. This social change in South Texas could not have developed without the influx of American capital through the Quartermaster's Department's use of private contractors. These contractors translated their wealth from army trade monopolies into massive territorial acquisitions, further shifting the power dynamic in the region.

With the "Double-Eagle," the hard coin that the army brought to the region, the Valley saw economic growth like never before. In the decades before the Mexican-American War, there had been some growth as Matamoros became an economic hub for much of northern Mexico, with Brazos Santiago as its port. With the end of the war and Brazos Santiago residing on the American side of the river, however, the economic landscape changed. The new towns that grew up beside the army forts supplied and supported the soldiers in them. Money from the army encouraged this settlement, making it the first nation-building program to succeed on a large scale. The infrastructure established by the Quartermaster's Department synergized with the entrepreneurship of American businessmen, which created new trade systems in South Texas. Furthermore, the close ties between the army and Anglo civilians led to a power shift in favor of these new Anglo settlers. Tejanos and Mexicans in Texas found themselves relegated to second-class-citizen status despite the agreed upon terms of equal citizenship in the Treaty of Guadalupe-Hidalgo.

The significance of the Mexican-American War cannot be overstated in the history of the Lower Rio Grande Valley and in the United States. The transfer of land in the Mexican Cession shifted the border across peoples who suddenly had a new country thrust upon them. The residents Texas and the Lower Rio Grande Valley experienced such changes first during Mexican Independence, then when the United States acquired the territory. The arrival of Anglo and European settlers before, during, and after the war caused significant social and economic upheaval in the postwar years. The ethnic demographics remained in favor of Hispanic peoples, but Anglo and European residents rose to prominence and wealth.

The Quartermaster's Department not only established a professional logistics organization to support the army, but it also built a mechanism allowing the armed forces to have dramatic influence on the area where they operated. The department and its quartermasters served as a catalyst for economic, social, and political change along the borderlands of the Lower Rio Grande Valley. The complicated issues of cultural and historical identity were only more muddied by the artificial economic support provided to Anglos by the army despite the ethnic Hispanic majority in South Texas. The Lower Rio Grande exemplifies the complicated nature of a borderland region and how unexpected results develop when outside influences such as the US Army's Quartermaster's Department enter and contribute to changing the pre-established social order. The US-Mexican War of 1846 to1848 may not have rivaled the scope of wars in Europe or Asia, but the war's results were monumental to the United States, Mexico, and their citizens. Thus, changes to the social order occurred in ways that were unanticipated when viewed from 1845, just before the war started. These changes had far-reaching results that lasted for decades and shaped the ultimate development of South Texas and the Rio Grande Valley.

Notes

Introduction

1. Peter Guardino, *Dead March: A History of the Mexican-American War* (Cambridge, MA: Harvard University Press, 2017).

2. Charles R. Shrader, *U.S. Military Logistics, 1607–1991: A Research Guide* (New York: Greenwood, 1992), 22.

3. Samuel Watson, ed., *Warfare in the USA 1784–1861* (Burlington, VT: Ashgate Publishing, 2005), *xxvii—xxviii*.

4. Risch, *Quartermaster Support of the Army*, 237–296; James A. Huston, *The Sinews of War: Army Logistics, 1775–1953* (Washington, DC: Office of the Chief of Military History, United States Army, 1966), 125–136.

5. Robert Wooster, The American Military Frontiers: The United States Army in the West, 1783–1900 (Albuquerque: University of New Mexico, 2009); Robert Wooster, *Soldiers, Sutlers, and Settlers: Garrison Life on the Texas Frontier* (College Station: Texas A&M University Press, 1987); W. Turrentine Jackson, *Wagon Roads West; a Study of Federal Road Surveys and Construction in the Trans-Mississippi West, 1846–1869* (New Haven: Yale University Press, 1965); Francis Paul Prucha, *Broadaxe & Bayonet: The Role of the United States Army in the Development of the Northwest, 1815–1860* (Lincoln: University of Nebraska Press, 1953); William A. Dobak, *Fort Riley and Its Neighbors: Military Money and Economic Growth, 1853–1895* (Norman: University of Oklahoma Press, 1998); Robert Walter Frazer, *Forts and Supplies: The Role of the Army in the Economy of the Southwest, 1846–1861* (Albuquerque: University of New Mexico Press, 1983); Darlis A. Miller, Soldiers and Settlers: Military Supply in the Southwest, 1861–1885 (Albuquerque: University of New Mexico Press, 1989); Michael L. Tate, *The Frontier Army in the Settlement of the West* (Norman: University of Oklahoma Press, 1999); Robert W. Frazer, Forts of the West: Military Forts and Presidios, and Posts Commonly Called Forts (Norman: University of Oklahoma Press, 1965). Herbert M. Hart, Old Forts of the Southwest (Seattle, Washington: Superior, 1964).

6. Frederick Jackson Turner, "The Significance of the Frontier in History," in *Selected Essays of Frederick Jackson Turner*, ed. Ray Allen Billington (Englewood Cliffs, N.J.:

Prentice-Hall, 1961), 37–62; Herbert Eugene Bolton, *The Spanish Borderlands* (Lexington: First Rate Publishers, 2017 Reprint); David J. Weber, *The Mexican Frontier, 1821–1846* (Albuquerque: University of New Mexico Press, 1982), xviii-xxii; David J. Weber, "Turner, the Boltonians, and the Borderlands," *The American Historical Review*, Vol. 91, No. 1 (Feb. 1986), 66–81; Pekka Hämäläinen and Samuel Truett, "On Borderlands," *The Journal of American History*, September 2011, 338–361; Jeremy Adelman and Stephen Aron, "From Borderlands to Borders: Empires, Nation-states, and the Peoples in between in North American History," *The American Historical Review*, Vol. 104, No. 3 (June 1999), 814–841; Benjamin Johnson and Andrew R. Graybill, *Bridging National Borders in North American: Transnational and Comparative Histories* (Durham: Duke University Press, 2010); James David Nichols, "The Line of Liberty: Runaway Slaves and Fugitive Peons in the Texas-Mexico Borderlands," *The Western Historical Quarterly*, Vol. 44, No. 4 (Winter 2013), 413–433.

7. Andrés Reséndez, *Changing National Identities at the Frontier: Texas and New Mexico, 1800–1850* (New York: Cambridge University Press, 2004); Arnoldo De Leon, *The Tejano Community, 1836–1900* (Albuquerque: University of New Mexico Press, 1982); David Montejano, *Anglos and Mexicans In the Making of Texas, 1836–1986* (Austin: University of Texas Press, 1999); Armando C. Alonzo, *Tejano Legacy: Rancheros and Settlers in South Texas, 1734–1900* (Albuquerque: University of New Mexico Press, 1998); Valerio-Jiménez, *River of Hope*; Omar S. Valerio-Jiménez, *River of Hope: Forging Identity and Nation in the Río Grande Borderlands* (Durham, NC: Duke University Press, 2013); Miguel Ángel González-Quiroga, *War and Peace on the Rio Grande Frontier, 1830–1880* (Norman, Ok: The University of Oklahoma Press, 2020).

8. Risch, *Quartermaster Support of the Army: A History of the Corps*, 237–238, 240; Russell F. Weigley, *The American Way of War: A History of United States Military Strategy and Policy* (Indianapolis: Indiana University Press, 1973), 59–68; Allan R. Millett and Peter Maslowski, *For the Common Defense: A Military History of the United States of America* (New York: The Free Press, 1984), 144–157; Samuel J. Watson, *Peacekeepers and Conquerors: The Army Officer Corps on the American Frontier, 1821–1846* (Lawrence: University of Kansas Press, 2013), 384–398; Hess, *Civil War Logistics*, 4–9; Risch, *Quartermaster Support of the Army*, 3–23; Huston, *The Sinews of War*, 3–5; Richard Peters, ed., *The Public Statutes at Large of the United States of America from the Organization of the Government in 1789, to March 3, 1845* (Boston: Charles C. Little and James Brown, 1850), 696–699; Risch, *Quartermaster Support of the Army*, 135–181; Huston, *The Sinews of War*, 102–125; Trueman Cross, *Military Laws of the United States; including those relating to the Marine Corps, to which is prefixed the Constitution of the Unites States* (Washington DC: George Templeman, 1838), 261–267.

See Ricardo A. Herrera, *Feeding Washington's Army: Surviving the Valley Forge Winter of 1778* (Chapel Hill: The University of North Carolina Press, 2023) for a detailed description of the hardships faced acquiring supplies during the Revolutionary War.

9. Chester L. Kiefer, *Maligned General: The Biography of Thomas Sidney Jesup* (San Rafael, CA: Presidio Press, 1979), 1–2, 4–5; James Ripley Jacobs, *Tarnished Warrior: Major-General James Wilkinson* (New York: Macmillan Company, 1938), 314–315.

10. Kiefer, *Maligned General*, 6–12, 26–29, 35–37, 39–40, 44–47, 61, 63–64, 65–66, 67; Noble E. Cunningham, Jr., *The Presidency of James Monroe* (Lawrence: University of Kansas, 1996), 12–13, 55–69, 110–111; John Missall and Mary Lou Missall, *The Seminole Wars: America's Longest Indian Conflict* (Gainesville: University of Florida, 2004), 121–122, 130–131, 134, 141, 151–152; John Niven, *John C. Calhoun and the Price of Union: A Biography* (Baton Rouge: Louisiana State University Press, 1988), 78; H. W. Brands, *Andrew Jackson: His Life and Times* (New York: Doubleday, 2005), 257–262. For more on the Quartermaster's Department prior to 1846 see Cynthia Ann Miller, "The United States Army logistics complex, 1818–1845: A case study of the northern frontier." PhD diss., Syracuse University, 1991.

11. Risch, *Quartermaster Support of the Army*, 240; Weigley, *The American Way of War*, 68.

Chapter 1

1. For a robust overview of the history of the Rio Grande in American history see, Paul Horgan, *Great River: The Rio Grande in North American History* (Middletown, CT: Wesleyan University Press, 1984); Oscar J. Martínez, *Troublesome Border* (Tucson: University of Arizona Press, 1988), 56.

2. Bernardo de Gálvez, Donald Emmet Worcester, trans., *Instructions for Governing the Interior Provinces of New Spain, 1786* (Quivira Society, 1951), xi.

3. Oakah Jones, Jr., *Los Paisanos: Spanish Settlers on the Northern Frontier of New Spain* (Norman: University of Oklahoma Press, 1996), 20; Brian Robertson, *Wild Horse Desert* (Edinburg, Texas: New Santander Press, 1985), 7; Harriett Denise Joseph and Donald E. Chipman, " Spanish Texas," *Handbook of Texas Online*, accessed June 14, 2019, https://www.tshaonline.org/handbook/entries/spanish-texas; Donald E. Chipman, *Spanish Texas: 1519–1821* (Austin: University of Texas Press, 1992), 60–67, 104–110.

4. Robertson, *Wild Horse Desert*, 8–9; Robert Wood, *Life in Laredo: A Documentary History from the Laredo Archives* (Denton: University of North Texas, 2004), 15–24; J.B. Wilkinson, *Laredo and the Rio Grande Frontier*, (Austin: Jenkins Book Pub. Co., 1975), 9–15; Jones, *Los Paisanos*, 65.

5. Robertson, *Wild Horse Desert*, 9, 11, 12; Jones, *Los Paisanos*, 65–66; Robert S. Weedle, *The French Thorn: Rival Explorers in the Spanish Sea, 1682–1762* (College Station: Texas A&M Press, 1991), 276–285; Pat Kelley, *River of Lost Dreams: Navigation on the Rio Grande*, (University of Nebraska Press: Lincoln, 1986), 5; Florence Johnson Scott, *Royal Land Grants North of the Rio Grande, 1777–1821: Early History of Large Grants Made by Spain to Families in Jurisdiction Reynosa*, (Rio Grande City, TX: La Retama Press, 1969), 1–5.

6. Robertson, *Wild Horse Desert*, 13–14, 15; Wilkinson, *Laredo and the Rio Grande*, 15–21; Scott, *Royal Land Grants*, 1–4, 8–9; Jones, *Los Paisanos*,66–68; Weddle, *The French Thorn*, 276–285.

7. Robertson, *Wild Horse Desert*, 17, 19, 20; Scott, *Royal Land Grants*, 21–26; Weedle, *The French Thorn*, 276–285.

8. Robertson, *Wild Horse Desert*, 21, 23; *Handbook of Texas Online*, Raúl A. Ramos, "Tienda de Cuervo, Jose," accessed June 17, 2019, https://www.tshaonline.org /handbook/entries/tienda-de-cuervo-jose; Wilkinson, *Laredo and the Rio Grande*, 26–31; Scott, *Royal Land Grants*, 9–12.

9. Chipman, *Spanish Texas*, 176; Donald E. Chipman, "Galvez Gallardo, Jose Bernardo de," *Handbook of Texas Online*, accessed February 17, 2019, https://www.tshaonline .org/handbook/entries/galvez-gallardo-jose-bernardo-de; Donald E. Chipman, "Provincias Internas," *Handbook of Texas Online*, accessed February 17, 2019, https://www.tshaonline.org/handbook/entries/provincias-internas.

Santa Fe de Nuevo México, Nueva Vizcaya, Sonora y Sinaloa, Alta California, and Baja California were included in the western portion called the *Provincias Internas De Occidente*. Texas, Coahuila, Nuevo Leon, and Nuevo Santander made up the eastern portion called *Provincias Internas de Oriente*. For more information see Herbert Ingram Priestley, *José De Gálvez: Visitor-general of New Spain (1765–1771)* (Berkeley: University of California Press, 1916) and Luis Navarro García, *Don José De Gálvez Y La Comandancia General De Las Provincias Internas Del Norte De Nueva España* (Sevilla: Consejo Superior De Investigaciones Científicas, 1964).

10. *Handbook of Texas Online*, Donald E. Chipman, "Rubi, Marques de," accessed June 17, 2019, https://www.tshaonline.org/handbook/entries/rubi-marques-de; Wilkinson, *Laredo and the Rio Grande*, 40–43; Jack Jackson, Ed., *Imaginary Kingdom: Texas as Seen by the Rivera and Rubí Military Expeditions, 1727 and 1767* (Austin: Texas State Historical Association, 1995), 171–173, 178–183, 187, 191, 199; Gary B. Starnes, "Juan de Ugalde (1729–1816) and the Provincias Internas of Coahuila and Texas" (MA Thesis, Texas Christian University, 1971), 23–24; Scott, *Royal Land Grants*, 12–13.

11. Robertson, *Wild Horse Desert*, 23, 24; Wilkinson, *Laredo and the Rio Grande*, 34–39, 40; John A. Adams, *Conflict and Commerce on the Rio Grande: Laredo, 1755–1955* (College Station: Texas A&M University Press, 2008, 10–29.

12. Gálvez, *Instructions for Governing*, xi; *Handbook of Texas Online*, Donald E. Chipman, "Provincias Internas," accessed June 18, 2019, https://www.tshaonline.org /handbook/entries/provincias-internas.

13. Galen D. Greaser, *New Guide to Spanish and Mexican Land Grants in South Texas* (Austin, TX: Texas General Land Office, 2009), 23–26; *Handbook of Texas Online*, Aldon S. Lang and Christopher Long, "Land Grants," accessed February 17, 2019, https://www.tshaonline.org/handbook/entries/land-grants; Adams, *Conflict and Commerce*, 20–21; Miguel Ángel Gonzalez-Quiroga, *War and Peace on the Rio Grande Frontier, 1830–1880* (Norman, OK: University of Oklahoma Press, 2020), 11; For more information on Teodoro de Croix's writings see Teodoro de

Croix, Alfred Barnaby Thomas, trans., *Teodoro de Croix and the Northern Frontier of New Spain, 1776–1783: From the Original Documents in the Archives of the Indies* (Norman: University of Oklahoma Press, 1968).

14. Brian DeLay, *War of a Thousand Deserts: Indian Raids and the U.S.-Mexican War* (New Haven: Yale University Press, 2008), 11–12; Lawrence Frances Hill, *José de Escandón and the Founding of Nuevo Santander* (Columbus: The Ohio State University Press, 1926), 46–55; Wood, *Life in Laredo*, 77–86. For more on the Comanche see Pekka Hämäläinen, *The Comanche Empire* (New Haven: Yale University Press, 2009); see also James F. Brooks, *Captives and Cousins: Slavery, Kinship, and Community in the Southwest Borderlands* (Chapel Hill: University of North Carolina Press, 2004); Gálvez, *Instructions*, 32, 34, 74–75; Starnes, "Juan de Ugalde," 44–45 ; Gilbert Hinojosa, *A Borderlands Town in Transition* (Austin: Texas A&M University, 1983), 5–7, 14.

15. Teodoro de Croix, Alfred Barnaby Thomas, trans., *Teodoro de Croix and the Northern Frontier of New Spain, 1776–1783: From the Original Documents in the Archives of the Indies* (Norman: University of Oklahoma Press, 1968), xi; Starnes, "Juan de Ugalde," iii; Robert S. Weddle, "Nuevo Santander," *Handbook of Texas Online*, accessed June 18, 2019, https://www.tshaonline.org/handbook/entries/nuevo-santander.

16. *Handbook of Texas Online*, Robert Bruce Blake, "Salcedo, Manuel Maria de," accessed February 17, 2019, https://www.tshaonline.org/handbook/entries/salcedo-manuel -maria-de; Chipman, *Spanish Texas*, 230, 243–247.

17. Robert H. Thonhoff, "Arredondo, Joaquin de," *Handbook of Texas Online*, accessed June 19, 2019, https://www.tshaonline.org/handbook/entries/arredondo-joaquin-de; Bradley Folsom, *Arredondo: The Last Ruler of Texas and Northeastern New Spain* (Norman: University of Oklahoma, 2017), 111, 139; *Handbook of Texas Online*, Robert Bruce Blake, "Salcedo, Manuel Maria de," accessed February 17, 2019, https://www .tshaonline.org/handbook/entries/salcedo-manuel-maria-de; Chipman, *Spanish Texas*, 230, 248–252; Jaime E. Rodríguez O. and Kathryn Vincent, eds., *Myths, Misdeeds, and Misunderstandings: The Roots of Conflict in U.S.-Mexican Relations* (Wilmington, DE: SR Books, 1997), 81.

18. Aldon S. Lang and Christopher Long, "Land Grants," *Handbook of Texas Online*, accessed February 17, 2019, https://www.tshaonline.org/handbook/entries/land -grants; David B. Gracy II, "Austin, Moses," *Handbook of Texas Online*, accessed February 17, 2019, https://www.tshaonline.org/handbook/entries/austin-moses: Eugene C. Barker, "Mexican Colonization Laws," *Handbook of Texas Online*, accessed February 17, 2019, https://www.tshaonline.org/handbook/entries/mexican -colonization-laws; Eugene C. Barker, "Austin, Stephen Fuller," *Handbook of Texas Online*, accessed February 17, 2019, https://www.tshaonline.org/handbook/entries /austin-stephen-fuller.

19. "Dictamen Presentado a la Soberana Junta Gobernativa del Imperio Mexicanos, por la Comision de Relaciones Exteriores," December 29, 1821, quoted in Joseph Carl McElhannon, "Imperial Mexico and Texas, 1821–1823," *The Southwestern Historical Quarterly*, 53, no. 2 (October 1949) 138–139; Andrew J. Torget, *Seeds of Empire: Cotton*,

Slavery, and the Transformation of the Texas Borderlands, 1800–1850 (Chapel Hill: University of North Carolina, 2015), 68; Mireles, "Social Life," 29.

20. José Barragan, ed., *Actas Constitucionales Mexicanas, 1821–1824* (Mexico: Instituto de Investigaciones Jurídicas. Universidad Nacional Autónoma de México, 1980), 165, 188, 220, quoted in Torget, *Seeds of Empire*, 68–69; Adams, *Laredo*, 43.

21. *The Imperial Colonization Law* in Ernest Wallace and David M. Vigness, eds., *Documents of Texas History* (Lubbock, TX: Library, Texas Technological College, 1960), 47–48; O. Rodríguez, Jaime E., and Kathryn Vincent, eds., *Myths, Misdeeds, and Misunderstandings: The Roots of Conflict in U.S.-Mexican Relations* (Wilmington, DE: SR Books, 1997), 85–86; *The National Colonization Law* in Wallace and Vigness, eds., *Documents of Texas History*, 48; *The Coahuila-Texas State Colonization Law*, 48–50; "Constitution of the State of Coahuila and Texas (1827)," Preamble and Preliminary Provisions, 2014, accessed March 22, 2016, http://tarlton.law.utexas .edu/constitutions/coahuila1827/preamble; Andrew Torget, "Decree No. 56," May 5, 1828," Texas Slavery Project, 2008, accessed March 22, 2016, http://www .texasslaveryproject.org/sources/LawsOfTexas/display.php?f=TSP0139.xml; Torget, *Seeds of Empire*, 129–133; Eugene C. Barker, "The Influence of Slavery in the Colonization of Texas," *The Southwestern Historical Quarterly* 28, no. 1 (July 1924): 15–18.

22. Juan N. Almonte, "Statistical Report on Texas (1835) by Juan N. Almonte," trans. Carlos E. Casteñeda, *The Southwestern Historical Quarterly* 28, no. 3 (January 1925): 179–180; Antonio López de Santa Anna and Ann Fears Crawford, ed., *The Eagle: The Autobiography of Santa Anna,* (Austin: State House Press, 1988), 48–51; Rodríguez, *Myths*, 89. For more on Almonte and his report see Juan Nepomuceno Almonte, *Almonte's Texas: Juan N. Almonte's 1834 Inspection, Secret Report, and Role in the 1836 Campaign,* ed. Jack Jackson, trans. John Wheat (Austin: Published by the Texas State Historical Association, 2003).

23. Randolph B. Campbell, *Gone to Texas: A History of the Lone Star State* (New York: Oxford University Press, 2018), 128–153.

24. Campbell, *Gone to Texas*, 153–158; Valerio-Jiménez, *Identity and Nation*, 204–205; Stephen L. Hardin, *Texian Iliad: A Military History of the Texas Revolution, 1835–1836* (Austin: University of Texas Press, 2015); Paul D. Lack, *The Texas Revolutionary Experience: a Political and Social History, 1835–1836* (College Station: Texas A & M University Press, 1992); For more on the Texas Revolution see: Richard Bruce Winders, *Crisis in the Southwest: The United States, Mexico, and the Struggle over Texas* (Lanham, MD: SR Books, 2004).

25. Mayfield to Webb, 22 March 1841, United States Department of State. *Diplomatic Correspondence of the Republic of Texas Part II.* Washington, DC. 1909; D. W. Smith to E. Livingston, August 21, 1832, cited in Leroy Graf, "The Economic History of the Lower Rio Grande Valley, 1820–1875," (PhD diss., Harvard University, 1942.), 93.

26. Wilkinson, *Laredo and the Rio Grande*, 154–174; Beatriz de la Garza, *From the Republic of the Rio Grande: A Personal History of the Place and the People* (Austin: University of Texas Press, 2013), 1–22; David M. Vigness, "Republic Of The Rio Grande," *Handbook*

of Texas Online, accessed June 17, 2019, https://www.tshaonline.org/handbook/entries /republic-of-the-rio-grande; Martínez, *Troublesome Border*, 108

27. Alice L. Baumgartner, *South to Freedom: Runaway Slaves to Mexico and the Road to Civil War*, New York: Basic Books, 2020, 165, 167, 175, 176; Quintard Taylor, *In Search of the Racial Frontier: African Americans in the American West, 1528–1990* (New York: W.W. Norton & Company, 1998), 37, 41, 60; Ronnie C. Tyler, "Fugitive Slaves in Mexico," *The Journal of Negro History*, Vol LVII, No. 1, January, 1992, 1, 4; Rosalie Schwartz, *Across the Rio to Freedom: U.S. Negroes in Mexico* (El Paso: Texas Western Press/The University of Texas El Paso, 1975), 25, 26–27, 32–33; Sean Kelley, "'Mexico in His Head': Slavery and the Texas-Mexico Border, 1810–1860," *Journal of Social History*, Vol. 37, No. 3 (Spring, 2004), 716, 717; Sarah E. Cornell, "Americans in the U.S. South and Mexico: A Transnational History of Race, Slavery, and Freedom, 1810–1910," PhD diss. (New York University, 2008), 93–94, 104, 111; Juan Mora-Torres, *The Making of the Mexican Border* (Austin: University of Texas Press, 2001), 23, 28.

28. Campbell, *Gone to Texas*, 159–186; Peter Guardino, *Dead March: A History of the Mexican-American War* (Cambridge, MA: Harvard University Press, 2017), 34–35; David M. Pletcher, *The Diplomacy of Annexation: Texas, Oregon, and the Mexican War* (Columbia: University of Missouri Press, 1975), 113–138; Martínez, *Troublesome Border*, 81, 91.

29. K. Jack Bauer, *The Mexican War: 1846–1848* (New York: Macmillan Publishing Co., 1974) 6–11; Pletcher, *The Diplomacy of Annexation*, 113–138.

30. For more on the *porciones* land grants see Galen D. Greaser and Jesus F. De La Teja, "Quieting Title to Spanish and Mexican Land Grants in the Trans-Nueces: The Bourland and Miller Commission, 1850–1852," *The Southwestern Historical Quarterly* 95 (April 1992). For more on the population of Tejanos before and after the Mexican-American War see Arnoldo De León and Kenneth L. Stewart, *Tejanos and the Numbers Game: A Socio-historical Interpretation from the Federal Censuses, 1850–1900* (Albuquerque: University of New Mexico Press, 1989).

Chapter 2

1. John S. D. Eisenhower, *So Far from God: The U.S. War with Mexico, 1846–1848* (New York: Random House, 1989), 30–32; Erna Risch, *Quartermaster Support of the Army: A History of the Corps, 1775–1939* (Washington, DC: Center of Military History, United States Army, 1989), 242; Thomas Jesup to D. D. Tompkins, 26 May 1846, Letters Sent by the Office of the Quartermaster General, microfilm no M745, Roll 21,583.

2. Bauer, *The Mexican War*, 11–13, 16–19, 21–23; Miguel Ángel González-Quiroga, *War and Peace on the Rio Grande Frontier, 1830–1880* (Norman: University of Oklahoma Press, 2020), 82.

3. Bauer, *The Mexican War*, 24–29; Douglas A. Murphey, *Two Armies on the Rio Grande: The First Campaign of the US-Mexican War* (College Station: Texas A&M Press, 2015), 14–19.

4. Eisenhower, *So Far from God*, 30–32; Risch, *Quartermaster Support of the Army*, 242; Thomas Jesup to D. D. Tompkins, 26 May 1846, *House Exec. Docs.*, 30th Cong., 1st Sess., No. 60, 583; Mark R. Wilson, *The Business of Civil War: Military Mobilization and the State, 1861–1865* (Baltimore: The Johns Hopkins University Press, 2006), 44–46.

5. Henry Stanton to Henry Lindsey, 1 November 1846, Henry Stanton to Lieut. S.L. Fremont, 30 November 1846, Henry Stanton to Thomas Jesup, 4 December 1846, Henry Stanton to Thomas Jesup, 14 January 1847, , Letters Sent by the Office of the Quartermaster General, microfilm no M745, Roll 21, 254, 306, 312, 384–385; Kieffer, *Maligned General*, 254, 255, 256; James A. Huston, *The Sinews of War: Army Logistics, 1775–1953* (Washington, DC: Office of the Chief of Military History, United States Army, 1966), 128, 132; Robert B. Roberts, *Encyclopedia of Historic Forts the Military Posts of the United States* (New York: Macmillan Publishing Company, 1988), 671.

6. Risch, *Quartermaster Support of the Army*, 241, 242; Henry Stanton to Trueman Cross, 9 September 1845, *House Exec. Docs.*, 30th Cong., 1st Sess., No. 60, 576–577.

7. González-Quiroga, *War and Peace*, 80–81, 92; Montejano, *Anglos and Mexicans*, 43.

8. Thomas Jesup to D. D. Tompkins, 5 September 1846, Letters Sent by the Office of the Quartermaster General, microfilm no M745, Roll 21, 112.

9. T. Cross to Henry Stanton, 10 September 1846, *House Exec. Docs.*, 30th Cong., 1st Sess., No. 60, Serial Set 520, 642; Thomas Jesup to M.M. Clark, 22 August 1846, Thomas Jesup to William P. Landing, NY, 29 August 1846, Thomas Jesup to S. B. Dusenbery, 4 September 1846, Thomas Jesup to D.H. Vinton, 5 September 1846, Henry Stanton to Thomas Jesup, 29 January 1847, Letters Sent by the Office of the Quartermaster General, microfilm no M745, Roll 21, 62, 88, 109, 114, 415–416.

10. Thomas Jesup to Francis Taylor, 26 August 1846, Thomas Jesup to Nathaniel Anderson, 22 September 1846, Thomas Jesup to J. L. Joulmin, 24 September 1846, Thomas Jesup to Charles Thomas, 25 September 1846, Letters Sent by the Office of the Quartermaster General, microfilm no M745, Roll 21, 80, 160–161, 170, 175.

11. William Marcy to Winfield Scott, 31 May 1847, Winfield Scott to William Marcy, 21 December 1846, *House Exec. Docs.*, 30th Cong., 1st Sess., No. 60, Serial Set 520, 692, 838; Thomas to Charles Thomas, 18 September 1846, Thomas Jesup to Samuel MacRee, 19 September 1846, Thomas Jesup to Thomas Hunt, 19 September 1846, Henry Stanton to M. M. Clark, 24 November 1846, Letters Sent by the Office of the Quartermaster General, microfilm no M745, Roll 21, 150, 152, 155, 295; J. Jacob Oswandel, *Notes of the Mexican War, 1846–1848*, ed. Timothy D. Johnson and Nathaniel Cheairs Hughes (Knoxville: University of Tennessee Press, 2010), 7.

12. Thomas Jesup to M. M. Clark, 22 August 1846, Thomas Jesup to D. D. Tompkins, 24 August 1846, Thomas Jesup to Hartman Bache, 24 August 1846, Henry Stanton to John Henderson, 30 October 1846, Henry Stanton to Thomas Jesup, 19 November 1846, Letters Sent by the Office of the Quartermaster General, microfilm no M745, Roll 21, 62, 67, 86, 253, 283.

13. Risch, *Quartermaster Support of the Army*, 243; Mexican War Correspondence, *House Executive Documents*, No. 60, 30th Congress, 1st Session, Serial Set 520, 584.

14. W. Smith, New Orleans 1847, Teamster Contracts (Record Group 92, Records of the Office of the Quartermaster General, 1774–1985, National Archives, Washington, DC), Folder 445.

15. Huston, *The Sinews of War*, 131–132.

16. González-Quiroga, *War and Peace*, 80–81, 92; Montejano, *Anglos and Mexicans*, 43.

17. Risch, *Quartermaster Support of the Army*, 243–244; George T. M. Davis, *Autobiography of the Late Col. Geo. T.M. Davis, Captain and Aide-de-camp Scott's Army of Invasion (Mexico), from Posthumous Papers*. New York: Press of Jenkins and McCowan, 1891, 119; Oswandel, *Notes*, 16, 29.

18. Martin Dugard, *The Training Ground: Grant, Lee, Sherman, and Davis in the Mexican War, 1846–1848* (New York: Little, Brown and Co, 2008), 165; Huston, *Sinews*, 145; Don Graham, *Kings of Texas: The 150-year Saga of an American Ranching Empire* (Hoboken, NJ: Wiley, 2003), 18–19; Tom Lea, *The King Ranch* (Boston: Little, Brown and, 1957), 20–22; Thomas T. Smith, *The U.S. Army and the Texas Frontier Economy, 1845–1900* (College Station: Texas A&M University Press, 1999), 80; David Montejano, *Anglos and Mexicans In the Making of Texas, 1836–1986* (Austin, TX: Univ. of Texas Press, 1999), 20.

19. Henry Stanton to D. H. Vinton, 8 October 1846, Henry Stanton to Thomas Hunt, 19 October 1846, Henry Stanton to S. B. Dusenbery, 15 December 1846, Henry Stanton to John Birmingham, 4 January 1847, Letters Sent by the Office of the Quartermaster General, microfilm no M745, Roll 21, 211, 231, 337, 369.

20. Thomas Jesup to Harman Bache, Philadelphia, 29 August 1846, Letters Sent by the Office of the Quartermaster General, microfilm no M745, Roll 21, 86.

21. Henry Stanton to S. B. Dusenbery, 8 October 1846, Henry Stanton to D. D. Tompkins, 7 November 1846, Henry Stanton to Thomas Jesup, 4 December 1846, Henry Stanton to S.B. Dusenbery, 8 December 1846, Letters Sent by the Office of the Quartermaster General, microfilm no M745, Roll 21, 210, 266, 312–313, 320.

22. Thomas Jesup to Samuel MacRee, 19 September 1846, Thomas Jesup to Thomas F. Hunt, 19 September 1846, Thomas Jesup to F. P. Heintzelman, 25 September 1846, Henry Stanton to Thomas Jesup, 6 November 1846, Henry Stanton to Thomas Jesup, 19 November 1846, Henry Stanton to S. B. Dusenbery, 24 November 1846, Henry Stanton to Henry Lindsey, 17 December 1846, Henry Stanton to Thomas Jesup, 22 January 1847, Letters Sent by the Office of the Quartermaster General, microfilm no M745, Roll 21, 152, 153, 177, 263, 283, 294, 339, 403; Guardino, *The Dead March*, 121, 144, 188.

23. Graham, *Kings of Texas*, 21–22, 30; Graf, "Economic History" 198–199; Sizer, *The King Ranch Story*, 14–15; Monday and Colley, *Voices from the Wild Horse Desert*, 9; Stambaugh, *The Lower Rio Grande Valley of Texas*, 73, 79.

24. John Robinson to Brother, 5 February 1846, 8 March 1846, 26 April 1846, Special Collections, University of Texas at Arlington.

25. John James Peck, *Sign of the Eagle: A View of Mexico, 1830–1855* (San Diego: Copley Books, 1970), 9; Samuel J. Watson, *Peacekeepers and Conquerors: The Army Officer*

Corps on the American Frontier, 1821–1846 (Lawrence: University of Kansas Press, 2013), 398–408.

26. James A. Huston, *The Sinews of War: Army Logistics 1775–1953* (Washington, DC: Office of the Chief of Military History, United States Army, 1966), 126, 128.

27. Eisenhower, *So Far from God*, 50–52; Mexican War Correspondence. *House Executive Documents*, No. 60, 30th Congress, 1st Session, Serial Set 520, 116–117; Risch, *Quartermaster Support of the Army*, 243.

28. Eisenhower, *So Far from God*, 53–57; Zachary Taylor to Adjutant General, 21 March 1846, 21 March 1846, Mexican War Correspondence. *House Executive Documents*, No. 60, 30ᵗʰ Congress, 1ˢᵗ Session, Serial Set 520, 123–125, 129; Risch, *Quartermaster Support of the Army*, 245–247; George Wilkins Kendall, *Dispatches from the Mexican War* (Norman: University of Oklahoma, 1999), 43.

29. Peck, *Sign of the Eagle*, 10.

30. Eisenhower, *So Far from God*,64, 66; United States Department of War, General and Special Orders Issued by General Zachary Taylor, Headquarters of the Army, War with Mexico, 1847–1848, Record Group 94: Records of the Adjutant General's Office, 1780s-1917, National Archives, Washington, D.C., Order 33 [1846]; Mexican War Correspondence. *House Executive Documents*, No. 60, 30th Congress, 1st Session, Serial Set 520, 138, 288; Risch, *Quartermaster Support of the Army*, 245; John Robinson to Brother, 26 April 1846, Special Collections, University of Texas at Arlington.

31. Francis Preston Blair et al., *The Congressional Globe . . . [23d Congress to the 42d Congress, Dec. 2, 1833, to March 3, 1873].* (Washington: Printed at the Globe Office for the Editors, 1833–1873), 783; Guardino, *The Dead March*, 205–207. For more on political resistance to the war see Amy S Greenberg. *A Wicked War: Polk, Clay, Lincoln, and the 1846 US Invasion of Mexico,* (New York: Vintage Books, 2013); Pletcher, *The Diplomacy of Annexation*, 352–360; Graf, "The Economic," 93.

32. Graf, "The Economic," 93, 145–146; Montejano, *Anglos and Mexicans*, 18–21.

33. Eisenhower, *So Far from God*, 71–76; United States Department of War, General and Special Orders, Orders 35, 45, 46, 58; Zachary Taylor to Adjutant General, 6 April 1846, J. Broan to W.W.S. Bliss, 4 May 1846, *House Exec. Docs.*, 30th Cong., 1st Sess., No. 60, Serial Set 520, 133–134, 293–294.

34. Mexican War Correspondence, *House Exec. Docs.*, 30th Cong., 1st Sess., No. 60, Serial Set 520, 294.

35. Risch, *Quartermaster Support of the Army*, 274–275.

36. An Act Providing for the Prosecution of the Existing War between the United States and the Republic of Mexico, Pub. L. Sess. No.1 Ch. 16, 9 Stat. 16 (1846); For numbers of soldiers that served during the war see K. Jack Bauer, *The Mexican War, 1846–1848* (New York: Macmillan Publishing Co., 1974) and Justing H. Smith, *The War with Mexico* (New York: Macmillian Publishing Co., 1919).

37. Henry Stanton to M. M. Clark, 24 November 1846, Letters Sent by the Office of the Quartermaster General, microfilm no M745, Roll 21, 295.

38. Thomas M. Davies Jr., "Assessments During the Mexican War: An Exercise in Futility," *New Mexico Historical Review* 41, no. 3, (1966), 197–199, 207, 211–212.

39. Risch, *Quartermaster Support of the Army*, 275.

40. [1] William Marcy to Zachary Taylor, 18 November 1846, Mexican War Correspondence, *House Executive Documents*, No. 60, 30th Congress, 1st Session, Serial Set 520, 479.

41. Oswandel, *Notes*, 7; Winfield Scott Memorandum, 15 May 1846, Mexican War Correspondence, *House Executive Documents*, No. 60, 30th Congress, 1st Session, Serial Set 520, 546.

42. Risch, *Quartermaster Support of the Army*, 250; W.W.S. Bliss Orders No. 94, 2 August 1846, Thomas Jesup to E. Harding, 27 May 1846, Mexican War Correspondence, *House Executive Documents*, No. 60, 30th Congress, 1st Session, Serial Set 520, 497, 584.

43. Risch, *Quartermaster Support of the Army*, 250; W.W.S. Bliss Orders No. 94, 2 August 1846, Mexican War Correspondence, *House Executive Documents*, No. 60, 30th Congress, 1st Session, Serial Set 520, 497

44. Risch, *Quartermaster Support of the Army*, 258; Thomas Jesup to H. Whiting, 3 June 1846, Mexican War Correspondence, *House Executive Documents*, No. 60, 30th Congress, 1st Session, Serial Set 520, 585–586.

45. Eisenhower, *So Far from God*, 87; Risch, *Quartermaster Support of the Army*, 264.

46. Bauer, *The Mexican War*, 46–63; Eisenhower, *So Far from God*, 54–56, 60–64, 98–100; For a detailed account of Taylor's movements and battles along the Rio Grande see Douglas A. Murphy, *Two Armies on the Rio Grande* (College Station, TX: Texas A&M University Press, 2015).

47. Risch, *Quartermaster Support of the Army*, 263–265.

Chapter 3

1. Eisenhower, *So Far from God*, 98–99; Risch, *Quartermaster Support of the Army*, 265–266; Mexican War Correspondence, *House Executive Documents*, No. 60, 30th Congress, 1st Session, Serial Set 520, 547; Kendall, *Dispatches*, 60.

2. E. T. Blamire to Friend, 19 March 1847, 5 February 1846, Special Collections, University of Texas at Arlington; Henry Stanton to Thomas Jesup, 7 November 1846, Henry Stanton to James Hill, 29 January 1847, Henry Stanton to Thomas Jesup, 17 February 1847, Letters Sent by the Office of the Quartermaster General, microfilm no M745, Roll 21, 264–265, 417, 438; Kendall, *Dispatches*, 76.

3. Graf, "Economic History," 178–179; 180–182; *American Flag*, October 14 1846, May 1, May 26, June 2, 1847; Justing H. Smith, *The War with Mexico* (New York: Macmillan Company, 1919), 261–262, 483.

4. *Senate Ex. Doc.* 80, 32d Cong., 1st Session, 57; J. Fred Rippy, "Border Troubles along the Rio Grande, 1848–1860," *The Southwestern Historical Quarterly*, 23, no. 2 (Oct. 1919): 94.

5. Risch, *Quartermaster Support of the Army*, 265; John S. D. Eisenhower, *Zachary Taylor* (New York: Times Books, 2008), 39, 52–58; K. Jack Bauer, *Zachary Taylor: Soldier, Planter, Statesman of the Old Southwest* (Baton Rouge: Louisiana State University Press, 1985), 172–175; Felice Flanery Lewis, *Trailing Clouds of Glory: Zachary*

Taylor's Mexican War Campaign and His Emerging Civil War Leaders (Tuscaloosa: The University of Alabama Press, 2010), 100–108.

6. Risch, *Quartermaster Support of the Army*, 267–268; Graham, *Kings of Texas*, 21–22, 30; Graf, "Economic History" 198–199; Sizer, *The King Ranch Story*, 14–15.

7. Thomas Jesup to Thomas Hunt, 4 September 1846, Letters Sent by the Office of the Quartermaster General, microfilm no M745, Roll 21, 107–108; Risch, *Quartermaster Support of the Army*, 271; *An Act to provide for the better Organization of the Treasury, and for the Collection, Safe-Keeping, Transfer, and Disbursement of the public Revenue. U.S. Statutes at Large* 9 (1845–1847): 59–66.

8. Thomas Jesup to Samuel MacRee, 19 September 1846, Thomas Jesup to Thomas Hunt, 19 September 1846, Letters Sent by the Office of the Quartermaster General, microfilm no M745, Roll 21, 152, 153.

9. Risch, *Quartermaster Support of the Army*, 265; Eisenhower, *So Far from God*, 98–99.

10. Risch, *Quartermaster Support of the Army*, 271; Eisenhower, *So Far from God*, 30–32.

11. Thomas Jesup to Theodore O'Hara, 1 September 1846, Letters Sent by the Office of the Quartermaster General, microfilm no M745, Roll 21, 98–99.

12. Thomas Jesup to Officer in Charge, 18 September 1846, Letters Sent by the Office of the Quartermaster General, microfilm no M745, Roll 21, 150–151.

13. Thomas Jesup to Thomas Eastland, 21 September 1846, Thomas Jesup to S. P. Huntington, 22 September 1846, Thomas Jesup to Stephen Long, 22 September 1846, Thomas Jesup to Henry Stanton, 22 September 1846, Thomas Jesup to Thomas Hunt, 28 September 1846, Letters Sent by the Office of the Quartermaster General, microfilm no M745, Roll 21, 158, 159–160, 162, 189.

14. Thomas Jesup to Nathaniel Anderson, 22 September 1846, Letters Sent by the Office of the Quartermaster General, microfilm no M745, Roll 21, 160.

15. Thomas Jesup to D.H. Vinton, 23 September 1846, Thomas Jesup to A.W. Hunter, 23 September 1846, Letters Sent by the Office of the Quartermaster General, microfilm no M745, Roll 21, 164, 165.

16. Thomas Jesup to M.M. Clark, New York, 24 September 1846, Thomas Jesup to J.L. Joulmin, 24 September 1846, Thomas Jesup to A Mackay, 25 September 1846, Letters Sent by the Office of the Quartermaster General, microfilm no M745, Roll 21, 168, 170, 172.

17. Sam W. Haynes, "The Battle of Monterrey, A Continent Divided: The U.S.-Mexico War," https://library.uta.edu/usmexicowar/item?content_id=144&format_id=1&ofst=1&ni=13 (accessed 2/11/2019).

18. Thomas Jesup to S.B. Dusenbery. 27 September 1846, Letters Sent by the Office of the Quartermaster General, microfilm no M745, Roll 21, 181–182.

19. Thomas Jesup to Thomas Hunt, 27 September 1846 Letters Sent by the Office of the Quartermaster General, microfilm no M745, Roll 21, 183–184.

20. Thomas Jesup to Thomas Hunt, 27 September 1846, Letters Sent by the Office of the Quartermaster General, microfilm no M745, Roll 21, 184.

21. Henry Stanton to George Gibson, 15 October 1846, Letters Sent by the Office of the Quartermaster General, microfilm no M745, Roll 21, 220.

22. Thomas Jesup to Thomas Hunt, 28 September 1846, Letters Sent by the Office of the Quartermaster General, microfilm no M745, Roll 21, 190.

23. Thomas Jesup to S.H. Drum, 30 September 1846, Letters Sent by the Office of the Quartermaster General, microfilm no M745, Roll 21, 197.

24. Thomas Jesup to Thomas Hunt, 1 October 1846, Thomas Jesup to S. B. Dusenbery, 1 October 1846, Letters Sent by the Office of the Quartermaster General, microfilm no M745, Roll 21, 201, 202.

25. Thomas Jesup to E.F. Steplie, 1 October 1846, Thomas Jesup to S.B. Dusenbery, 2 October 1846, Letters Sent by the Office of the Quartermaster General, microfilm no M745, Roll 21, 202, 203.

26. Henry Stanton to S. B. Dusenbery, 1 October 1846, Henry Stanton to Joshua Beech, 13 October 1846, Letters Sent by the Office of the Quartermaster General, microfilm no M745, Roll 21, 202, 216.

27. Henry Stanton to Thomas Hunt, 13 October 1846, Henry Stanton to D. H. Vinton, 13 October 1846, Letters Sent by the Office of the Quartermaster General, microfilm no M745, Roll 21, 229, 230.

28. Henry Stanton to Thomas Hunt, 19 October 1846, Henry Stanton to Samuel Dusenbery, 28 October 1846, Letters Sent by the Office of the Quartermaster General, microfilm no M745, Roll 21, 231, 243.

29. Circular, Quartermasters, 15 October 1846, Letters Sent by the Office of the Quartermaster General, microfilm no M745, Roll 21, 240–242; *An Act concerning the disbursement of public money. U.S. Statutes at Large* 3 (1821–1823): 723–724.

30. Richard K. Fleischman and Thomas N. Tyson, "Developing Expertise: Two Episode in Early Nineteenth Century U.S. Management Accounting History, *"Business and Economic History,* Vol. 26, No. 2 (Winter 1997), 371–372, 377; Darwin L. King, Kathleen M. Premo, Carl J. Case, "Historical Influence on Modern Cost Accounting Practices," *Academy of Accounting and Financial Studies Journal,* Col. 13, No. 4 (2009), 22–24; Christopher McGregory Klyza, "The United States Army, Natural Resources, and Political Development in the Nineteenth Century," *Polity,* Vol. 35, No. 1 (Autumn, 2002), 2–4, 8–10, 13–14; Keith W. Hoskin and Richard H. Macve, "The Genesis of Accountability: The West Point Connections," *Accounting, Organizations, and Society,* Vol. 13, No. 1 (1988), 38, 46, 49–53; Keith Hoskin and Richard Macve, "Reappraising the genesis of managerialism: A reexamination of the role of accounting at the Springfield Armory, 1815–1845," *Accounting, Auding, & Accountability Journal,* Vol. 7, No. 2 (1994), 5, 7, 14, 17.

31. The Saffir-Simpson Hurricane Scale was not created until the 1970s, but it is used here anachronistically to provide a context to the reader of the severity of the storm.

32. Henry Stanton to Henry Lindsey, 1 November 1846, Letters Sent by the Office of the Quartermaster General, microfilm no M745, Roll 21, 254.

33. Henry Stanton to Thomas Jesup, 6 November 1846, Letters Sent by the Office of the Quartermaster General, microfilm no M745, Roll 21, 263; Peter Guardino, *Dead March: A History of the Mexican-American War* (Cambridge: Harvard University Press, 2017), 134–141.

34. Anne Chase to My Beloved, Tampico, 21 October 1846, Special Collections, University of Texas at Arlington, F10–1; "A Daily Lesson in History. Mrs. Ann Chase, The Heroine of Tampico in the Mexican War," Special Collections, University of Texas at Arlington, F11–2; Anne Chase to B.M. Norman, Tampico, 17 April 1847, Special Collections, University of Texas at Arlington, F11–4; R.W. to Mr. Chase, Tampico, 7 February 1847, Special Collections, University of Texas at Arlington, F5–21; William Gates to Franklin Chase, Tampico, 3 December 1846, Special Collections, University of Texas at Arlington, F5–10; William Gates to W.L. Marcy, Tampico, 8 July 1847, Special Collections, University of Texas at Arlington, F7–1; United States Department of War, Tampico, Mexico Custom House Collector's Record of Customs Revenues Collected, Record Group 94: Records of the Adjutant General's Office, 1780s-1917, National Archives, Washington, D.C., Box 145 [1847–1848].

35. Henry Stanton to Benjamin Graham, 18 November 1846, Letters Sent by the Office of the Quartermaster General, microfilm no M745, Roll 21, 275; United States War Department, *General Regulations for the Army of the United States, 1841* (Washington, DC: United States War Department, J. and G. S. Gideon, 1841), 191.

36. K. Jack Bauer, *The Mexican War: 1846–1848* (New York: Macmillan Publishing, 1974), 202.

37. The Quartermaster's Department eventually purchased the *Eudora*. The proposed price was $20,000. See Henry Stanton to Thomas Jesup, 19 November 1846, Letters Sent by the Office of the Quartermaster General, microfilm no M745, Roll 21, Roll 21, 282.

38. Henry Stanton to Thomas Jesup, 19 November 1846, Letters Sent by the Office of the Quartermaster General, microfilm no M745, Roll 21, 281, 282.

39. Henry Stanton to D.H. Vinton, 19 November 1846, Letters Sent by the Office of the Quartermaster General, microfilm no M745, Roll 21, 282–283.

40. Henry Stanton to S.B. Dusenbery, 24 November 1846, Letters Sent by the Office of the Quartermaster General, microfilm no M745, Roll 21, 294.

41. Risch, *Quartermaster Support of the Army*, 269–270.

42. Henry Stanton to M.M. Clark, 24 November 1846, Henry Stanton to Thomas Hunt, 26 November 1846, Letters Sent by the Office of the Quartermaster General, microfilm no M745, Roll 21, 295, 297.

43. Guardino, *The Dead March*, 147–155.

Chapter 4

1. William Patrick O'Brien, *Merchants of Independence: International Trade on the Santa Fe Trail, 1827–1860* (Kirksville, MO: Truman State University Press, 2014), 14–16, 17, 31, 32–33, 46, 64–65; William F. Switzler, *Report on Internal Commerce of the United State for the Fiscal Year 1886* (Washington, D.C.: Department of the Treasury, 1889) 265–266.

2. Patricia Joy Richmond, *Trail to Disaster: The Route of John C. Frémont's Fourth Expedition from Big Timbers, Colorado, through the San Luis Valley, to Taos, New Mexico* (Niwot: University Press of Colorado, 1989), v.

3. Erna Risch, *Quartermaster Support of the Army: A History of the Corps, 1775–1939* (Washington, DC: Center of Military History, US Army, 1989), 277; William Elsey Connelley, *Doniphan's Expedition: War with Mexico, 1846–1847, & the Conquest of New Mexico & California* (Topeka, Kansas: William Connelley, 1907), 256; Jacob Robinson, *A Journal of the Santa Fe Expedition Under Colonel Doniphan* (Princeton: Princeton University Press, 1932), xix.

4. Norma B. Ricketts, *The Mormon Battalion: U.S. Army of the West, 1846–1847* (Logan: Utah State University Press, 1996), 12, 15, 35.

5. Frank S. Edwards, A Campaign in New Mexico with Colonel Doniphan (Philadelphia: Carey and Hart, 1847), 20–21; Joseph G. Dawson, *Doniphan's Epic March: The 1st Missouri Volunteers in the Mexican War* (Lawrence: University Press of Kansas, 1999), 28–29; Dwight L. Clarke, *Stephen Watts Kearny: Soldier of the West* (Norman: Oklahoma University Press, 1961), 106–107, 111.

6. Ricketts, *The Mormon Battalion*, 35–36, 41, 42.

7. Ricketts, *The Mormon Battalion*, 35–36, 41, 42; Connelley, *Doniphan's Expedition*, 139; Roger D. Launius, *Alexander William Doniphan: Portrait of a Missouri Moderate* (Columbia: University of Missouri Press, 1997), 93; Dawson, *Doniphan's Epic March*, 44–45, 52–53; Clarke, *Stephen Watts Kearny*, 108–109.

8. Ricketts, *The Mormon Battalion*, 35–36, 41, 42; Connelley, *Doniphan's Expedition*, 139; Launius, *Alexander William Doniphan*, 93; Dawson, *Doniphan's Epic March*, 44–45, 52–53.

9. Dawson, *Doniphan's Epic March*, 45; John S. D. Eisenhower, *So Far From God: The U.S. War with Mexico, 1846–1848* (New York: Random House, 1989), 211–216.

10. Richmond, Trail to Disaster, 2; Edwards, A Campaign in New Mexico, 23; Connelley, *Doniphan's Expedition*, 147–148; George Rutledge Gibson, Ralph P. Bieber, Ed., *Journal of a Soldier Under Kearny and Doniphan, 1846–1847*, (The Arthur C. Clark Company: Glendale, California, 1935), 121, 165–170.

11. Risch, *Quartermaster Support of the Army*, 278; Thomas Jesup to Henry Stanton, New York, 11 September 1846, Letters Sent by the Office of the Quartermaster General, microfilm no M745, Roll 21, 133–134.

12. Risch, *Quartermaster Support of the Army*, 278–279; Thomas Jesup to A. Mackay, 20 September 1846, Letters Sent by the Office of the Quartermaster General, microfilm no M745, Roll 21, 172; Connelley, *Doniphan's Expedition*, 263–264; Launius, *Alexander William Doniphan*, 93–94; Robinson, *A Journal of the Santa Fe*, 7; Clarke, *Stephen Watts Kearny*, 118.

13. Edwards, A Campaign in New Mexico, 28–31; Connelley, *Doniphan's Expedition*, 139–140, 161; Robinson, *A Journal of the Santa Fe*, 15; Dawson, *Doniphan's Epic March*, 58; Clarke, *Stephen Watts Kearny*, 122.

14. Edwards, A Campaign in New Mexico, 36–38; Connelley, *Doniphan's Expedition*, 178–180; Launius, *Alexander William Doniphan*, 99; Susan Shelby Magoffin, *Down the Santa Fe Trail and into Mexico: The Diary of Susan Shelby Magoffin, 1846–1847*, ed. Stella M. Drumm (New Haven: Yale University Press, 1962), 60–61; Dawson, *Doniphan's Epic March*, 59, 70; Clarke, *Stephen Watts Kearny*, 126.

15. Launius, *Alexander William Doniphan*, 95; Eisenhower, *So Far From God*, 195, 205–206.

16. Connelley, *Doniphan's Expedition*, 183; Clarke, *Stephen Watts Kearny*, 132; Gibson, *Journal of a Soldier*, 173–192.

17. This is from a third hand account of Frank Edwards, who escorted a Mexican man claiming to be a general to see Kearny. The man claimed there had been an army of some four thousand Mexican troops positioned in a pass that the Army of the West planned to cross. If true, it would have been a hard-fought contest for Kearny to have prevailed and continued to Santa Fe. Whether the story is true or not, the army marched into the city uncontested. Frank S. Edwards, *A Campaign in New Mexico with Colonel Doniphan* (Philadelphia: Carey and Hart, 1847). The account by Hughes has the number of Mexicans at two thousand.

18. Eisenhower, *So Far From God*, 105, 195, 207–210.

19. Edwards, A Campaign in New Mexico, 45–47, 53, 65; Connelley, *Doniphan's Expedition*, 194–201, 245–246; Launius, *Alexander William Doniphan*, 107, 108; Clarke, *Stephen Watts Kearny*, 141–145.

20. Connelley, *Doniphan's Expedition*, 207; Eisenhower, *So Far From God*, 219–226.

21. Thomas Jesup to Henry Stanton, 4 September 1846, Letters Sent by the Office of the Quartermaster General, microfilm no M745, Roll 21, 108.

22. Thomas Jesup to Henry Stanton, 5 September 1846, Thomas Jesup to Henry Stanton, 11 September 1846, Letters Sent by the Office of the Quartermaster General, microfilm no M745, Roll 21, 115, 133–134.

23. Thomas Jesup to Henry Stanton, 11 September 1846, Thomas Jesup to J. L. Folsom, 14 September 1846, Thomas Jesup to Henry Stanton, 15 September 1846, Letters Sent by the Office of the Quartermaster General, microfilm no M745, Roll 21, 133–134, 137–138, 139–140.

24. Thomas Jesup to S. B. Dusenbery, 4 September 1846, Thomas Jesup to Henry Stanton, 20 September 1846, Thomas Jesup to Henry Stanton, 22 September 1846, Letters Sent by the Office of the Quartermaster General, microfilm no M745, Roll 21,109, 156, 158.

25. Thomas Jesup to D. H. Vinton, 5 September 1846, Letters Sent by the Office of the Quartermaster General, microfilm no M745, Roll 21,114.

26. Thomas Jesup to G. Griswold, 18 September 1846, Thomas Jesup to Henry Stanton, 18 September 1846, Letters Sent by the Office of the Quartermaster General, microfilm no M745, Roll 21, 149.

27. Henry Stanton to D. H. Vinton, 8 October 1846, Henry Stanton to D. H. Vinton, 15 October 1846, Henry Stanton to Richard Mason, 2 November 1846, Letters Sent by the Office of the Quartermaster General, microfilm no M745, Roll 21, 211, 218–219, 256.

28. Clarke, *Stephen Watts Kearny*, 156–157, 158.

29. Connelley, *Doniphan's Expedition*, 260.

30. Ricketts, *The Mormon Battalion*, 62–63, 68–69; Edwards, A Campaign in New Mexico, 69–70.

31. Edwards, A Campaign in New Mexico, foreword, 70; Launius, *Alexander William Doniphan*, 125; Clarke, *Stephen Watts Kearny*,160–162; Eisenhower, *So Far From God*, 219.

32. Ricketts, *The Mormon Battalion*, 71–72, 79; Eisenhower, *So Far From God*, 219–221.

33. Edwards, A Campaign in New Mexico, 72; Connelley, *Doniphan's Expedition*, 317.

34. Clarke, *Stephen Watts Kearny*, 180, 183, 185–186.

35. Clarke, *Stephen Watts Kearny*, 187–188, 195–232, 234.

36. Launius, *Alexander William Doniphan*, 134–137.

37. Launius, *Alexander William Doniphan*, 137–139; Robinson, *A Journal of the Santa Fe*,64; Dawson, *Doniphan's Epic March*, 107–108.

38. Dawson, *Doniphan's Epic March*, 110–119, 120–121; Launius, *Alexander William Doniphan*, 142–150.

39. Edwards, A Campaign in New Mexico, 90–91, 92, 96–97; Dawson, *Doniphan's Epic March*, 125; Launius, *Alexander William Doniphan*,152–153.

40. Steve Inskeep, *Imperfect Union* (New York: Penguin Books, 2021), 153, 155–157, 159–161, 162, 176; Adrew F. Rolle, *Character as Destiny* (Norman: University of Oklahoma Press, 1991), 79, 80, 85, 90–93; John Charles Frémont, *Memoirs of My Life and Times* (New York: Belford, Clarke and Co., 1886), 504–505, 531–532, 582–583; Tom Chaffin, *Pathfinder: John Charles Frémont and the Course of American Empire* (Norman: University of Oklahoma Press, 2014), 330–331, 341–342, 349–350, 361–363, 368–371; John Charles Frémont, Donald Jackson, ed., Mary Lee Spence, ed. *The Expeditions of John Charles Frémont* (Urbana: University of Illinois Press, 1970), 80, 139, 174, 255–257; Ricketts, *The Mormon Battalion*, 131; Clarke, *Stephen Watts Kearny*,233–244.

41. The Sandwich Islands at this point in time was the name given to the Hawaiian Islands. The name Hawaii was just beginning to be used more regularly in the 1840s. Captain James Cook named the Hawaiian Islands after his sponsor John Montagu, 4th Earl of Sandwich. This leads to a bit of misunderstanding reading records from the time.

42. Clarke, *Stephen Watts Kearny*, 235, 245–255, 256–287; Ricketts, *The Mormon Battalion*, 143, 147, 148, 152.

43. Dawson, *Doniphan's Epic March*, 132–135.

44. Edwards, A Campaign in New Mexico, 112–120, 122, 128, 131–132; Robinson, *A Journal of the Santa Fe*, 83–84; Dawson, *Doniphan's Epic March*,144–159, 178–179; Launius, *Alexander William Doniphan*,156–160.

45. This is the spelling Frank Edwards used in his diary A Campaign in New Mexico, the city's name is usually spelled Reynosa.

46. Edwards, A Campaign in New Mexico, 149, 150, 151, 152, 158, 162, 164–165: Robinson, *A Journal of the Santa Fe*, 88–89; Dawson, *Doniphan's Epic March*, 180–183, 184; Launius, *Alexander William Doniphan*,182–191.

47. Richard W. Amero, "The Mexican-American War in Baja California," *The Journal of San Diego History*, 30, no. 1 (1984). http://www.sandiegohistory.org/journal/1984/january/war/ (Accessed 2/11/2019).

Chapter 5

1. K. Jack Bauer, *The Mexican War, 1846–1848* (New York: Macmillan, 1974), 243–261; John S. D. Eisenhower, *So Far From God: The U.S. War with Mexico, 1846–1848* (New York: Random House, 1989), 253–265; Peter Guardino, *The Dead March: A History of the Mexican-American War* (Cambridge: Harvard University Press, 2017), 150, 187–188, 190–192.

2. Bauer, *The Mexican War*, 233.

3. Winfield Scott, *Memoirs of Lieut.-General Winfield Scott*, edited by Timothy D. Johnson (Knoxville: University of Tennessee Press, 2015), 210; K. Jack Bauer, *Surfboats and Horse Marines: U.S. Naval Operations in the Mexican War, 1846–48* (Annapolis: US Naval Institute, 1969), 63–64, 66; Mexican War Correspondence, *House Executive Documents*, No. 60, 30th Congress, 1st Session, Serial Set 520, 1,268–1,270.

4. Bauer, *Surfboats*, 63–64, 66; Memorandum by Winfield Scott, 12 November 1846, Mexican War Correspondence, *House Executive Documents*, No. 60, 30th Congress, 1st Session, Serial Set 520, 1,270–1,274.

5. Winfield Scott to William Marcy, 16 November 1846, Mexican War Correspondence, *House Executive Documents*, No. 60, 30th Congress, 1st Session, Serial Set 520, 1,274.

6. Bauer, *Mexican War*, 232, 236.

7. Mexican War Correspondence, *House Executive Documents*, No. 60, 30th Congress, 1st Session, Serial Set 520, 1,275–1,276.

8. Bauer, *Surfboats*, 63–64, 66; Mexican War Correspondence, *House Executive Documents*, No. 60, 30th Congress, 1st Session, Serial Set 520, 1,268–1,274.

9. John Lenthall Papers, Independence Seaport Museum, Philadelphia; Bauer, *Surfboats*, 66; Chester L. Kiefer, *Maligned General: The Biography of Thomas Sidney Jesup*, (San Rafael, CA: Presidio Press, 1979), 285; Bauer, K. Jack. "The Veracruz Expedition of 1847." *Military Affairs* 20 (Fall 1956), 164; Mexican War Correspondence, *House Executive Documents*, No. 60, 30th Congress, 1st Session, Serial Set 520, 1274.

   Within the sources the boats are referred to by several names all referring to long, flat-bottomed boats used to transfer men and supplies from ship to shore. Some of the names include surfboats, longboats, whale boats, and beach boats. The sources use these names interchangeably and most of the correspondence understood the type of boat being discussed despite the rotation of names.

   For more information on the surfboats see William G. Temple, "Memoir of the Landing of the United States Troops at Veracruz in 1847," in David Conner, *The Home Squadron Under Commodore Conner*, with Philip S. P. Conner (Philadelphia: P. S. P. Conner, 1896), 60–62i.

10. Henry Stanton to R. F. Loper, 29 November 1846, Letters Sent by the Office of the Quartermaster General, microfilm no M745, Roll 21, 302–303.

11. Henry Stanton to D. H. Vinton, 5 December 1846, Henry Stanton to R. F. Loper, 7 December 1846, Henry Stanton to R. F. Loper, 8 December 1846, Letters Sent by the Office of the Quartermaster General, microfilm no M745, Roll 21, 314, 319–320, 322.

12. Ivor Debenham Spencer, *The Victor and the Spoils: A Life of William L. Marcy*, (Providence, RI: Brown University Press, 1959), 147, 164; Temple, "Memoir of the Landing," 60–62; Bauer, *Surfboats*, 66; Kieffer, *Maligned General*, 285; Bauer, "The Veracruz Expedition," 164; Mexican War Correspondence, *House Executive Documents*, No. 60, 30th Congress, 1st Session, Serial Set 520, 1,274.

13. Bauer, *Mexican War*, 239; Thomas Jesup to M.M. Clark, 22 August 1846, Henry Stanton to Thomas Jesup, 13 December 1846, Henry Stanton to Thomas Jesup, 14 January 1847, Henry Stanton to Thomas Jesup, 22 January 1847, Letters Sent by the Office of the Quartermaster General, microfilm no M745, Roll 21, 62, 331, 384–385, 404.

14. Henry Stanton to B. Alvoro, 3 December 1846, Henry Stanton to John Goolrick, 3 December 1846, Henry Stanton to Thomas Jesup, 3 December 1846, Letters Sent by the Office of the Quartermaster General, microfilm no M745, Roll 21, 309, 310, 311.

15. Henry Stanton to Thomas Jesup, 4 December 1846, Letters Sent by the Office of the Quartermaster General, microfilm no M745, Roll 21,312–313; Theodore J. Karamanski, *Schooner Passage: Sailing Ships and the Lake Michigan Frontier* (Detroit: Wayne State University Press, 2000), 29.

16. It is unclear what type of steamship the *Virginia* was, but she was most likely screw driven because of Stanton dislike of sidewheel ships by this point in the war. He felt the latter were unsafe on the open sea.

17. Henry Stanton to Thomas Jesup, 4 December 1846, Henry Stanton to D. D. Thompkins, 12 December 1846, Henry Stanton to D. H. Vinton, 13 December 1846, Letters Sent by the Office of the Quartermaster General, microfilm no M745, Roll 21, 312–313, 328, 329–330.

18. Henry Stanton to D. H. Vinton, 7 December 1846, Letters Sent by the Office of the Quartermaster General, microfilm no M745, Roll 21, 318–319.

19. Edward J. Nichols, *Zach Taylor's Little Army* (Garden City, NY: Doubleday, 1963), 194; Zachary Taylor, *Letters of Zachary Taylor from the Battle-fields of the Mexican War: Reprinted from the Originals in the Collection of Mr. William K. Bixby, of St. Louis, Mo.*, William K. Bixby and William Holland Samson, ed. (New York: Kraus Reprint, 1970),104; J. Jacob Oswandel, *Notes of the Mexican War, 1846–1848*, ed. Timothy D. Johnson and Nathaniel Cheairs Hughes (Knoxville: University of Tennessee Press, 2010), 26; Mexican War Correspondence, *House Executive Documents*, No. 60, 30th Congress, 1st Session, Serial Set 520, 365–366; Thomas T. Smith, *The U.S. Army and the Texas Frontier Economy, 1845–1900* (College Station: Texas A & M University Press, 1999), 16, 20, 24, 71, 112, 138.

20. Mexican War Correspondence, *House Executive Documents*, No. 60, 30th Congress, 1st Session, Serial Set 520, 882–884; Bauer, *Surfboats*, 70; Henry Stanton to D.H. Vinton, 19 January 1847, Letters Sent by the Office of the Quartermaster General, microfilm no M745, Roll 21, 393.

21. Henry Stanton to S. P. Heintzelman, 15 December 1846, Henry Stanton to D. H. Vinton, 15 December 1846, Henry Stanton to R. F. Loper, 20 December 1846, Letters

Sent by the Office of the Quartermaster General, microfilm no M745, Roll 21, 335, 336, 342.

22. Henry Stanton to S. B. Dusenbery, 15 December 1846, Henry Stanton to R. F. Loper, 20 December 1846, Henry Stanton to S. B. Dusenbery, 26 December 1846, Henry Stanton to D. D. Vinton, 27 December 1846, Letters Sent by the Office of the Quartermaster General, microfilm no M745, Roll 21, 337, 343, 352, 353.

23. Henry Stanton to R. F. Loper, 20 December 1846, Henry Stanton to R. F. Loper, 20 December 1846, Henry Stanton to George Totton, 21 December 1846, Letters Sent by the Office of the Quartermaster General, microfilm no M745, Roll 21, 342, 343, 343–344.

24. Henry Stanton to Samuel Dusenbery, 2 January 1847, Henry Stanton to John Goolrick, 4 January 1847, 369; Henry Stanton to R. F. Loper, 4 January 1847, Henry Stanton to D. H. Vinton, 9 January 1847, Letters Sent by the Office of the Quartermaster General, microfilm no M745, Roll 21, 368, 369, 370, 382.

25. Bauer, *Mexican War*, 238; Mexican War Correspondence, *House Executive Documents*, No. 60, 30th Congress, 1st Session, Serial Set 520, 391; Henry Stanton to R.F. Loper, 4 January 1847, Letters Sent by the Office of the Quartermaster General, microfilm no M745, Roll 21, 370.

26. Henry Stanton to D. H. Vinton, 5 January 1847, Letters Sent by the Office of the Quartermaster General, microfilm no M745, Roll 21, 373.

27. Thomas T. Smith, *The U.S. Army and the Texas Frontier Economy, 1845–1900* (College Station: Texas A&M University Press, 1999), 27; Henry Stanton to Thomas Hunt, 21 December 1846, Henry Stanton to D.H. Vinton, 5 January 1847, Letters Sent by the Office of the Quartermaster General, microfilm no M745, Roll 21, 346, 373.

28. Henry Stanton to Thomas Hunt, 14 January 1847, Letters Sent by the Office of the Quartermaster General, microfilm no M745, Roll 21, 383.

29. Henry Stanton to Thomas Jesup, 14 January 1847, Henry Stanton to D. H. Vinton, 19 January 1847, Henry Stanton to Thomas Jesup, 22 January 1847, Henry Stanton to Thomas Jesup, 29 January 1847, Letters Sent by the Office of the Quartermaster General, microfilm no M745, Roll 21, 384–385, 393, 404, 415–416.

30. Henry Stanton to James McKay, 19 January 1847, Letters Sent by the Office of the Quartermaster General, microfilm no M745, Roll 21, 394–398.

31. Henry Stanton Circular to Quartermaster Officers, 22 January 1847, Letters Sent by the Office of the Quartermaster General, microfilm no M745, Roll 21, 407–408.

32. Henry Stanton Circular to Quartermaster Officers, 22 January 1847, Letters Sent by the Office of the Quartermaster General, microfilm no M745, Roll 21, 407–408.

33. Henry Stanton to H. D. Grafton, 5 February 1847, Letters Sent by the Office of the Quartermaster General, microfilm no M745, Roll 21, 426.

34. Winfield Scott to William Marcy, 12 January 1847, Winfield Scott to Commodore Connor, 26 December 1846, Winfield Scott to W. O. Butler, 3 January 1847, Mexican War Correspondence, *House Executive Documents*, No. 60, 30th Congress, 1st Session, Serial Set 520, 844–846, 846–847, 851–852; Bauer, *Surfboats*, 71, 72.

35. Henry Stanton to Thomas Jesup, 16 February 1847, Henry Stanton to Thomas Jesup, 18 February 1847, Letters Sent by the Office of the Quartermaster General, microfilm no M745, Roll 21, 437–438, 445.

36. A main-truck is a circular or rectangular piece of wood near the top of the mast with holes or sheaves to reeve signal halyards. Scott's pennant was displayed on the truck of the mainmast.

37. Bauer, *Surfboats*, 75–76; Henry Stanton to B. E. Bee, 2 March 1847, Letters Sent by the Office of the Quartermaster General, microfilm no M745, Roll 21, 472.

38. Bauer, *Surfboats*, 76; William H. Parker, *Recollections of a Naval Officer, 1841–1865* (New York: Charles Scribners' Sons), 82; Temple, "Memoir," 63–64.

39. Henry Stanton to Morris Miller, 5 March 1847, Letters Sent by the Office of the Quartermaster General, microfilm no M745, Roll 21, 479.

40. United States Department of War, General and Special Orders Issued by General Winfield Scott, Headquarters of the Army, Roll 1: 45.

41. Bauer, *Mexican War*, 241; Bauer, *Surfboats*, 77; Conner, *Home Squadron*, 19; Temple, "Memoir," 64.

42. Bauer, *Mexican War*, 242, 244; Bauer, *Surfboats*, 81–82 ; Oswandel, *Notes*, 35–36; Davis, *Autobiography*, 125; Raphael Semmes, *Service Afloat and Ashore during the Mexican War* (Cincinnati: W. H. Moore & Co., 1851), 128.

   The number of troops landed at Collado Beach during these five hours varies between 8,600 and around 13,000 men, depending on the source.

43. Bauer, *Mexican War*, 249–253.

44. Ebbert to Sister, 30 March 1847, Ebbert to Sister, 5 April 1847, Special Collections, University of Texas at Arlington, GA 51.

45. Timothy D. Johnson, *A Gallant Little Army: The Mexico City Campaign* (Lawrence: University of Kansas Press, 2007), 66–101.

46. Johnson, *A Gallant Little Army*, 119–150.

47. Peter Guardino, *Dead March: A History of the Mexican-American War* (Cambridge, MA: Harvard University Press, 2017), 220, 226, 229–231; Ebbert to Sister, 21 May 1847, Special Collections, University of Texas at Arlington, GA 51; Irving W. Levinson, *Wars within War: Mexican Guerrillas, Domestic Elites, and the United States of America, 1846–1848* (Canada: Irving Levinson, 2005), 34–40.

48. Levinson, *Wars within War*, 41–43.

49. Johnson, *A Gallant Little Army*, 171–193.

50. Johnson, *A Gallant Little Army*, 210–226; Eisenhower, *So Far From God*, 345–350.

51. Treaty of Guadalupe-Hidalgo, *National Archives*, https://www.archives.gov/education/lessons/guadalupe-hidalgo (Accessed 2/12/2019)

52. Quoted in Marjory M. Moody, "The Evolution of Emerson as an Abolitionist," *American Literature* 17:1 (March 1945), 11fn41.

Chapter 6

1. Miguel Ángel Gonzalez-Quiroga, *War and Peace on the Rio Grande Frontier, 1830–1880* (Norman, OK: University of Oklahoma Press, 2020), 91–92, 107; US

Census Bureau, *Census of 1850*, Statistics of Texas; US Census Bureau, *Census of 1860*, Statistics of Texas.

2. Arnoldo De León, *The Tejano Community, 1836–1900* (Albuquerque: University of New Mexico Press, 1982), 17; Paul S. Taylor, *An American Mexican Frontier: Nueces County, Texas*, (Chapel Hill: University of North Carolina Press, 1934), 180; *American Flag*, August 20, 1856; Roberto Ramón Calderón, "Mexican politics in the American era, 1846–1900: Laredo, Texas," PhD diss., 1993, 249–250; Oscar J. Martínez, *Troublesome Border* (Tucson: University of Arizona Press, 1988), 91–92; Gonzalez-Quiroga, *War and Peace on the Rio Grande Frontier, 1830–1880*, 96.

3. Leroy Graf, "The Economic History of the Lower Rio Grande Valley, 1820–1875," PhD diss., Harvard University, 1945, 369–380; Arnoldo De León, *They Called Them Greasers: Anglo Attitudes toward Mexicans in Texas, 1821–1900* (Austin: University of Texas Press, 1983), 54–55, 83–85.

4. Quoted in Andrés Reséndez, *Changing National Identities at the Frontier: Texas and New Mexico, 1800–1850* (Cambridge: Cambridge University Press, 2004), 3; Jane Monday and Frances Vick, *Petra's Legacy: The South Texas Ranching Empire of Petra Vela and Mifflin Kenedy* (College Station: Texas A&M University Press, 2007), 1–6; Jane Clements Monday and Betty Baily Colley, *Voices from the Wild Horse Desert: The Vaquero Families of the King and Kenedy Ranches* (University of Texas Press: Austin, 1997), 46–48; Walker D, Wyman, *The Wild Horse of the West* (The Caxton Printers :Caldwell, Ohio, 1945), 99.

5. Omar Valerio-Jiménez, *River of Hope: Forging Identity and Nation in the Rio Grande Borderlands* (Durham, NC: Duke University Press, 2013), 130–131; Richard T. Marcum, "Fort Brown, Texas: The History of a Border Post," PhD diss., Texas Technical College, Lubbock, 1964, 52; Reginald Horseman, *Race and Manifest Destiny: The Origins of American Racial Anglo-Saxonism* (Cambridge: Harvard University Press, 1981), 219–221.

6. Valerio-Jiménez, *River of Hope*, 135; *American Flag*, December 30, 1847, January 3, 1848, February 2, 1848; Montejano, *Anglos and Mexicans*, 37–38; Juan Mora-Torres, *The Making of the Mexican Border* (Austin: University of Texas Press, 2001), 31.

7. de León, *Tejano Community*, 17, 63; Andrés Tijerina, *Tejanos and Texas under the Mexican Flag, 1821–1836* (College Station: Texas A&M University Press, 1994), 5 ,141; Frank Cushman Pierce, *Texas' Last Frontier: A Brief History of the Lower Rio Grande Valley* (Menahsa, Wisconsin: Collegiate Press, 1917), 138; J. Lee and Lillian J. Stambaugh, *The Lower Rio Grande Valley of Texas* (San Antonio: Naylor Company, 1954), 88–92; Jovita González, "Social Life in Cameron, Starr, and Zapata Counties," M.A. thesis, University of Texas at Austin, 1930, 26.

8. Kenneth L. Stewart and Arnoldo De León, *Not Enough Room: Mexicans, Anglos, and Socioeconomic Change in Texas, 1850–1900* (Albuquerque: University of Mexico Press, 1993), 10–13.

9. Valerio-Jiménez, *River of Hope*, 140; Graf, "Economic,"153–155, 168–69; Gilberto Hinojosa, *A Borderlands Town in Transition: Laredo, 1755–1870* (College Station:

Texas A&M Press, 1983), 59; Alexander Mendoza, "'For Our Own Best Interests':
Nineteenth-Century Laredo Tejanos, Military Service, and the Development of
American Nationalism," *Southwestern Historical Quarterly* 115, no. 2 (2011): 127, 131,
133; Calderón, "Mexican politics in the American era," 1993, 217–220, 240–242,

10. Armando C. Alonzo, *Tejano Legacy: Rancheros and Settlers in South Texas, 1734–1900*
(Albuquerque: University of New Mexico Press, 1998), 96–97; Randolph B. Camp-
bell, *Gone to Texas: A History of the Lone Star State* (New York: Oxford University
Press, 2003), 207; de León and Stewart, *Tejanos and the Numbers Game*, 12, 19, 24;
Alicia A. Garza and Christopher Long, "Cameron County," *Handbook of Texas
Online*, accessed August 25, 2023, https://www.tshaonline.org/handbook/entries
/cameron-county.

11. Alonzo, *Tejano Legacy*, 162–163, 265–268; Hinojosa, *A Borderlands Town*, 61, 82–83.

12. Tax Rolls, Cameron County, 1852, 1856, 1860; Tax Rolls, Starr County, 1852, 1856,
1860; Tax Rolls, Hidalgo County, 1852, 1856, 1860.

13. Valerio-Jiménez, *River of Hope*, 148–149; David Montejano, *Anglos and Mexicans
in the Making of Texas, 1836–1986* (Austin, TX: Univ. of Texas Press, 1999), 34–35,
43–44.

14. Greaser, Galen D., and Jesus F. De La Teja, "Quieting Title to Spanish and Mexican
Land Grants in the Trans-Nueces: The Bourland and Miller Commission, 1850–1852."
The Southwestern Historical Quarterly 95, No. 4 (April 1992): 449, 454, 456, 457,
461–462.

15. González-Quiroga, *War and Peace*, 122–123, 130–131, 165–166; *Telegraph and Texas
Register*, October 7, 1846, 5; Rippy, "Border Troubles," 100.

16. Graf, "Economic History," 148–149, 168; Frederick Zeh, *An Immigrant Soldier in
the Mexican War*, ed. William Orr (Texas A&M University Press: College Station, 1995), 39; Ralph Kirkham, *The Mexican War Journal and Letters of Ralph W.
Kirkham*, ed. Robert Miller (Texas A&M University Press: College Station, 1991),
38; Philip Barbour and Martha Barbour, *Journals of the Late Brevet Major Philip
Barbour . . . and his wife, Martha Isabella Hopkins Barbour: Written during the War
with Mexico—1846*, ed. Rhoda van Vivver Tanner Doubleday (G. P. Putnam's Sons:
New York, 1936), 25, 92; J. Jacob Oswandel, *Notes of the Mexican War, 1846–1848*,
ed. Timothy Johnson (Philadelphia, 1885), 107.

17. Arnoldo De León, *The Tejano Community, 1836–1900* (Albuquerque: University
of New Mexico Press, 1982), 62, 79; San Antonio *Express*, December 4, 1877, 2;
Montejano, *Anglos and Mexicans*, 43–44, 59–60.

18. Thomas T. Smith, *The U.S. Army and the Texas Frontier Economy, 1845–1900* (College
Station: Texas A&M University Press, 1999), 11; David Montejano, *Anglos and
Mexicans In the Making of Texas, 1836–1986* (Austin: University of Texas Press,
1999), 40–41; James Thompson, "A 19th Century History of Cameron County"
(M.A. Thesis), 80–82.

19. "Report of the Quartermaster General" *Message from the President of the United
States*, 32nd Congress, 1st Session, House Exec. Doc. 2, Serial Set 634, 253–269.

20. Smith, *The U.S. Army*, 131–133, 138–139, 144; Crimmins, ed., "Colonel Mansfield's Report," 141; Dan R. Manning, "The Mexican War Journal of Jahn James Dix: A Texian," *Military History of the West* 23 (Spring, 1993): 46–74.

21. Smith, *The U.S. Army*, 131–133, 138–139, 144; Crimmins, ed., "Colonel Mansfield's Report," 141; Thomas T. Smith, *Under the Double Eagle: Citizen Employees of the U.S. Army on the Texas Frontier, 1846–1899* (Austin: Texas State Historical Association, 2023), 15.

22. Smith, *The U.S. Army*, 13; Edmund Thomas Miller, *A Financial History of Texas, 1519–1970*, (Austin: University of Texas Bulletin no. 37, 1916), 252–53, 396.

23. Reséndez, *Changing National Identities*, 4; Graf, "Economic," 204; Valerio-Jiménez, "Identity and Nation," 222; *American Flag*, March 8, 11, July 13, 1848.

24. Alonzo, *Tejano Legacy*, 109–110.

25. Starr County Historical Society, *When Rio Grande City*, I, II, 43–46; Stambaugh, *The Lower Rio Grande Valley of Texas*, 82, 88, 89, 105; Caleb Coker, ed., *News From Brownsville*, 107, 133; Allhands, *Gringo Builders*, 57; Audubon, *Audubon's Western Journal*, 59, 63–64, 71, 82; Oats, ed., *Rip Ford's Texas*, 204, 211; González-Quiroga, *War and Peace*, 81, 93.

26. Graf, "Economic History," 404; Stambaugh, *The Lower Rio Grande Valley of Texas*, 92, 168, 172, 287; J.L. Allhands, *Gringo Builders* (Iowa City: Private Print., 1931), 28. 160, 184; Amberson, *I Would Rather Sleep in Texas*, 123–124.

27. Reséndez, *Changing National Identities*, 4–5; Andrés Reséndez, "National Identity on a Shifting Border: Texas and New Mexico in the Age of Transition, 1821–1848," *Journal of American History* 86:2 (Sep. 1999), 668–688.

28. Reséndez, *Changing National Identities*, 128–129, 131; Valerio-Jiménez, *River of Hope*, 149, 178–179; Hans Peter Nielsen Gammel, comp. *Laws of Texas, 1822–1897*, 10 vols (Austin: Gammel, 1898), 1:32; Hinojosa, *A Borderlands Town*, 71–72; Montejano, *Anglos and Mexicans in the Making of Texas*, 36, 40; González-Quiroga, *War and Peace*, 17–18.

29. Mireles, "Social Life," 101–103, 108.

30. Montejano, *Anglos and Mexicans*, 41–42; Graf, "Economic History," 129, 150, 207; Scott, "Spanish Land Grants," 125–126; J. Thompson, "A 19th Century History," 80–82; B. P. Tilden, Jr., *Notes on the Upper Rio Grande*, (Philadelphia: Lindsay & Blakiston, 1847), 30; Starr County Historical Society, *When Rio Grande City*, I, II, 43–46; Stambaugh, *The Lower Rio Grande Valley of Texas*, 82, 88, 89, 105; Caleb Coker, ed., *News From Brownsville*, 107, 133; Allhands, *Gringo Builders*, 57; Audubon, *Audubon's Western Journal*, 59, 63–64, 71, 82; Oats, ed., *Rip Ford's Texas*, 204, 211; Gonzalez-Quiroga, *War and Peace*, 81, 93; Jovita González Mireles, "Social Life," MA Thesis, University of Texas Austin, 1930, 25–27; Paul Horgan, *Great River: The Rio Grande in North American History* (Middletown, CT: Wesleyan University Press, 1984), 152.

31. Montejano, *Anglos and Mexicans*, 41–42; Graf, "Economic History," 129, 150, 207; Scott, "Spanish Land Grants," 125–126; J. Thompson, "A 19th Century History," 80–82; B. P. Tilden, Jr., *Notes on the Upper Rio Grande*, (Philadelphia: Lindsay & Blakiston, 1847), 30; Starr County Historical Society, *When Rio Grande City*, I, II,

43–46; Stambaugh, *The Lower Rio Grande Valley of Texas*, 82, 88, 89, 105; Caleb Coker, ed., *News From Brownsville*, 107, 133; Allhands, *Gringo Builders*, 57; Audubon, *Audubon's Western Journal*, 59, 63–64, 71, 82; Oats, ed., *Rip Ford's Texas*, 204, 211; Gonzalez-Quiroga, *War and Peace*, 81, 93; Jovita González Mireles, "Social Life," 25–27; Horgan, *Great River*, 152; "Contracts—War Department," *Letter from the Secretary of War*, House Exec. Doc. 17, 34th Congress 1st Session, 7.

32. A. A. Champion, "Champion, Albert," *Handbook of Texas Online*, accessed July 14, 2023, http://www.tshaonline.org/handbook/entries/champion-albert; Allhands, *Gringo Builders*, 39, 160–161; "General Index to Deeds—Grantee, 1830–1912," *Deed Records*, Cameron County, Texas County Clerk, 38.

33. Graf, "Economic History," 360, 404, 686, 687; Roberto Mario Salmón, "San Roman, Jose," *Handbook of Texas Online*, accessed July 17, 2023, https://www.tshaonline.org/handbook/entries/san-roman-jose; Stambaugh, *The Lower Rio Grande Valley of Texas*, 112; González-Quiroga, *War and Peace*, 160; Mary Margaret McAllen Amberson, James A McAllen, and Margaret H. McAllen, *I Would Rather Sleep in Texas: A History of the Lower Rio Grande Valley & the People of the Santa Anita Land Grant* (Austin, TX: Texas State Historical Association, 2003), 123.

34. Alonzo, *Tejano Legacy*, 128–129; Sarah Deutsch, "Landscape of Enclaves: Race Relations in the West," in *Under and Open Sky: Rethinking America's Western Past*, ed. William Cronon, George Miles, and Jay Gitlin (New York, 1992), 113; Frances Leon Swadesh, *Los primeros pobladores: Hispanic Americans of the Ute Frontier* (Notre Dame, Indiana: University of Notre Dame Press, 1974), 199.

35. deGarmo, *Pathfinders of Texas*, 146–148; John Salmon Ford & Stephen B. Oats, ed., *Rip Ford's Texas*, (Austin: University of Texas Press, 1963) 350, 363, 402.

36. Maria Augusta Von Blücher, *Maria Von Blücher's Corpus Christi: Letters from the South Texas Frontier, 1849–1879*, ed. Bruce S. Cheeseman (College Station: Texas A&M University Press, 2002), 79, 119; Valerio-Jiménez, *River of Hope*, 182–183; Jane Monday and Frances Vick, *Petra's Legacy: The South Texas Ranching Empire of Petra Vela and Mifflin Kenedy* (College Station: Texas A&M University Press, 2007), 189–198; Samuel J. Watson, *Peacekeepers and Conquerors: The Army Officer Corps on the American Frontier, 1821–1846* (Lawrence: University of Kansas Press, 2013), 408–415.

37. Emmanuel Domenech, *Missionary Adventures in Texas and Mexico.: A Personal Narrative of Six Years' Sojourn in Those Regions.*, ed. Henry Cohen (London: Longman, Brown, Green, Longmans, and Roberts., 1858), 129–130.

38. Karl Jacoby, *Shadows at Dawn: A Borderlands Massacre and the Violence of History* (New York: Penguin Press, 2008), 107, 115; Valerio-Jiménez, *River of Hope*, 142; Armando C. Alonzo, *Tejano Legacy: Rancheros and Settlers in South Texas, 1734–1900* (Albuquerque: University of New Mexico, 1998), 85.

    For more on Comanche and Apache actions against U.S. and Mexican citizens see Brian DeLay, *War of a Thousand Deserts: Indian Raids and the U.S.-Mexican War* (New Haven: Yale University Press, 2008) and Pekka Hämäläinen, *The Comanche Empire* (New Haven: Yale University Press, 2008).

39. Jerry D. Thompson, *Cortina: Defending the Mexican Name in Texas* (College Station: Texas A&M University Press, 2007), 34; Chapman, *Notes*, 328–329; von Blücher, *Corpus Christi*, 6, 69; Domenech, *Missionary Adventures*, 176; de León, *They Called Them Greasers*, 54–55, 83–85.

40. Valerio-Jiménez, *River of Hope*, 136–139.

     For examples of court martial cases see: United States Department of War, *General and Special Orders Issued by General Zachary Taylor, Headquarters of the Army, War with Mexico, 1847–1848*. Record Group 94, Records of the Adjutant General's Office, 1780s-1917. National Archives and Records Administration, Washington, D.C and United States Department of War, *General and Special Orders Issued by General Winfield Scott, Headquarters of the Army, War with Mexico, 1847–1848*. Record Group 94, Records of the Adjutant General's Office, 1780s-1917. National Archives and Records Administration, Washington, D.C.

41. Alexander Mendoza, "'For Our Own Best Interests': Nineteenth-Century Laredo Tejanos, Military Service, and the Development of American Nationalism," *Southwestern Historical Quarterly* 115, no. 2 (2011): 134–135; Arnoldo De León, *The Tejano Community, 1836–1900* (Albuquerque: University of New Mexico Press, 1982), 15–16; De León, *They Called Them Greasers*, 82–83; González-Quiroga, *War and Peace*,126, 170; Rippy, "Border Troubles," 103–104; Larry Knight, "The Cart War: Defining American in San Antonio in the 1850s," *The Southwestern Historical Quarterly*, 109, no. 3 (January 2006): 326, 328, 335.

     For more information on the Cortina War see Jerry D. Thompson, *Cortina: Defending the Mexican Name in Texas* (College Station: Texas A & M University Press, 2007).

     For more information on the influence of historical memory on violence against Tejanos during the nineteenth century see William D. Carrigan, *The Making of a Lynching Culture: Violence and Vigilantism in Central Texas, 1836–1916* (Urbana: University of Illinois Press, 2004).

42. Chapman, *Notes*, 295; Robert J. Rosenbaum, *Mexicano Resistance in the Southwest* (Dallas: Southern Methodist University Press, 1998), 41; William D. Carrigan, *The Making of a Lynching Culture: Violence and Vigilantism in Central Texas, 1836–1916* (Urbana: University of Illinois Press, 2004), 24–30.

Chapter 7

1. Treaty of Guadalupe-Hidalgo, *National Archives*, https://www.archives.gov /education/lessons/guadalupe-hidalgo (accessed 2/12/2019).

2. Arnoldo de León and Kenneth L. Stewart, "Lost Dreams and Found Fortunes: Mexican and Anglo American Immigrants in South Texas, 1850–1900," *Western Historical Quarterly*, Vol. 14 (July 1983), 295; US Census Bureau, *Census of 1850, Statistics of Texas*.

3. General Orders no. 49, August 31, 1848, General Orders No. 58, November 7, 1848, United States, Department of War, General and Special Orders Issued by General Zachary Taylor, Headquarters of the Army, War with Mexico, 1847–1848, Record

Group 94, Records of the Adjutant General's Office, 1780s-1917, National Archives and Records Administration, Washington, DC; Smith, *The U.S. Army*, 28.

General Orders No. 49 defined the 8th Military District as "That part of Texas lying south and east of a line drawn from a point on the Río Grande south of El Paso at the 32d degree of north latitude, to the junction of the *Ensenada Choctau;* (Choctaw creek,) with the Colorado or Red river, and down said river to Arkansas."

4. Smith, *The U.S. Army*, 30; Robert Walter Frazer, *Forts and Supplies: The Role of the Army in the Economy of the Southwest, 1846–1861* (Albuquerque: University of New Mexico Press, 1983), 160. Thomas T. Smith, *The Old Army in Texas: A Research Guide to the U.S. Army in Nineteenth-Century Texas* (Austin: Texas State Historical Association, 2000), 82; Mark R. Wilson, *The Business of Civil War: Military Mobilization and the State, 1861–1865* (Baltimore: The Johns Hopkins University Press, 2006), 47.

5. Smith, *The U.S. Army*, 33–34; Smith, *The Old Army in Texas*, 53, 60, 68; Martin L. Crimmins, ed., "W. G. Freeman's Report on the Eighth Military Department," *Southwestern Historical Quarterly* 51 (October 1947): 168; Martin L. Crimmins, ed., "Colonel J. F. K. Mansfield's Report of the Inspection of the Department of Texas in 1856," *Southwestern Historical Quarterly* 42 (October 1938): 134–135.

6. Leroy Graf, "The Economic History of the Lower Río Grande Valley, 1820–1875," PhD diss., Harvard University, 1945, 180–185, 186, 187–188, 190; *American Flag*, May 1, June 2, August 21, 1847.

7. Smith, *The U.S. Army*, 18–19, 27; Stephen A. Townsend, *The Yankee Invasion of Texas* (College Station,: Texas A&M University Press, 2006), 19; Wooster, *Soldiers, Sutlers, and Settlers*, 111.

8. Smith, *The U.S. Army*, 37–38; Graf, "Economic History," 192–194. Both the Rio Grande Line and the Santa Fe Trail existed prior to the war. The aftereffects of the war pushed the army to secure and expand the trade along these two systems. For more on the Santa Fe Trail see William Patrick O'Brien, *Merchants of Independence: International Trade on the Santa Fe Trail, 1827–1860* (Kirksville, MO: Truman State University Press, 2014).

9. Graf, "Economic History," 273–275; *American Flag*, August 23, 1846.

10. M. L. Crimmins, ed., "Colonel J. K. F. Mansfield's Report of the Inspection of the Department of Texas in 1856," *Southwestern Historical Quarterly* 42, no. 2 (October 1938): 130; Omar Santiago Valerio-Jiménez, *Indios Bárbaros, Divorcées, and Flocks of Vampires: Identity and Nation on The Río Grande, 1749–1894*, PhD diss., University of California, Los Angeles, 2001, 224–226; Omar S. Valerio-Jiménez, *River of Hope: Forging Identity and Nation in the Río Grande Borderlands* (Durham, NC: Duke University Press, 2013), 147; Daniel D. Arreola, *Tejano South Texas: A Mexican American Cultural Province* (Austin: University of Texas Press, 2002), 41; Arnoldo De León, *The Tejano Community, 1836–1900* (Albuquerque: University of New Mexico Press, 1982), 17.

Colonel Mansfield was ordered by the US Army to inspect all of the forts and supply depots in Texas. His report provided a good insight into the status of the installations along the Rio Grande and the towns that grew up around them. His report, paired with George McClellan's survey of the ports and rivers, give two, often opposing, views of the army presence in South Texas. W. G. Freeman also produced another survey for the army of the installations along the border. Between these three surveys, a very complete image of the region is possible.

11. For more information on settlements growing near army bases see: Robert Wooster, *The American Military Frontiers: The United States Army in the West, 1783–1900* (Albuquerque: University of New Mexico Press, 2009); Robert M. Utley, *Frontiersmen in Blue* (Lincoln: University of Nebraska Press, 1967); Francis Paul Prucha, *Broadaxe and Bayonet: The Role of the United States Army in the Development of the Northwest, 1815–1860* (Lincoln: University of Nebraska Press, 1953); Robert Wooster, *Soldiers, Sutlers, and Settlers: Garrison Life on the Texas Frontier* (College Station: Texas A&M University Press, 1987).

12. Martin Dugard, *The Training Ground: Grant, Lee, Sherman, and Davis in the Mexican War, 1846–1848* (New York: Little, Brown and Co, 2008), 165; James A. Huston, *The Sinews of War: Army Logistics, 1775–1953* (Washington, DC: Office of the Chief of Military History, United States Army, 1966), 145; Don Graham, *Kings of Texas: The 150-year Saga of an American Ranching Empire* (Hoboken, NJ: Wiley, 2003), 18–19; Tom Lea, *The King Ranch* (Boston: Little, Brown and, 1957), 20–22; Smith, *The Old Army in Texas*, 80; David Montejano, *Anglos and Mexicans In the Making of Texas, 1836–1986* (Austin, TX: Univ. of Texas Press, 1999), 20; Joe B. Frantz, "The Significance of Frontier Forts to Texas," *The Southwestern Historical Quarterly*, Vol. 74, No. 2 (Oct., 1970): 205; James A. Huston, *The Sinews of War: Army Logistics, 1775–1953* (Washington: Office of the Chief of Military History, United States Army, 1966), 139; Thomas Jesup to Henry Stanton, 11 September 1846 Letters Sent by the Office of the Quartermaster General, microfilm no M745, Roll 21, 134; Smith, *The Old Army in Texas*, 56.

13. Montejano, *Anglos and Mexicans*, 19–20; Alonzo, *Tejano Legacy*, 73–74, 103–104; *River of Hope*, 35–36, 44–46.

14. Crimmins, "Mansfield's Report," 130; Alonzo, *Tejano Legacy*,100; Robert Frazer, *Forts of the West: Military Forts and Presidios and Posts Commonly Called Forts West of the Mississippi River to 1898* (Norman: University of Oklahoma Press, 1965), 144–145, 157; Helen Chapman, *The News from Brownsville: Helen Chapman's Letters from the Texas Military Frontier, 1848–1852*, ed. Caleb Coker (Austin: Published for the Barker Texas History Center by the Texas State Historical Association, 1992), 18; Smith, *The Old Army in Texas*, 56, 77–78.

15. United States, Congress. *Report on the United States Boundary Survey.* Senate Executive Document No. 108, 34th Congress, 1st Session.Washington, D.C., [Serial Set 520], 60; Crimmins, "Mansfield's Report," 130; Chapman, *Notes*,24, 81, 87, 130; Tate, *Frontier Army*, 128; Frazer, *Forts of the West*, 144–145; Graf, *The Economic History*, 232–233; *American Flag*, September 12, 1848, May 5, August 11, 1847; Arnoldo de León and Kenneth L. Stewart, "Lost Dreams and Found Fortunes: Mexican and

Anglo Immigrants in South Texas, 1850–1900," *Western Historical Quarterly*, Vol. 14, No. 3 (Jul., 1983): 295; González-Quiroga, *War and Peace*, 94; US Census Bureau, *Census of 1860*, Cameron County, Fort Brown Garrison.

16. *Boundary Survey*, 62; Frazer, *Forts of the West*, 1158–159; *Boundary Survey*, 62; Graf, *The Economic History*, 257–258.

17. *Boundary Survey*, 9; De León, *Tejano Community*, 17; Lea, *The King Ranch*, 43; Graf, *The Economic History*, 259, 261; *American Flag*, June 10, 1848; *Rio Grande Sentinel* (Brownsville), December 25, 1850; Kelley, *River of Lost Dreams*, 38; US Census Bureau, *Census of 1860*, Starr County, Ringgold Barracks; Juan Mora-Torres, *The Making of the Mexican Border* (Austin: University of Texas Press, 2001), 32.

18. *Boundary Survey*, 67; Crimmins, "Mansfield's Report," 130; Valerio-Jiménez, *Identity and Nation*, 222–223; Frazer, *Forts of the West*, 154; Smith, *The Old Army in Texas*, 72. For more on Laredo in the nineteenth century see John A. Adams, *Conflict and Commerce on the Río Grande: Laredo, 1755–1955* (College Station: Texas A&M University Press, 2008); US Census Bureau, *Census of 1860*, Webb County, Fort McIntosh.

19. Crimmins, "Mansfield's Report," 131; *Boundary Survey*, 68; Frazer, *Forts of the West*, 1148–149; Smith, *The Old Army in Texas*, 63; Kelley, *River of Lost Dreams*, 35, 40, 42; González-Quiroga, *War and Peace*, 93–94, 134; William T. Kerrigan, "Race, Expansion, and Slavery in Eagle Pass, Texas, 1852," *The Southwestern Historical Quarterly*, 101, no. 3 (January 1998): 280, 282, 286, 291, 295; US Census Bureau, *Census of 1860*, Maverick County, Fort Duncan.

20. Smith, *The U.S. Army*, 36; Frazer, *Forts of the West*, 150, 156. Quoted in Frazer, *Forts of the West*, 150; Smith, *The Old Army in Texas*, 64, 74; De León, *The Tejano Community*, 17.

21. De León, *Tejano Community*, 87–89, 118; Smith, *The U.S. Army*, 8; Frederick Law Olmstead, *A Journey Through Texas, or, A saddle-trip on the southwestern frontier: with a statistical appendix*, (New York: Dix, Edwards & Co., 1857), 160; *San Antonio Herald*, March 13, 1858, 2; Teresa Griffin Vielé, *Following the Drum: A Glimpse of the Frontier*, (Lincoln: University of Nebraska Press, 1984), 148; González-Quiroga, *War and Peace*, 121–122, 161.

22. Graf, *The Economic History*, 175–176; *American Flag*, August 26, August 29, 1846; Samuel E. Bell and James M. Smallwood, "Zona Libre: Trade and Diplomacy on the Mexican Border 1858–1905," *Arizona and the West*, Vol. 24, No. 2 (Summer, 1982): 120, 124–125.

23. Mora-Torres, *The Making of the Mexican Border*, 13.

24. Stambaugh, *The Lower Rio Grande Valley of Texas*, 92, 94, 103, 161, 162; Caleb Coker, ed., *News From Brownsville*, 106–107, 307, 311; J. L. Allhands, *Gringo Builders*, (Privately Printed, 1931), 19, 104–105; Oats, ed., *Rip Ford's Texas*, 475, 458, 461, 463, 465, 469; Marilyn McAdams Sibley, "Charles Stillman: A Case Study of Entrepreneurship on the Rio Grande, 1861–1865," The Southwestern Historical Quarterly, 77, no. 2 (October 1973): 222–223; Paul Horgan, *Great River: The Rio Grande in North American History* (Middletown, CT: Wesleyan University Press, 1984), 105–106.

25. Graham, *Kings of Texas*, 21–22, 30; Graf, "Economic History" 198–199; Sizer, *The King Ranch Story*, 14–15; Monday and Colley, *Voices from the Wild Horse Desert*, 9; Stambaugh, *The Lower Rio Grande Valley of Texas*, 73, 79.

26. Caleb, Coker, "Chapman, William Warren," *Handbook of Texas Online*, accessed July 18, 2023, https://www.tshaonlin.org/handbook/entries/chapman-william -warren; Caleb Coker, ed., *News From Brownsville*, xxi, 56, 61, 307, 361–362; John Woodhouse Audubon, *Audubon's Western Journal, 1849–1850* (Tucson, Arizona: The University of Arizona Press, 1984), 50–51, 55.

27. Jovita González Mireles, "Social Life in Cameron, Starr, and Zapata Counties," MA Thesis, University of Texas Austin, 1930, 84; Stambaugh, *The Lower Rio Grande Valley of Texas*, 79, 161, 162; Allhands, *Gringo Builders*, 106; Horgan, *Great River*, 100–101.

28. Natalie Ornish, "Mussina, Simon," *Handbook of Texas Online, accessed July 17, 2023,* https://www.tshaonline.org/handbook/entires/mussina-simon; Graf, "Economic History," 233; Caleb Coker, ed., *News From Brownsville*, 16, 50, 102, 107, 339; Allhands, *Gringo Builders*, 104; Ira Rosenwaike, "The Mussina Family: Early American Jews?," *American Jewish History*, Vol. 75, No. 4 (June 1986): 400–401.

29. Grace Edman, "Woodhouse, Humphrey Eugene," *Handbook of Texas Online*, accessed July 14, 2023, https://www.tshaonline.org/handbook/entries/woodhouse -humphrey-eugene; Graf, "Economic History," 404, 693; Allhands, *Gringo Builders*, 110; John Henry Brown, *Indian Wars and Pioneers of Texas*, (Austin: L. E. Daniel,), 584–584; Amberson, *I Would Rather Sleep in Texas*, 122.

30. Graf, "Economic History," 208, 404; Stambaugh, *The Lower Rio Grande Valley of Texas*, 99, 161, 162; Allhands, *Gringo Builders*, 104.; Oats, ed., *Rip Ford's Texas*, 327, 460; Amberson, *I Would Rather Sleep in Texas*, 122; Alicia A. Garza and Christopher Long, "Cameron County." *Handbook of Texas Online*, accessed July 17, 2023, http:// www.tshaonline.org/handbook.entries/cameron-county; Stambaugh, *The Lower Rio Grande Valley of Texas*, 92; González-Quiroga, *War and Peace*, 155–156.

31. Graham, *Kings of Texas*, 21–22, 30; Graf, "Economic History" 198–199; Sizer, *The King Ranch Story*, 14–15; Monday and Colley, *Voices from the Wild Horse Desert*, 9; Stambaugh, *The Lower Rio Grande Valley of Texas*, 73, 79.

32. Graham, *Kings of Texas*, 37, 38. Letter cited in Lea, *The King Ranch*, 43; Graf, "Economic History," 360–361; Mona D. Sizer, *The King Ranch Story: Truth and Myth*, (Republic of Texas Press: Plano, Texas, 1999), 13; Stambaugh, *The Lower Rio Grande Valley of Texas*, 106.

33. Graf, "Economic History," 214–218, 222, 263–265; Valerio-Jiménez, *River of Hope*, 178–179; *Corpus Christi Star*, August 4, 1849; M. W. Martin, "California Emigrant Roads through Texas," *Southwestern Historical Quarterly*, 28 (April 1925): 290.

34. Graham, *Kings of Texas*, 38–39; Caleb Coker, "Chapman, Willam Waren," *Handbook of Texas Online*, accessed February 17, 2019, https://www.tshaonline.org/handbook /entries/chapman-william-warren; Lea, *The King Ranch*, 59, 72–73; Allhands, *Gringo Builders*, 19–20.

35. "Contracts—War Department—For 1856," *Letter from the Secretary of* War, House Exec. Doc. 59, 34th Congress, 3rd Session, 30, 31; Kelley, *River of Hope,* 58–59.

36. Graham, *Kings of Texas,* 38–40; Lea, *The King Ranch,* 87–89; Graf, "Economic History," 214, 227–228; *American Flag,* May 17, 1848; *Corpus Christi Star,* November 21, 1848; Caleb Coker, ed., *News From Brownsville,* 192, 326.

37. Graham, *Kings of Texas,* 60–61, 65–67; Lea, *The King Ranch,* 103; Valerio-Jiménez, *River of Hope,*142–144; Sizer, *The King Ranch Story,* 29, 51; Stambaugh, *The Lower Rio Grande Valley of Texas,* 145; Allhands, *Gringo Builders,* 21–23, 27, 106; Oats, ed., *Rip Ford's Texas,* 461; Gonzalez-Quiroga, *War and Peace,* 31.

38. Graf, "Economic History," 404.

39. Tax Rolls, Cameron County, 1852, 1856, 1860; Tax Rolls, Starr County, 1852, 1856, 1860; Horgan, *Great River,* 99–100.

40. Arnoldo de León and Kenneth L. Stewart, "Lost Dreams and Found Fortunes: Mexican and Anglo Immigrants in South Texas, 1850–1900," *Western Historical Quarterly,* Vol. 14, No. 3 (Jul., 1983): 296–297, 304; US Census Bureau, *Census of 1860,* Statistics of Texas; US Census Bureau, *Census of 1870,* Statistics of Texas.

41. Mireles, "Social Life," 85–88.

42. Gonzalez-Quiroga, *War and Peace,* 23–24.

Conclusion

1. "Receipts and Expenditures," *Letter from the Secretary of the Treasury,* Treasury Department, 1848, 1849, 1853, 1857, 1860, Library of Congress.

Bibliography

Archives and Documents

John Lenthall Papers. Independence Seaport Museum, Philadelphia, PA.

Library of Congress

  Receipts and Expenditures. Letters of the Secretary of the Treasury.

Mexican War Collection. Special Collections, University of Texas at Arlington.

National Archives and Records Administration, Washington, DC (hereafter cited as NARA). Records of the US Army Adjutant General's Office, 1780–1917. Record Group (hereafter cited as RG 94).

  General and Special Order, 1847–1860

    Orders of Gen. Zachary Taylor to the Army of Occupation in the Mexican War, 1845–1847. M 29.

    General and Special Orders Issued by General Winfield Scott, Headquarters of the Army, War with Mexico, 1845–1847. M 2125.

    Mexico Custom House Collector's Record of Customs Revenue Collected, 1847–1848.

NARA, Washington, DC Records of the Office of the Quartermaster General, 1774–1985. RG 92.

  Letters Sent by the Office of the Quartermaster General 1818–1870. M 745.

  Letters Received by the Office of the Quartermaster General 1818–1870.

    Teamster Contracts

U.S. Senate and Congressional Records

Correspondence with General Taylor. *House Documents*, No. 119, 29th Congress, 2nd Session, Serial Set 500.

  Mexican War Correspondence. *House Executive Documents*, No. 60, 30th Congress, 1st Session, Serial Set 520.

  Report on the United States Boundary Survey. Senate Executive Documents, No. 108, 34th Congress, 1st Session, Serial Set 833.

Congressional Globe: 23d Congress to the 42d Congress, Dec. 2, 1833, to March 3, 1873.

Cross, Trueman. *Military Laws of the United States; including those relating to the Marine Corps, to which is prefixed the Constitution of the United States.* Washington, DC: George Templeman, 1838.

Peters, Richard, ed. *The Public Statutes at Large of the United States of America from the Organization of the Government in 1789, to March 3, 1845.* Boston: Charles C. Little and James Brown, 1850.

    An Act to provide for the better Organization of the Treasury, and for the Collection, Safe-Keeping, Transfer, and Disbursement of the public Revenue. US Statutes at Large 9 (1845–1847): 59–66.

    An Act concerning the disbursement of public money. US Statutes at Large 3 (1821–1823): 723–724.

    Reports of the Committee of Investigation Sent in 1873 by the Mexican Government to the Frontier of Texas. New York: Printed by Baker & Godwin, 1875.

Switzler, William F. *Report on Internal Commerce of the United State for the Fiscal Year 1886.* Washington, DC: Department of the Treasury, 1889.

United States Census Bureau, 1850 Census, digital image, *FamilySearch.org.*

United States Census Bureau, 1860 Census, *FamilySearch.org.*

United States War Department. *General Regulations for the Army of the United States, 1841.* Washington, DC: J. and G. S. Gideon, 1841.

United States. Department of State. *Consular Despatches, Matamoros.* Washington, DC, 1909.

United States. Department of State. *Diplomatic Correspondence of the Republic of Texas Part II.* Washington, DC, 1909.

United States. Department of War. *Military Laws of the United States; including those relating to the Marine Corps, to which is prefixed the Constitution of the Unites States.* Compiled by Colonel Trueman Cross. Washington, DC: George Templeman, 1838.

United States. Department of War. *Official Army Register for 1847.* Washington, DC: Adjutant General's Office and C. Alexander, Printer, 1847.

Newspapers
San Antonio Express
American Flag
Rio Grande Sentinel (Brownsville)
San Antonio Herald
Nueces Valley (Corpus Christi)
Corpus Christi Star

Books
Adams, John A. *Conflict and Commerce on the Río Grande: Laredo, 1755–1955.* College Station: Texas A&M University Press, 2008.

Allhands, J. L. *Gringo Builders.* Iowa City: Private Print., 1931.

Almonte, Juan Nepomuceno. *Almonte's Texas: Juan N. Almonte's 1834 Inspection, Secret Report, and Role in the 1836 Campaign.* ed. Jack Jackson, trans. John Wheat. Austin: Published by the Texas State Historical Association, 2003.

Alonzo, Armando C. *Tejano Legacy: Rancheros and Settlers in South Texas, 1734–1900.* Albuquerque: University of New Mexico Press, 1998.

Amberson, Mary Margaret McAllen, James A. McAllen, and Margaret H. McAllen, *I Would Rather Sleep in Texas: A History of the Lower Rio Grande Valley & the People of the Santa Anita Land Grant* (Austin, TX: Texas State Historical Association, 2003).

Arreola, Daniel D. *Tejano South Texas: A Mexican American Cultural Province.* Austin: University of Texas Press, 2002.

Barragan, José, ed. *Actas Constitucionales Mexicanas (1821–1824).* Mexico: Instituto de Investigaciones Jurídicas. Universidad Nacional Autónoma de México, 1980.

Bauer, K. Jack. *The Mexican War, 1846–1848.* New York: Macmillan, 1974.

———. *Surfboats and Horse Marines: U.S. Naval Operations in the Mexican War, 1846–48.* Annapolis: US Naval Institute, 1969.

———. *Zachary Taylor: Soldier, Planter, Statesman of the Old Southwest.* Baton Rouge: Louisiana State University Press, 1985.

Baumgartner, Alice L. *South to Freedom: Runaway Slaves to Mexico and the Road to Civil War.* New York: Basic Books, 2020.

Blücher, Maria Augusta Von. *Maria Von Blücher's Corpus Christi: Letters from the South Texas Frontier, 1849–1879,* ed. Bruce S. Cheeseman. College Station: Texas A&M University Press, 2002.

Bolton, Herbert Eugene. *The Spanish Borderlands.* Reprint. Lexington: First Rate Publishers, 2017 (1921).

Brands, H. W. *Andrew Jackson: His Life and Times.* New York: Doubleday, 2005.

Campbell, Randolph B. *Gone to Texas: A History of the Lone Star State.* New York: Oxford University Press, 2003.

Carrigan, William D. *The Making of a Lynching Culture: Violence and Vigilantism in Central Texas, 1836–1916.* Urbana: University of Illinois Press, 2004.

Chaffin, Tom. *Pathfinder: John Charles Frémont and the Course of American Empire.* Norman: University of Oklahoma Press, 2014.

Chapman, Helen. *The News from Brownsville: Helen Chapman's Letters from the Texas Military Frontier, 1848–1852,* ed. Caleb Coker. Austin: Published for the Barker Texas History Center by the Texas State Historical Association, 1992.

Chipman, Donald E. *Spanish Texas: 1519–1821.* Austin: University of Texas Press, 1992.

Clarke, Dwight L. *Stephen Watts Kearny: Soldier of the West.* Norman: Oklahoma University Press, 1961.

Connelley, William Elsey. *Doniphan's Expedition: War with Mexico, 1846–1847, & the Conquest of New Mexico & California.* Topeka: William Connelley, 1907.

Coulter, Richard and Thomas Barclay. *Volunteers: The Mexican War Journals of Private Richard Coulter and Sergeant Thomas Barclay, Company E, Second Pennsylvania Infantry,* ed. Allan Peskin. Kent, OH: Kent State University Press, 1991.

Croix, Teodoro de, Alfred Barnaby Thomas, trans. *Teodoro de Croix and the Northern Frontier of New Spain, 1776–1783: From the Original Documents in the Archives of the Indies.* Norman: University of Oklahoma Press, 1968.

Cunningham, Jr., Noble E. *The Presidency of James Monroe.* Lawrence: University of Kansas Press, 1996.

Davis, George T. M. *Autobiography of the Late Col. Geo. T. M. Davis, Captain and Aide-de-camp Scott's Army of Invasion (Mexico), from Posthumous Papers.* New York: Press of Jenkins and McCowan, 1891.

Dawson, Joseph G. *Doniphan's Epic March: The 1st Missouri Volunteers in the Mexican War.* Lawrence: University Press of Kansas, 1999.

DeGarmo, Frank. *Pathfinders of Texas, 1836–1846.* Austin: Press of Von Boeckmann-Jones Co., 1951.

de León, Arnoldo. *The Tejano Community, 1836–1900.* Albuquerque: University of New Mexico Press, 1982.

———. *They Called Them Greasers: Anglo Attitudes toward Mexicans in Texas, 1821–1900.* Austin: University of Texas Press, 1983.

———. and Kenneth L. Stewart. *Tejanos and the Numbers Game: A Socio-historical Interpretation from the Federal Censuses, 1850–1900.* Albuquerque: University of New Mexico Press, 1989.

DeLay, Brian. *War of a Thousand Deserts: Indian Raids and the U.S.-Mexican War.* New Haven: Yale University Press, 2008.

Deutsch, Sarah. "Landscape of Enclaves: Race Relations in the West" in *Under and Open Sky: Rethinking America's Western Past.* ed. William Cronon, George Miles, and Jay Gitlin (New York: W.W. Norton, 1992).

Dobak, William A. *Fort Riley and Its Neighbors: Military Money and Economic Growth, 1853–1895.* Norman: University of Oklahoma Press, 1998.

Domenech, Emmanuel. *Missionary Adventures in Texas and Mexico.: A Personal Narrative of Six Years' Sojourn in Those Regions.*, ed. Henry Cohen. London: Longman, Brown, Green, Longmans, and Roberts, 1858.

Dugard, Martin. *The Training Ground: Grant, Lee, Sherman, and Davis in the Mexican War, 1846–1848.* New York: Little, Brown and Co, 2008.

Dusinberre, William. *Slavemaster President: The Double Career of James Polk.* Oxford: Oxford University Press, 2003.

Edwards, Frank S. *A Campaign in New Mexico.* Ann Arbor: University Microfilms, 1974 (1966).

Eisenhower, John S. D. *Agent of Destiny: The Life and Time of General Winfield Scott.* New York: The Free Press, 1997.

———. *So Far from God: The U.S. War with Mexico, 1846–1848.* New York: Random House, 1989.

———. *Zachary Taylor.* New York: Times Books, 2008.

Elliot, Charles Winslow. *Winfield Scott: The Soldier and the Man.* New York: Macmillan Company, 1937.

Finer, S. E. *The Man on Horseback; the Role of the Military in Politics.* New York: Praeger, 1962.

Folsom, Bradley. *Arredondo: The Last Ruler of Texas and Northeastern New Spain.* Norman: University of Oklahoma, 2017.

Frazer, Robert Walter. *Forts and Supplies: The Role of the Army in the Economy of the Southwest, 1846–1861.* Albuquerque: University of New Mexico Press, 1983.

Frémont, John Charles. *Memoirs of My Life and Times.* New York: Belford, Clarke and Co., 1886.

———. Donald Jackson and Mary Lee Spence, eds. *The Expedition of John Charles Frémont.* Urbana: University of Illinois Press, 1970.

Gálvez, Bernardo de, Donald Emmet Worcester, trans. *Instructions for Governing the Interior Provinces of New Spain, 1786.* Berkely: Quivira Society, 1951.

Gammel, Hans Peter Nielsen, comp. *Laws of Texas, 1822–1897.* Austin: Gammel, 1898.

García, Luis Navarro. *Don José De Gálvez Y La Comandancia General De Las Provincias Internas Del Norte De Nueva España.* Sevilla: Consejo Superior De Investigaciones Científicas, 1964.

de la Garza, Beatriz. *From the Republic of the Rio Grande: A Personal History of the Place and the People.* Austin: University of Texas Press, 2013.

Gibson, George Rutledge and Ralph P. Bieber, Ed., *Journal of a Soldier under Kearny and Doniphan, 1846–1847,* (The Arthur C. Clark Company: Glendale, California, 1935).

Gillett, Mary C. *The Army Medical Department, 1818–1865.* Washington, DC: Center of Military History, United States Army, 1987.

González-Quiroga, Miguel Ángel. *War and Peace on the Rio Grande Frontier, 1830–1880.* Norman: University of Oklahoma Press, 2020.

Graham, Don. *Kings of Texas: The 150-year Saga of an American Ranching Empire.* Hoboken, NJ: John Wiley & Sons, 2003.

Greaser, Galen D. *New Guide to Spanish and Mexican Land Grants in South Texas.* Austin: Texas General Land Office, 2009.

Greenberg, Amy S. *A Wicked War: Polk, Clay, Lincoln, and the 1846 US Invasion of Mexico.* New York: Vintage Books, 2013.

Guardino, Peter. *Dead March: A History of the Mexican-American War.* Cambridge: Harvard University Press, 2017.

Hämäläinen, Pekka. *The Comanche Empire.* New Haven: Yale University Press, 2008.

Hardin, Stephen L. *Texian Iliad: A Military History of the Texas Revolution, 1835–1836.* Austin: University of Texas Press, 2015.

Hart, Herbert M. *Old Forts of the Southwest.* Seattle, Washington: Superior, 1964.

Henry, Robert Selph. *The Story of the Mexican War.* New York: Bobbs-Merrill Company., 1950.

Hess, Earl J. *Civil War Logistics: A Study of Military Transportation.* Baton Rouge: Louisiana State University Press, 2017.

Hitchcock, Ethan Allen. *Fifty Years in Camp and Field.* New York: Putnam, 1909.

Hinojosa, Gilbert. *A Borderlands Town in Transition*. Austin: Texas A&M University Press, 1983.

Horgan, Paul. *Great River: The Rio Grande in North American History*. Middletown, CT: Wesleyan University Press, 1984.

Huston, James A. *The Sinews of War: Army Logistics, 1775–1953*. Washington, DC: Office of the Chief of Military History, United States Army, 1966.

Inskeep, Steve. *Imperfect Union*. New York: Penguin Books, 2021.

Jackson, Jack, ed. *Imaginary Kingdom: Texas as Seen by the Rivera and Rubí Military Expeditions, 1727 and 1767*. Austin: Texas State Historical Association, 1995.

Jacobs, James Ripley. *Tarnished Warrior: Major-General James Wilkinson*. New York: Macmillan Company, 1938.

Jacoby, Karl. *Shadows at Dawn: An Apache Massacre and the Violence of History*. New York: Penguin Books, 2009.

Jackson, W. Turrentine. *Wagon Roads West; a Study of Federal Road Surveys and Construction in the Trans-Mississippi West, 1846–1869*. New Haven: Yale University Press, 1965.

Johnson, Benjamin, and Andrew R. Graybill. *Bridging National Borders in North America: Transnational and Comparative Histories*. Durham, NC: Duke University Press, 2010.

Johnson, Timothy D. *A Gallant Little Army: The Mexico City Campaign*. Lawrence: University Press of Kansas, 2007.

Johnson, Timothy. *Winfield Scott: The Quest for Military Glory*. Lawrence: University Press of Kansas, 1998.

Jones, Oakah L. *Los Paisanos: Spanish Settlers on the Northern Frontier of New Spain*. Norman: University of Oklahoma Press, 1978.

Karamanski, Theodore J. *Schooner Passage: Sailing Ships and the Lake Michigan Frontier*. Detroit: Wayne State University Press, 2000.

Kelley Pat. *River of Lost Dreams: Navigation on the Rio Grande*. University of Nebraska Press: Lincoln, 1986.

Kendall, George Wilkins. *Dispatches from the Mexican War*. Norman: University of Oklahoma Press, 1999.

Kiefer, Chester L. *Maligned General: The Biography of Thomas Sidney Jesup*. San Rafael, CA: Presidio Press, 1979.

Lack, Paul D. *The Texas Revolutionary Experience: A Political and Social History, 1835–1836*. College Station: Texas A&M University Press, 1992.

Launius, Roger D. *Alexander William Doniphan: Portrait of a Missouri Moderate*. Columbia: University of Missouri Press, 1997.

Lewis, Felice Flanery. *Trailing Clouds of Glory: Zachary Taylor's Mexican War Campaign and His Emerging Civil War Leaders*. Tuscaloosa: The University of Alabama Press, 2010.

Lynn, John A. *Feeding Mars: Logistics in Western Warfare from the Middle Ages to the Present*. Boulder, CO: Westview Press, 1993.

Lea, Tom. *The King Ranch*. Boston: Little, Brown and, Co., 1957.

Levinson, Irving W. *Wars within War: Mexican Guerrillas, Domestic Elites, and the United States of America, 1846–1848*. Fort Worth: TCU Press, 2005.

Magoffin, Susan Shelby. *Down the Santa Fe Trail and into Mexico: The Diary of Susan Shelby Magoffin, 1846–1847*, ed. Stella M. Drumm. Bethesda, MD: Microfiche Project of University Publications of America, 1998.

Martínez, Oscar J. *Troublesome Border*. Tucson: University of Arizona Press, 1988.

McCaffrey, James. *Army of Manifest Destiny: The American Soldier in the Mexican War, 1846–1848*. New York: New York University Press, 1992.

Members of Starr County Historical Society. *When Rio Grande City Was Young*. Pan American University, Edinburg, Texas, 1986.

Monday, Jane Clements, and Betty Baily Colley, *Voices from the Wild Horse Desert: The Vaquero Families of the King and Kenedy Ranches*, (University of Texas Press: Austin, 1997).

Monday, Jane Clements, and Frances Brannen Vick. *Petra's Legacy: The South Texas Ranching Empire of Petra Vela and Mifflin Kenedy*. College Station: Texas A&M University Press, 2007.

Mora-Torres, Juan. *The Making of the Mexican Border*. Austin: University of Texas Press, 2001.

Mier y Terán, Manuel de, *Texas by Terán: The Diary Kept by General Manuel De Mier Y Terán on His 1828 Inspection of Texas*, ed. Jack Jackson, trans. John Wheat. Austin: University of Texas Press, 2000.

Miller, Darlis A. *Soldiers and Settlers: Military Supply in the Southwest, 1861–1885*. Albuquerque: University of New Mexico Press, 1989.

Miller, Edmund Thomas. *A Financial History of Texas, 1519–1970*. Austin: University of Texas Bulletin no. 37, 1916.

Missall, John and Mary Lou Missall, *The Seminole Wars: America's Longest Indian Conflict*. Gainesville: University Press of Florida, 2004.

Montejano, David. *Anglos and Mexicans In the Making of Texas, 1836–1986*. Austin: University of Texas Press, 1999.

Murphey, Douglas A. *Two Armies on the Rio Grande: The First Campaign of the US-Mexican War*. College Station: Texas A&M Press, 2015.

Nichols, Edward J. *Zachary Taylor's Little Army*. Garden City, NY: Doubleday, 1963.

Niven, John. *John C. Calhoun and the Price of Union: A Biography*. Baton Rouge: Louisiana State University Press, 1988.

O'Brien, William Patrick. *Merchants of Independence: International Trade on the Santa Fe Trail, 1827–1860*. Kirksville, MO: Truman State University Press, 2014.

Olmstead, Frederick Law. *A Journey Through Texas, or, A saddle-trip on the southwestern frontier: with a statistical appendix*. New York: Dix, Edwards & Co., 1857.

Oswandel, J. Jacob. *Notes of the Mexican War, 1846–1848*, ed. Timothy D. Johnson and Nathaniel Cheairs Hughes. Knoxville: University of Tennessee Press, 2010.

Parker, William H. *Recollections of a Naval Officer, 1841–1865*. New York: Charles Scribners' Sons, 1883.

Peck, John James. *Sign of the Eagle: A View of Mexico, 1830–1855*. San Diego: Copley Books, 1970.

Peskin, Allan. *Winfield Scott and the Profession of Arms.* Kent, OH: Kent State University Press, 2003.

Pierce, Frank Cushman. *Texas' Last Frontier: A Brief History of the Lower Rio Grande Valley.* Menahsa, Wisconsin: Collegiate Press, 1917.

Pletcher, David M. *The Diplomacy of Annexation: Texas, Oregon, and the Mexican War.* Columbia: University of Missouri Press, 1975.

Priestley, Herbert Ingram. *José De Gálvez: Visitor-general of New Spain (1765–1771).* Berkeley: University of California Press, 1916.

Prucha, Francis Paul. *Broadaxe and Bayonet: The Role of the United States Army in the Development of the Northwest, 1815–1860.* Lincoln: University of Nebraska Press, 1953.

Remini, Robert V. *Andrew Jackson and the Course of American Democracy, 1833–1845, Vol. III.* New York: Harper & Row, Publishers, 1984.

Reséndez, Andrés. *Changing National Identities at the Frontier: Texas and New Mexico, 1800–1850.* Cambridge, UK: Cambridge University Press, 2005.

Richmond, Patricia Joy. *Trail to Disaster: The Route of John C. Frémont's Fourth Expedition from Big Timbers, Colorado, through the San Luis Valley, to Taos, New Mexico.* Niwot: University Press of Colorado, 1989.

Richardson, James D., ed. *A Compilation of the Messages and Papers of the Presidents, 1789–1897.* 10 vols. New York: Bureau of National Literature, 1897.

Ricketts, Norma B. *The Mormon Battalion: U.S. Army of the West, 1846–1847.* Logan: Utah State University Press, 1996.

Risch, Erna. *Quartermaster Support of the Army: A History of the Corps, 1775–1939.* Washington, DC: Center of Military History, United States Army, 1989.

Roberts, Robert B. *Encyclopedia of Historic Forts the Military Posts of the United States.* New York: Macmillan Publishing Company, 1988.

Robertson, Brian. *Wild Horse Desert.* Edinburg, TX: New Santander Press, 1985.

Robinson, Jacob. *A Journal of the Santa Fe Expedition Under Colonel Doniphan.* Princeton: Princeton University Press, 1932.

Rodríguez O., Jaime E., and Kathryn Vincent, eds., *Myths, Misdeeds, and Misunderstandings: The Roots of Conflict in U.S.-Mexican Relations.* Wilmington, DE: SR Books, 1997.

Rolle, Andrew F. *John Charles Frémont: Character as Destiny.* Norman: University of Oklahoma Press, 1991.

Rosenbaum, Robert J. *Mexicano Resistance in the Southwest.* Dallas: Southern Methodist University Press, 1998.

Santa Anna, Antonio López de. *The Eagle: The Autobiography of Santa Anna,* ed. Ann Fears Crawford. Austin: State House Press, 1988.

Schwartz, Rosalie, *Across the Rio to Freedom: U.S. Negroes in Mexico.* El Paso: Texas Western Press/The University of Texas El Paso, 1975.

Scott, Florence Johnson. *Royal Land Grants of the Río Grande, 1777–1821: Early History of Large Grants Made by Spain to Families in Jurisdiction of Reynosa.* Rio Grande City: La Retama Press, 1969.

Scott, Winfield. *Memoirs of Lieut.-General Scott, LL. D.* 2 Vols. New York: Sheldon, 1864.

Semmes, Raphael. *Service Afloat and Ashore during the Mexican War.* Cincinnati: W. H. Moore & Co., 1851.

Shrader, Charles R. *U.S. Military Logistics, 1607–1991: A Research Guide.* New York: Greenwood Press, 1992.

Sizer, Mona D., *The King Ranch Story: Truth and Myth.* Republic of Texas Press: Plano, Texas, 1999.

Smith, Justin Harvey. *The War with Mexico,* 2 vols. New York: Macmillan Company, 1919.

Smith, Thomas T. *The U.S. Army and the Texas Frontier Economy, 1845–1900.* College Station: Texas A&M University Press, 1999.

Spencer, Ivor Debenham. *The Victor and the Spoils: A Life of William L. Marcy.* Providence, RI: Brown University Press, 1959.

Stambaugh, J. Lee, and Lillian J. Stambaugh, *The Lower Rio Grande Valley of Texas.* San Antonio: Naylor Company, 1954.

Stewart, Kenneth L., and Arnoldo De León, *Not Enough Room: Mexicans, Anglos, and Socioeconomic Change in Texas, 1850–1900.* Albuquerque: University of Mexico Press, 1993.

Swadesh, Frances Leon. *Los primeros pobladores: Hispanic Americans of the Ute Frontier.* Notre Dame, Indiana: University of Notre Dame Press, 1974.

Tate, Michael L. *The Frontier Army in the Settlement of the West.* Norman: University of Oklahoma Press, 1999.

Taylor, Paul S. *An American Mexican Frontier: Nueces County, Texas.* Chapel Hill: University of North Carolina Press, 1934.

Taylor, Quintard, *In Search of the Racial Frontier: African Americans in the American West, 1528–1990.* New York: W. W. Norton & Company, 1998.

Taylor, Zachary. *Letters of Zachary Taylor from the Battle-fields of the Mexican War: Reprinted from the Originals in the Collection of Mr. William K. Bixby, of St. Louis, Mo.,* ed. William K. Bixby and William Holland Samson. New York: Kraus Reprint, 1970.

Temple, William G. "Memoir of the Landing of the United States Troops at Veracruz in 1847," in David Conner, *The Home Squadron Under Commodore Conner,* with Philip S. P. Conner. Philadelphia: P. S. P. Conner, 1896.

Thompson, Jerry D. *Cortina: Defending the Mexican Name in Texas.* College Station: Texas A&M University Press, 2007.

Tijerina, Andrew. *Tejanos and Texas under the Mexican Flag: 1821–1836.* College Station: Texas A&M University Press, 1994.

Torget, Andrew J. *Seeds of Empire: Cotton, Slavery, and the Transformation of the Texas Borderlands, 1800–1850.* Chapel Hill: University of North Carolina Press, 2015.

Townsend, Stephen A. *The Yankee Invasion of Texas.* College Station: Texas A&M University Press, 2006.

Turner, Frederick Jackson, Ray Allen Billington ed. *Selected Essays of Frederick Jackson Turner.* Englewood Cliffs, NJ: Prentice-Hall, 1961.

Utley, Robert M. *Frontiersmen in Blue: The United States Army and the Indian, 1848–1865.* Lincoln: University of Nebraska Press, 2014.

Valerio-Jiménez, Omar S. *River of Hope: Forging Identity and Nation in the Río Grande Borderlands*. Durham: Duke University Press, 2013.

Vielé, Teresa Griffin. *Following the Drum: A Glimpse of the Frontier*. Lincoln: University of Nebraska Press, 1984.

Waddell, Steve R. *United States Army Logistics: From the American Revolution to 9/11*. Santa Barbara: Praeger, 2010.

Wallace, Ernest, and David M. Vigness, eds., *Documents of Texas History*. Lubbock: Library, Texas Technological College, 1960.

Watson, Samuel. *Peacekeepers and Conquerors: The Army Officer Corps on the American Frontier, 1821–1846*. Lawrence: University of Kansas Press, 2013.

———, ed. *Warfare in the USA 1784–1861*. Burlington, VT: Ashgate Publishing, 2005.

Weber, David J. *The Mexican Frontier, 1821–1846*. Albuquerque: University of New Mexico Press, 1982.

Weddle, Robert S. *The French Thorn: Rival Explorers in the Spanish Sea, 1682–1762*. College Station: Texas A&M University Press, 1991.

Weigley, Russell F. *The American Way of War: A History of United States Military Strategy and Policy*. Bloomington: Indiana University Press, 1977.

Wilkinson, J. B. *Laredo and the Rio Grande Frontier*. Austin: Jenkins Book Pub. Co., 1975.

Wilson, Mark R. *The Business of Civil War: Military Mobilization and the State, 1861–1865*. Baltimore: The Johns Hopkins University Press, 2006.

Winders, Richard Bruce. *Crisis in the Southwest: The United States, Mexico, and the Struggle over Texas*. Lanham, MD: SR Books, 2004.

Wood, Robert. *Life in Laredo: A Documentary History from the Laredo Archives*. Denton: University of North Texas Press, 2004.

Wooster, Robert. *The American Military Frontiers: The United States Army in the West, 1783–1900*. Albuquerque: University of New Mexico Press, 2009.

———. *Soldiers, Sutlers, and Settlers: Garrison Life on the Texas Frontier*. College Station: Texas A&M University Press, 1987.

Woltjer, Rodger. *American Civil War: Support Services of the Union Army*. Hoosick Falls, NY: Merriam Press, 2017.

Wyman, Walker D. *The Wild Horse of the West*. The Caxton Printers: Caldwell, Ohio, 1945.

Articles, Thesis, and Dissertations

Adelman, Jeremy and Stephen Aron. "From Borderlands to Borders: Empires, Nation-states, and the Peoples in between in North American History." *The American Historical Review* 104, no. 3 (June 1999), 814–841.

Almonte, Juan N. "Statistical Report on Texas (1835) by Juan N. Almonte," trans. Carlos E. Casteñeda, *The Southwestern Historical Quarterly* 28, no. 3 (January 1925): 177–222.

Amero, Richard W. "The Mexican-American War in Baja California." *The Journal of San Diego History* 30, no. 1 (Winter 1984), 49–64.

Barker, Eugene C. "The Influence of Slavery in the Colonization of Texas." *The Southwestern Historical Quarterly* 28, no. 1 (July 1924), 3–36.

Barker, Stockbridge H. "Blueprint for Victory." *Army Logistician* 3 no. 4 (July/August 1971), 18–22.

Bauer, K. Jack. "The Veracruz Expedition of 1847." *Military Affairs* 20 no. 3 (Autumn 1956), 162–169.

Bell, Samuel E. and James M. Smallwood, "Zona Libre: Trade and Diplomacy on the Mexican Border 1858–1905," *Arizona and the West*, 24, no. 2 (Summer, 1982): 119–152.

Calderón, Roberto Ramón. "Mexican politics in the American era, 1846–1900: Laredo, Texas," PhD diss., 1993.

Cirillo, Vincent J. "'More Fatal than Powder and Shot': Dysentery in the U.S. Army during the Mexican War, 1846–48." *Perspectives in Biology and Medicine* 52, no. 3 (2009), 400–413.

Cornell, Sarah E. "Americans in the U.S. South and Mexico: A Transnational History of Race, Slavery, and Freedom, 1810–1910," PhD diss., New York University, 2008.

Crimmins, M. L. ed., "Colonel J. K. F. Mansfield's Report of the Inspection of the Department of Texas in 1856." *Southwestern Historical Quarterly* 42, no. 2 (October 1938), 122–148.

Davies Jr., Thomas M. "Assessments during the Mexican War: An Exercise in Futility." *New Mexico Historical Review* 41, no. 3 (1966).

"Dictamen Presentado a la Soberana Junta Gobernativa del Imperio Mexicanos, por la Comision de Relaciones Exteriores, December 29, 1821," quoted in Joseph Carl McElhannon, "Imperial Mexico and Texas, 1821–1823," *The Southwestern Historical Quarterly*, 53, no. 2 (October 1949), 117–150.

Fleischman, Richard K. and Thomas N. Tyson, "Developing Expertise: Two Episodes in Early Nineteenth Century U.S. Management Accounting History," *Business and Economic History*, 26, no. 2 (Winter 1997): 365–380.

Frantz, Joe B., "The Significance of Frontier Forts to Texas," *The Southwestern Historical Quarterly*, 74, no. 2 (October 1970): 204–222.

González, Jovita, "Social Life in Cameron, Starr, and Zapata Counties," M.A. thesis, University of Texas at Austin, 1930.

Graf, Leroy. "The Economic History of the Lower Río Grande Valley, 1820–1875." PhD diss., Harvard University, 1945.

Greaser, Galen D. and Jesus F. De La Teja, "Quieting Title to Spanish and Mexican Land Grants in the Trans-Nueces: The Bourland and Miller Commission, 1850–1852." *The Southwestern Historical Quarterly* 95, no. 4 (April 1992), 445–464.

Hämäläinen, Pekka, and Samuel Truett, "On Borderlands." *The Journal of American History* 98 no. 2 (September 2011), 338–361.

Hoskin, Keith W., and Richard H. Macve, "The Genesis of Accountability: The West Point Connections," *Accounting, Organizations, and Society*, 13, no. 1 (1988): 37–73.

Hoskin, Keith, and Richard Macve, "Reappraising the Genesis of Managerialism: A Reexamination of the Role of Accounting at the Springfield Armory, 1815–1845," *Accounting, Auditing, & Accountability Journal* 7, no. 2 (1994): 4–29.

Janicek, Ricki Shults. "The Development of Early Mexican Land Policy: Coahuila and Texas, 1810–1825." PhD diss., Tulane University, 1985.

Kelley, Sean. "'Mexico in His Head': Slavery and the Texas-Mexico Border, 1810–1860," *Journal of Social History* 37, no. 3 (Spring 2004), 709–723.

Kerrigan, William T., "Race, Expansion, and Slavery in Eagle Pass, Texas, 1852," *The Southwestern Historical Quarterly* 101, no. 3 (January 1998): 275–301.

King, Darwin L., Kathleen M. Premo, Carl J. Case, "Historical Influence on Modern Cost Accounting Practices," *Academy of Accounting and Financial Studies Journal*, 13, no. 4 (2009): 21–40.

Knight, Larry, "The Cart War: Defining American in San Antonio in the 1850s," *The Southwestern Historical Quarterly* 109, no. 3 (January 2006): 319–336.

Klyza, Christopher McGregory, "The United States Army, Natural Resources, and Political Development in the Nineteenth Century," *Polity* 35, no. 1 (Autumn 2002): 1–28.

de León, Arnoldo and Kenneth L. Stewart, "Lost Dreams and Found Fortunes: Mexican and Anglo American Immigrants in South Texas, 1850–1900," *Western Historical Quarterly* 14 (July 1983), 291–310.

Miller, Cynthia Ann. "The United States Army Logistics Complex, 1818–1845: A Case Study of the Northern Frontier." PhD diss., Syracuse University, 1991.

Mireles, Jovita González. "Social Life in Cameron, Starr, and Zapata Counties." MA Thesis, University of Texas Austin, 1930.

Mendoza, Alexander. "'For Our Own Best Interests:' Nineteenth-Century Laredo Tejanos, Military Service, and the Development of American Nationalism." *Southwestern Historical Quarterly* 115, no. 2 (2011), 125–152.

Moody, Marjory M. "The Evolution of Emerson as an Abolitionist." *American Literature* 17, no. 1 (March 1945), 1–21.

Nichols, James David. "The Line of Liberty: Runaway Slaves and Fugitive Peons in the Texas-Mexico Borderlands." *The Western Historical Quarterly* 44, no. 4 (Winter 2013), 413–433.

Reséndez, Andrés, "National Identity on a Shifting Border: Texas and New Mexico in the Age of Transition, 1821–1848," *Journal of American History* 86:2 (1999), 668–688.

Rosenwaike, Ira, "The Mussina Family: Early American Jews?" *American Jewish History*, 75, no. 4 (June 1986): 397–404.

Rippy, J. Fred, "Border Troubles along the Rio Grande, 1848–1860," *The Southwestern Historical Quarterly*, 23, no. 2 (Oct. 1919): 91–111.

Sibley, Marilyn McAdams, "Charles Stillman: A Case Study of Entrepreneurship on the Rio Grande, 1861–1865," *The Southwestern Historical Quarterly*, 77, no. 2 (October 1973): 227–240.

Starnes, Gary B., "Juan de Ugalde (1729–1816) and the Provincias Internas of Coahuila and Texas." MA Thesis, Texas Christian University, 1971.

Tyler, Ronnie C., "Fugitive Slaves in Mexico," *The Journal of Negro History* 57, no. 1, (January 1992), 1–12.

Valerio-Jiménez, Omar Santiago. "Indios Bárbaros, Divorcées, and Flocks of Vampires: Identity and Nation on The Río Grande, 1749–1894." PhD. diss., University of California, Los Angeles, 2001.

Weber, David J. "Turner, the Boltonians, and the Borderlands." *The American Historical Review* 91, no. 1 (February 1986), 66–81.

Websites

"Bustamante Decree 1830 & Turtle Bayou Resolutions." Accessed March 22, 2016. http://www.tamu.edu/faculty/ccbn/dewitt/consultations1.htm.

"Constitution of the State of Coahuila and Texas (1827), Preamble and Preliminary Provisions, 2014." Accessed March 22, 2016. http://tarlton.law.utexas.edu/constitutions/coahuila1827/preamble.

Handbook of Texas Online. https://www.tshaonline.org/handbook.

Haynes, Sam W. "The Battle of Monterrey." A Continent Divided: The U.S.-Mexico War. Accessed February 11, 2019. https://library.uta.edu/usmexicowar/item?content_id=144&format_id=1&ofst=1&ni=13.

Torget, Andrew, ed. "Decree No. 56, May 5, 1828," Texas Slavery Project, 2008. Accessed March 22, 2016. http://www.texasslaveryproject.org/sources/LawsOfTexas/display.php?f=TSP0139.xml

Treaty of Guadalupe-Hidalgo, *National Archives*. Accessed February 12, 2019. https://www.archives.gov/education/lessons/guadalupe-hidalgo.

.

Index

The manufacturer's authorized representative in the EU for product safety is Mare Nostrum Group B.V., Mauritskade 21D, 1091 GC Amsterdam, The Netherlands email: gpsr@mare-nostrum.co.uk